ADVANCE PRAISE

Bill Bradley personified an exceptional athleticism as a free safety in pro football. My only disappointment...I arrived in Philadelphia at the end of Bill's great career. Fortunately, I have been able to reconnect with Bill when he coached my secondary when I coached the NFL's College All-Star Game, three years in a row. A gifted communicator and a vibrant personality.

— DICK VERMEIL, HALL OF FAME NFL HEAD
COACH AND SUPER BOWL XXXIV CHAMPION

Joe Zagorski's book on Bill Bradley accurately captures the many great accomplishments of the former NFL free safety and assistant coach. Bradley had a keen sense for how to effectively shut down an opponent's passing attack, something that he did on a regular basis all throughout his career. His ability to work with athletes and coaches is even more amazing!

— WADE PHILLIPS, NFL HEAD COACH AND
SUPER BOWL 50 CHAMPION

Joe Zagorski is a master storyteller and this book is a perfect example. A leading authority on football in the 1970s, Zagorski weaved his knowledge and expertise to set the stage to talk about Bill Bradley and his career. Colorful quotes from Bradley provided an insight into his personality and gives the reader first-hand accounts of his life and career. Another great work by Joe Zagorski!

— KEN CRIPPEN, FOUNDER, LEAD
INSTRUCTOR, AND PODCASTER AT THE
FOOTBALL LEARNING ACADEMY

Whether you're a die-hard Eagles football fan like me or simply love a story of determination and excellence, *Free Spirit at Free Safety: The Incredible (But True!) Football Journey of Bill Bradley* is a must-read. Before reading this book, I knew Bill Bradley's stats and reputation, but within these pages, I felt like I was right there with Bill Bradley on and off the field during all his amazing adventures!

— JENNIFER NICHOLS, SOCIAL MEDIA
CONFIDENCE COACH

FREE SPIRIT
AT FREE SAFETY

ALSO BY JOE ZAGORSKI

*The 2,003-Yard Odyssey: The Juice, The Electric Company,
and an Epic Run for a Record*

*America's Trailblazing Middle Linebacker:
The Story of NFL Hall of Famer Willie Lanier*

The Year the Packers Came Back: Green Bay's 1972 Resurgence

The NFL in the 1970s: Pro Football's Most Important Decade

FREE SPIRIT
AT FREE SAFETY

THE INCREDIBLE (BUT TRUE!) FOOTBALL
JOURNEY OF BILL BRADLEY

AN AUTHORIZED BIOGRAPHY

JOE ZAGORSKI

Foreword by
RAY DIDINGER

HIGHLANDER
PRESS

Paperback ISBN: 978-1-956442-35-9
Ebook ISBN: 978-1-956442-36-6
Library of Congress Control Number: 2024939662

Published by Highlander Press
A division of Highlander Enterprises, LLC
501 W. University Pkwy, Ste. B2
Baltimore, MD 21210

Cover design: Hanne Broter
Author photo: Matt Hudson

CONTENTS

For everyone who loves life, humor, football...and free spirits.

FOREWORD

Before there was *Friday Night Lights*, there was Super Bill Bradley.

Some may think the cult of Texas high school football began with Buzz Bissinger's best-selling book, which spawned a major motion picture and popular television series. But long before we were introduced to the Panthers of Odessa Permian, there was a kid in Palestine, Texas, who wrote a legend of his own.

His name was Bill Bradley, but somewhere along the line he became Super Bill. That's what folks called him when he led Palestine High to the state championship, that's what the headline writers called him at the University of Texas, and that's what the fans called him when he led the NFL in interceptions in back-to-back years. It was a pretty weighty name to carry around, but he wore it well.

He wasn't very big. He was listed at 5-11 and 185 pounds, but even in uniform he looked smaller. We met in Philadelphia in 1970, when he was a second-year player with the Eagles and I was a rookie sportswriter assigned to cover the team for the *Philadelphia Bulletin*. He had an air of confidence that he brought with him from Palestine, along with his boots and blue jeans.

Bill was a fascinating character. He grew up in a small town in Texas, but when he came to Philadelphia he chose to live in the heart of the city, embracing the culture and history. He took up painting; living in a world that extended far beyond football.

He only knew success in high school and college, so losing in Philadelphia frustrated him. The defense generally played well, and Bill's performance as free safety was a big part of that, but they never could figure it out on offense. In Bill's eight seasons with the Eagles, the team went through four head coaches and six starting quarterbacks. They never finished with a winning record, and yet Bill came to play every week.

He was one of the most versatile players in the league. In addition to playing defense, he also punted, returned punts and kickoffs, and held for placekicks. Coach Ed Khayat once said, "If anything ever happens to Billy, it will take five players to replace him." He wasn't kidding.

The first time Bill intercepted a pass in the NFL, he returned it 56 yards for a touchdown. It was his rookie year, 1969, and the game was in the Cotton Bowl where he played so many times in college. The pass was thrown by Roger Staubach and intended for Mike Ditka, both future Hall of Famers, but Bill got the better of them. It was a preview of what was to come.

He was the first NFL player to lead the league in interceptions two years in a row. He picked off eleven passes in 1971, and nine more in 1972. It is even more impressive when you consider the Eagles were a losing team both years. Most players that win the interception title play on winning teams. They benefit from opponents having to play catch up and throw more passes. With the Eagles, Bill had fewer opportunities, but he made them count.

He still holds the club record for career interceptions (34), interceptions in a season (11), career return yardage (536), and return yardage in a season (248 in 1971). He appeared in three Pro Bowls and was voted into the Eagles Hall of Fame. When he finished his career, Eagles equipment manager Rusty Sweeney put Bill's No. 28 jersey on the shelf.

"If any players ask for it, I tell 'em it's retired," Sweeney said. "I think there are certain guys who deserve that kind of respect and Bill is one of them."

Anyone who saw him play—in high school, college, or the pros—would agree.

Ray Didinger

PREFACE

William "Bill" Bradley is a free spirit. There is no question about that. But being a free spirit is not a bad thing. In fact, it is a badge of honor that the former pro football player and assistant coach wears proudly. In a world where going along with the masses seems to be the safest and surest route to take in life, Bill Bradley is happy to avoid such normalcy, and this was the case even before his playing days in the National Football League ever began. He often displayed his willingness to "push the envelope," as it were, and in many instances, he still does. He is a product of the state of Texas, a state where legends sometime seem to figuratively grow as big as the state itself. Bill Bradley's legendary status in his home state may not be as big as some, but it is still rather large, with loads of stories surrounding it, and his reputation as a favorite son of the Lone Star State is certainly deserved.

One of the biggest challenges with writing this book comes in his name. There was an extraordinary professional basketball player whose name was also Bill Bradley, and that man would eventually become a United States Senator. Although these two athletes owned vastly different personalities and backgrounds, both still get confused with the other because of their identical name. This narrative will hopefully expand upon the achievements of the football player Bill Bradley, to separate the individualities of these two noteworthy men.

I had heard through an acquaintance in the pro football writing circles, in the early 2000s, that Mr. Bradley was interested in finding someone to write his story. At that time, I was working on several projects simultaneously, so I did not have any free time to follow up on the idea of writing a book on Bradley. But the idea certainly intrigued me. I was born and raised in the small town of Pottstown, Pennsylvania, a nearby suburb of Philadelphia, and I watched many of the football games that Bill Bradley played. As I recall, he was practically a beacon of light in a cloudy and rainy sky for Eagles fans. The Eagles teams of the early 1970s were well acquainted with losing. There is no kinder way to put it. The closest that they came to a winning season during those times was in 1974, when they finished 7-7. Bill Bradley suffered through those failing years, along with his teammates, and with the thousands of diehard Eagles fans. But he also managed to succeed as an individual in the sport during that time. Some would say that he exhibited the only element of success worthy of the Green and White (and later the Green and Silver) during a most trying era in Eagles history. The 5-foot-11, 185-pound Bradley, became the first man in history to lead the NFL in interceptions in two consecutive years (1971 and 1972). On a team starving for heroes, Bill Bradley was ripe for that title.

But Bradley was given much more than an appreciative designation by the Philly fans. Those folks gleefully gave their love to a player who reminded them so much of themselves. Bradley wore his emotions on his sleeve in every game. He was always willing to display his excitement—and his frustration—with the results of every play from scrimmage. Philadelphians are much the same way. They always voice their pleasure or displeasure with every struggle that they face in their daily lives, and with the challenges found in every situation. They took to Bill Bradley as if he were one of their kin, even though he hailed from a far-away place. Those Eagles fans who were cheering for the team back in the early-to-mid 1970s still regard Bill Bradley as a legend in "The City of Brotherly Love" to this day.

I sent Mr. Bradley a copy of my first book, *The NFL in the 1970s: Pro Football's Most Important Decade*, back in 2019. I then asked him if he was still interested in having his unique and incredible football story told, and to my delight and happiness, he was. A book on Bill Bradley is long overdue, because he was a man and a player many years ahead of his time. He was unique in numerous tangible and intangible ways. Bradley gave Philadelphians a glimpse of excitement as they attended games at the venerable Franklin Field on the University of Pennsylvania's campus, and at the now flattened parking lot where Veterans Stadium used to stand in South Philadelphia. Those fans knew that they were going to see a free safety chock-filled with ability and intensity. A free safety who could steal the ball out of the air at any moment, and then return it swiftly with the skill of a great open-field runner. The emotional fan base in Philadelphia would also see Bradley play key roles as a punt and kickoff returner for the team, and as a punter, a holder, and an emergency quarterback. A triple threat in pro football? Try quintuple threat! That was Bill Bradley, a multi-purpose player, times four or five. He could do a lot of specific things on a football field really well, because he was such a great athlete. But there is so much more to him than just what he could do as an athlete.

Old pro football players from a bygone era are often relegated to the attics of history, where they are seemingly no longer relevant to the game, or to today's fans. I dislike this current trend immensely, because today's NFL fans (and the current players) can learn so much about the game from these former athletes, and not just from a historical or a strategical perspective. A man like Bill Bradley has lived a truly incredible life, and one well worth exploring. The stories that he tells about his vivacity, and about the sport itself, breathe new life into the game that today's fans would enjoy immeasurably...if they would only take the time to discover. And Bradley is not alone in that regard. Many former NFL players have hundreds of unique and exciting narratives to tell about their gridiron experiences, and many of these men are surprisingly accessible to the public today. The Facebook webpage is an excellent tool with which to contact some of these former players, and quite a few of them are willing to talk to anyone—not just pro football writers—about their days in the NFL.

After my first telephone conversation with Bill Bradley, three things happened in my mind. One, I was immediately enthralled by his ability to remember his time in pro football, even though it is more than 40 years since he last suited up for a game. It is true that people who play contact sports like football often suffer debilitating concussions participating in such athletics, which in turn will unfortunately lead to an inability to remember the past. Bradley sustained concussions like most of his peers in football, but luckily, he still has been able to recall many specific details of a great number of his gridiron exploits. That fact alone is worth celebrating.

Two, his sense of humor is as ribald and as hilarious today as it was in the 1970s while he was an active player. He told me on numerous occasions in our discussions that he "...had more fun playing and coaching football than the law should have allowed," and he enjoyed revealing some of those fun moments with me in our subsequent conversations. It is hard to imagine that a

Bill Bradley and Joe Zagorski, holding a painting of Bill by Gene Sanny of Oakland, Iowa. Photo by Susan Bradley.

player on a perennially losing team can find *any* fun playing the game, but the unapologetic subject of this book certainly did, and what is more, the stories and anecdotes that he shared with me are ones that may never have been heard of before. I am happy to include many of them in this book.

And three, after our first conversation ended, I knew that I *had* to write this book. A guy like Bill Bradley needs to be remembered by longtime football fans like myself. The story of his career is indeed an entertaining chapter in the momentous annals of the NFL. But what could be even more important is the fact that a guy like Bill Bradley needs to be introduced to today's younger fans, if for no other reason than for them to see how important he was to the history of the sport. I have always felt that fans and players who love this game certainly owe a token of thanks to the league's former players like Bill Bradley. It was those men who made the sport what it is today…a super game played by unique men, some with undeniably free spirits.

Joe Zagorski
October 9, 2019

1

A TEXAS TWISTER

He emerged out of his mother's womb on January 24, 1947, and began an extraordinary life in the east Texas hillside town of Palestine, which is roughly 112 miles southeast of the big city metropolis of Dallas. The son of a railroad worker, the youngster would one day become famous in the world of professional football. And he would achieve notoriety in his own way, and by his own standards and beliefs, in an era when originality and eccentricity was often shunned upon. He grew up and lived fiercely individualistically, and his style and mannerisms had only rarely been seen before by others in the stoic sports in which he excelled. As a young adult, he was somewhat emblematic of the new decade of the 1970s, the "me" decade to beat all "me" decades. But he was not really a role model for anyone. He enjoyed searching for his own answers to life's daily questions in his own charismatic way. As he aged, he became a person who could be comfortable in virtually any situation, and within the company of any class of people. He was a free spirit in all its intended definitions.

William Calvin Bradley lived his formative years as commonly as most of the youngsters would in Palestine, a small town which served as the southern terminal of the Missouri Pacific Railroad. Even so, there were numerous times where he would display his uniqueness to many folks. Throughout his younger years, Bradley was blessed with the physical gifts of speed and quickness, which are commonly the requisite elements for success in any sport. He could also throw a baseball and a football with the best of the neighborhood kids that he grew up with in the open fields near his home. Moreover, he could also punt a football high and far, often with distances in height and length that astounded many who saw him in his early years. He loved the sports that he participated in, be it baseball, football, or track, as he paraded into and through his youth. It did not take long before his athletic exploits got noticed by many.

Today in his mid-70s, Bill Bradley has lived a life of few regrets. He has made the most of his God-given physical abilities, as evidenced by his nine years of playing pro football, at a time when the physicality of the game was the most presentable part of the sport. Like all former grid athletes, Bradley today endures the effects of hitting his opponents, and being hit in return. He would not trade his past, however. That is because, over the years, Bradley's participation in sports permitted him to live a life where he could express his own individuality to his teammates, to the fans, and to the television cameras whenever they were focused on him. That is worth quite a lot to him. He was his own man, as unique as they come. He has been faced with numerous situations that run the gamut of life's emotions, from fear, to pain, to anguish, to failure, to happiness, to joy, to ribald celebrations. He has seen it, he has embraced it, he has learned from it, and he has made his mark in life. In the end, he has remained the same person that he was when he was young. That kind of consistency, despite life's curveballs, bad breaks, and unforeseen moments, is admirable for any person. For Bradley, he just goes with the flow, which seems to be the common refrain of most free spirits.

Bill Bradley was—and still is—one of a kind. One of a kind in so many ways. He was the kind of guy that you would be proud of, and that you would be happy to be friends with. He was a born leader, and as time went by, and with his accomplishments growing in number, Bradley got bolder with age. The foundation of his youth, like all young men, stemmed from the many examples bestowed upon him by his parents and family, and from the daily camaraderie of his friends. In the years that he attended Palestine High School, he was lauded as one of the best pure athletes that had ever come out of the Lone Star State. He seemingly could do it all. He could run fast...*very* fast. He had great leaping ability. He had superior hand-eye coordination. He had exceptional quickness and range, and probably what is even more important, he could play several sports, and quite a few different positions in those sports, exceedingly well. He was what a later generation would describe as "a natural." The doors to opportunity began to spring open for him in the 1960s, and with all his talents, Bill Bradley's options for his future in sports grew in number. Every sport in which he played seemed to benefit from his multitude of physical abilities.

"I was a baseball nut," said Bradley. "There wasn't a day that went by, ever since I was six or seven years old, that I didn't go out pitching the ball with my dad (Joe Bradley), who was an outstanding baseball coach. So I learned all angles of balls...every ball that could be...the spin...everything. My dad taught me that. And then all my other buddies who were my age...we all played a lot of sports together. Track helped for my speed. Basketball helped for my moves and quickness. It just all coincided. I wouldn't trade the training of four different sports in high school for all the money in the world. It allowed me to allow football to be easy."[1]

The supposed "ease" of the sport of football had its roots for Bradley in athleticism, which served as a foundation for future success in all organized sports. Football involved a lot of running, and Bradley's stamina and swiftness were on display all throughout his scholastic days. His best 100-yard dash time in high school was 9.8 seconds, and his 40-yard dash time during those years was clocked at an astounding 4.4. For the mid-1960s, without the quality track shoes that are available to runners today, those times of his were rather eye-opening, to say the least. It was on his high school track team that he first learned of the importance of developing techniques, which could result in faster times in his races, and longer distances in several other track and field events.

"I think that anything under 4.5 (in the 40-yard dash) is pretty good," said Bradley. "But I played at 4.3 (in football) by the anticipation and by the knowledge and tendencies, and this, that and the other. I did mostly field events (in track). High jump, broad jump, and pole vault. They were my main events. So I would win first or second (place) in all of our track meets in high school. I'm not braggadocios or overconfident, but we were all confident in high school. We played all the sports. You get your work in. A lot of time, a lot of hours you put in, just to be a starter in high school. And then to win things...track meets, high point man in basketball...it takes a lot of concentration and a lot of dedication. In track, I practiced coming out of the blocks, and I practiced the techniques."[2]

Bradley's techniques in track, however, were not going to result in any scholarship offers from any college. That fact did not really bother him all that much though. His indifference to that reality was because his abilities and successes on the baseball diamond were much more promising and evident for many observers to see. He loved baseball, and that sport may have been declared as his first love. It was certainly one of his most favorite activities. He got to play it at a very young age, and in his adolescence, he had what many folks would consider a rare opportunity to play the sport with older players who were earning a paycheck on the baseball diamond.

"Heck, when I was 15, me and my buddies on my old high school baseball team played semi-pro baseball with the Palestine team," remembered Bradley. "We got taught how to play real big-time baseball. I mean baseball was *our* game. We travelled around the state of Texas on Sundays and played in games that were similar to Double A or Triple A baseball today. We could not get paid, but we were playing against real pro baseball players. It was the experience of my life."[3]

Bradley's baseball exploits during his youth earned him some keen attention from several scouts who roamed the southwest. The young pitcher and sometimes shortstop was targeted for a minor league baseball contract by a farm team of the Detroit Tigers upon his graduation from high school.

"I was drafted in the fifth round by the Tigers to play Double A baseball in Montgomery, Alabama with Denny McClain (a future star in Major League Baseball)," recalled Bradley. "The contract that they offered me was for $25,000, which was a lot of money back then."[4]

The lure of an instant payment of such a sum had to weigh heavily on Bradley's mind. He did not come from a wealthy background. Few people in the Hill Country of Texas did. His parents worked hard every day at blue collar jobs, where sweat, muscle, determination, and responsibility were the accepted ingredients needed to produce a weekly paycheck. They set a positive example for Bill to follow and aspire to as he developed his own hard work ethic. But the temptation to claim a bunch of money...much more than he had ever owned before...had to get him thinking. Nevertheless, he tabled the decision on his future for some time, as he thought on the life lessons that he got from his parents and siblings.

"My dad was a hard-drinking railroad man and a baseball coach," Bradley recalled. "He worked for the railroad since he was 13. My dad was a dispatcher, and his brothers were conductors, and his uncles were engineers."[5] We got a baseball field, which I thought was one of the best things that ever happened to our family, because I was still young and in school. My dad touched so many young lives as a baseball coach. They named the baseball field in Palestine after him.

"My mom (Mildred Bradley) worked at a grocery store, then she went to beauty school and became a beautician. And so we had a beauty shop in our house. And then when I was around age 13 or 14, I got to wash hair. We had two sinks downstairs in the utility room. She (Bradley's mom) would also work at the Piggly Wiggly supermarket, where she was a grocery checker to make ends meet. All my folks were hard working. I was a hard-working athlete. My sister (Rosemay Bradley) was a drum major, so she was active. She taught me music, the old soul music. She taught me rhythm...she did everything. And of course, Dad played the drums. And so we were a musical and an athletic family, but we were also a hard-working family. Everybody worked. I had summer jobs. I had football and the other sports, (which) was my deal. And so to relieve my parents, all I really got from them was clothes...a couple of pairs of jeans, some boots, and some t-shirts. And then for school every day I would get 25 cents for lunch money."[6]

The daily grind of attending school and staying busy with sports after school would become second nature for Bradley by the time he got to high school. He was not completely sure of his future path during his adolescence, but he knew that deep down, there was something more to be gained out of life than what he was witnessing in Palestine. In fact, if it was not for the excitement that sports provided, Bradley's youth might be considered by some to be quite boring. But Bradley did not see his efforts as unexciting. He saw athletics as a ticket to a better and more interesting life.

"I did all the sports, and that was my way out," Bradley explained. "And I enjoyed the hell out of it. I was busy all the time."[7]

One activity that nearly every young kid in the Lone Star State got at least somewhat involved in, did not have anything to do with scoring touchdowns on the gridiron and shooting jump shots on the basketball court, however. Like most youngsters in the 1950s in the environs of Palestine, Texas, Bill Bradley also took advantage of what the great outdoors in a wilderness setting offered, namely hunting and fishing. True, those occupations were more like hobbies to him, but they were still a pastime...a rite of passage for kids in Texas. Indeed, it was during these moments that the adolescent Bradley first developed his love for the great outdoors, something that was never lost on him.

"My dad was a hunter and a fisherman, so we did quite a bit of that," recalled Bradley. "We duck hunted, we dove hunted, we went fishing a lot...in rivers, and ponds, and lakes. I can remember one time we went down to a river, and my dad knew where the bass was going to spawn, because the river was up. We didn't even have to use any type of utensils to fish with. We were just standing there by the waterfall, just a little trickle at that time to the main body of the river. And we just threw in our buckets, we caught about I'd say maybe 150 bass, just with our hands throwing them in buckets. But the thing about that is that he (Bradley's dad) had to teach me how to clean fish. And you're cleaning 150 fish! That wasn't much fun."[8]

Because he took sports in high school much more seriously than he did fishing, Bradley was also forced to take several injuries that he sustained during that time more seriously. The sport of football was big in Texas, and it always has been. But the quality of the equipment and the number of medical supplies at that time were certainly not what one can find in the current day and age. Bradley's speed and his willingness to hustle on every play resulted in some very hard hits on the Texas scholastic football fields, both given and endured.

"My very first injury, other than sprains or bumps and bruises, was actually concussions in high school," remembered Bradley, who would also have to deal with at least one knee injury in high school. "I had three major concussions. Nowadays, you would be on protocol, and probably wouldn't play in two or three games."[9]

The daily life of a high school student/athlete in East Texas would lend elements that would help the youngster become the young man that he eventually became. He learned how to think for himself, how to become an individual, and how to develop his own unique personality. In the realm of pro football, Bradley was never afraid to voice his own opinion to his teammates, to his opponents, to his coaches, and even to the referees. And by the time that he started playing in the NFL, Bradley typically was not going to deliver his responses in a soft-spoken manner. He established his willingness to ask questions and to deliver answers in his high school years.

"Well first of all, we had tremendous mentors at Palestine High School, which of course was in a small town," said Bradley. "It was the only school for quite some time (in that area), and we were not integrated. We had great teachers in every type of subject. I was just a good student. Not only did we win the state football championship, but we were good in competing for state notoriety through academics, theater, and band and speech. We finished second in the state in debate (a subject in which Bradley excels in to this day), and our band finished third or something in their competition."[10]

While many schools at that time kept the races separate, one chapter during Bradley's early years which definitely did not discriminate between skin colors or religious creed or any other measuring label, was integration into the military. During the mid-1960s, the Vietnam War was in full swing, and young men all across the nation were being looked upon to fill the ranks. The draft was unavoidable by many, and for some, it resulted in a preliminary death sentence. But where many kids had come up with phony reasons to avoid the draft, Bill Bradley had the truth and legitimacy going for him.

"My hometown of Palestine was one of the number one draft boards," observed Bradley. "Some of my buddies got caught doing some illegal things to scratch some money. They would steal a mailbox, and because they planned to go to college on a football scholarship, they would lose the scholarship. So, you would either have to go to Vietnam, or you went to jail.

"And so, I went and took a physical in our bus. I was leaning on the bus when we went from Palestine to Dallas to take an Army physical to be inducted. But I already had some knee injuries, and I had a little bit of high blood pressure, so they didn't take me. But all of my buddies went. Some of them didn't come back from Vietnam.[11] They're the real heroes. They try to make football players into heroes. Football is just a game. It's pretty much a theatrical production. Now it's violent, mind you, but the real heroes back then were the guys who went to Vietnam, and I'm sure that was the prior case with World War I and II. They're the real heroes, and I keep saying that every time that I speak at a banquet."[12]

An ongoing war a whole world away is more than enough to get a young man thinking about the brevity of life, where the unknown specter of death can claim you at a moment's notice. But Bill Bradley put his Army physical experience in the back of his mind as he neared his high school graduation. He still had a pressing choice to make which would affect his immediate future. Would he decide to accept the cash offer from the Detroit Tigers to play pro baseball? Or would he instead decide to attend college with the hopes of playing college football, baseball, and perhaps performing for the school's track team? He had received scholarship letters from a bunch of Division One colleges, including the likes of Notre Dame, Alabama, the University of Southern California, and practically every college south of the Mason-Dixon Line. He took the time to look over all of those letters, which promised him quite a bit. But as with many of his choices at that time of his life, he relied on the knowledge of his elders, namely, his father.

"My dad wanted me to go to college," Bradley said. "He knew that I could stay close to home if I accepted a football scholarship. I could have gone to any college, because I got offers from quite a few of them. But there was never any wavering on my part. I was going to go to the University of Texas in Austin."[13]

Bill Bradley knew that the sum of money that the Tigers baseball team offered him would come and go, but a college degree—and the many different experiences that several years at college would provide him—would be his forever. Those diverse experiences would certainly be at least a little more interesting than fielding ground ball after ground ball in the minor leagues, and Bradley in his teenage years definitely needed something more than baseball to stimulate his mind. That weighed down the scales toward attending college in his mind. Attending a prestigious university like the University of Texas would also open a lot of future doors for him.

"It ultimately turned out that I made the right choice," said a contemplative Bradley. "I chose to go to the University of Texas on a football scholarship. I went in with a handshake from (Texas) head coach Darrell Royal that I could (still) play baseball (at college). Back then we had a freshman (football) team, and a freshman schedule. So I ended up lettering in three sports (football, baseball and track) at the University of Texas in my freshman year for the freshmen people across the Southwest Conference (the conference which included the University of Texas). And everybody had to play freshman ball...you couldn't be propped up to the varsity. That's just the rule back then. I thought it was a good rule."[14]

But before Bradley stepped foot as a freshman on the college campus at Austin, he had some final high school obligations to fulfill. The Palestine football team had to play for the state championship, which they won thanks in part to the efforts of head coach Luke Thornton and offensive coordinator Marion Turner. Then Bradley was chosen to play in several prestigious All-Star Football games. He was going to be a very busy young man in the summer of 1965. One of the most noteworthy contests that he took part in was the Big-33 Game, held annually in the faraway state of Pennsylvania. It is a game that is still played today between the best high school seniors from Pennsylvania, and the best high school seniors from Maryland. But back in Bradley's day, it was the best of Texas versus the best of Pennsylvania. If you were to list every NFL player who previously participated in the Big-33 Game (up to the present day), it would literally be recorded as a "who's who" directory of famous or noteworthy pro football players, some of whom have a bust of themselves today at the Pro Football Hall of Fame in Canton, Ohio. But Bradley and his contemporaries were not thinking too much about the game's significance in history, however.

"No, we never thought about that, but thinking about it now, there's a list as long as your arm (of eventual NFL players) for both teams (Texas and Pennsylvania) from the Big-33 Game," said Bradley. "Mike Reid (a former Cincinnati Bengals defensive tackle and a Grammy award-winning concert pianist) was on the Pennsylvania team. He was their kicker and their fullback. And he went on to make All-Pro as a defensive lineman. Terry Hanratty (a future All-American quarterback at Notre Dame and a future Super Bowl-winning quarterback for the Pittsburgh Steelers) played left corner-back for the Pennsylvania team. He didn't play that much at quarter-back (in the Big-33 Game). Norm Bulaich (a future running back for both the Baltimore Colts, the Philadelphia Eagles, and the Miami Dolphins) played for the Texas team with me. Ted Kwalick (a future tight end for the San Francisco 49ers and the Oakland Raiders) was also on the Pennsylvania team. If you look at each picture of those players, about half of both teams (Texas and Pennsylvania), or at least a third of both teams, went on to play professional football. And then 10-12 of them went on to make All-Pro."[15]

Today, Bradley and Hanratty remain good friends, as do some of the other players, which is not uncommon. Many former pro grid stars who can trace their relationships back to their youth often keep in touch with each other many years later. But back in 1965, the players in the Big-33 Game were certainly not looking too far into their futures. They were busy getting ready for the big game, and being surrounded by all the hype and hoopla that seemed to become a part of the contest, and a part of the events that led up to the game. The attention that the young athletes received was probably much more than many of them had ever seen in their lives. When asked how big it was to win the game, Bradley did not hesitate in his response.

"Oh, it was huge," he said. "Somebody wrote an article about it many, many years ago. I don't know if it was *Sports Illustrated*, but some big sportswriter said that it (the Big-33 Game) was like a Super Bowl. It was a big-time competition between the states in high school football. In the beginning, Pennsylvania played the neighboring states. And then finally, they decided that they wanted to have a big game with Texas. It all started with the governors of the two states. That game got competitive when the governors bet (on the outcome). Of course Pennsylvania has apples, and Texas has pecans. So I remember when the game really got heated, it was so many bushels of apples bet against so many bushels of pecans for whoever won the game."[16]

The Big-33 Game almost did not happen the way it eventually did, however. A scheduling conflict kept the Texas team in the Big-33 tilt in a state of limbo, due to another important game being held on the same day in the Lone Star State. Bill Bradley relates the story of the situation here:

"The first year that they played the Big-33 Game (versus Texas), Pennsylvania won," recalled Bradley. "But that coincided with the North-South high school All-Star game in Texas. I can remember playing in front of 30,000 people in that All-Star game in Texas. If you made it as a high school player, you got elected to play on the North or the South. That game (unfortunately) was scheduled to be played on the same weekend as the Big-33 Game (up in Pennsylvania)."[17]

It took a lot of wheeling and dealing to change the date of one of those two games in order for the best Texas high school football players to be able to play in both games, which in turn would give Texas a decent chance of winning against a northern rival such as Pennsylvania. Addressing that diplomatic effort and enterprise were some fairly famous people...some of whom also happened to be fairly famous football players.

"In the first game against Pennsylvania," remembered Bradley, "the Texas head coach was (former pro quarterback and Hall of Famer) Bobby Layne. And some of the assistant coaches were people like Doak Walker, who went on to play at SMU (Southern Methodist University) and who was a Heisman Trophy winner back in the day."[18]

As a young teenager, playing football under the tutelage of such esteemed gridiron stars as Layne and Walker must have been awe-inspiring for Bradley. Layne himself at that time was just two years away from being enshrined in the Pro Football Hall of Fame. The youthful Bradley probably had to pinch himself to make sure that he was not dreaming at the time. As one might suspect, it was one of the first great and memorable moments of his life.

"It was unbelievable," said Bradley of playing for Layne and Walker, and of the whole high school football All-Star game situation. "I mean it was a blast. Bobby lost that first (Big-33) game (in 1964), and if you know Bobby Layne like we all knew him, and like everybody from this state (Texas) and Detroit and Pittsburgh (where Layne played in the pros) knew him, we all knew how competitive he was. He **hated** to lose. I mean losing to him was **despicable**! And so, after he lost that first Big-33 Game, he went into the Texas governor's office and mandated the governor (John Connally...the same Texas governor who was wounded in the assassination of President John F. Kennedy in 1963) to change the date of the Texas high school All-Star game. And that was like an act of Congress. So he (Layne) stormed in there and just took over his (Connally's) office! I know how Bobby was, and I ended up being friends with him for the rest of his life after the All-Star game.

"So anyway, Bobby basically didn't have the best Texas players. The best players went to the North-South high school All-Star game (which Layne did not coach). He somehow got the state (Texas) to change the date of the All-Star football contest, which is a hard thing to do a week prior to the Big-33 Game. And it (the North-South game) was still a big hit, but now Bobby's got other picks of guys. He's definitely now got the best players from the North-South All-Star game. We got on a plane right after that (North-South All-Star) game and flew to Pennsylvania. Then after that particular game (the Big-33 Game), we flew back down south and played Oklahoma in the Oil Bowl. So for three weeks there, we were a traveling group of football players in high school. From Dallas, for the North-South game at the Cotton Bowl (Stadium), to Pennsylvania at Hershey, and then to western Texas to play the Oil Bowl at Wichita Falls. We were like *Bingo Long and the Traveling All-Stars*. We were actually introduced to some big-time, fan-based football. It was a big deal."[19]

The big deal to Bradley, in retrospect, also involved the many different stories that surrounded those games; stories that he lived through, in particular during the week prior to the Big-33 Game. His remembrances and depictions of those stories come from a distant memory from his past, and they are almost as entertaining as was the game itself. Chalk some of those tales up to the shenanigans, and perhaps the devil-may-care attitudes of youth, and of young men growing up in a nation which was still in the midst of growing up itself. America during the mid-1960s was dealing with a costly war in a foreign land, ugly episodes of racial strife in many of her states, and loud and sometimes violent protests from many factions on causes that were numerous and varied in their platforms and promises. Bradley simply found himself in the midst of all the morass of events, but still not thinking too much about those existing issues that dominated the headlines. He had to deal with what was in front of him, namely the experiences that he would enjoy just before attending college. In truth, he never could have predicted that his senior year in high school would have ended the way that it did, but he also could never have come up with a better way in his mind for it to end either.

For instance, Bradley and Texas teammates Norm Bulaich and Jerry LeVias borrowed a friend's car one night prior to the Big-33 Game, met some Pennsylvania girls—who just happened to be dating a couple of the players from the Pennsylvania team—and enjoyed their company that night. Suffice it to say that they had a *really* good time. That was a rather unique conquest for the representatives of the Texas team to get a laugh over for many years. Then came the drinking. True, young boys sow their wild oats every year in America with the aid of liquid refreshment. That fact will never change. Drinking certainly had its role for the players of the Texas team prior to the Big-33 Game. Then came the pregame practices for both the Texas and Pennsylvania teams. All of those moments were humorous in and of themselves.

"It was just amazing to me," Bradley related of the days leading up to the Big-33 Game. "When we get to the Big-33 Game, we stayed as a team in one of Layne's farmhouses in Hershey. Four to a room, or six to a room, with cots and bunkbeds. So when we first got there, there's two cases of beer iced down on the back porch...for the players! And they had water and cokes and soft drinks and fruit drinks, and this, that, and the other.

"And I can remember our first practice. We had to practice on the same field that the Pennsylvania team was practicing...at the same time! They were practicing at one end, and we (the Texas team) were practicing at the other end. And they had a real hard-nosed, strict coach. They're down there (at their end of the field) getting physical, and almost scrimmaging. They're at their first practice, and they're having a full-padded practice. And we're up at the other end (of the field). Our offense is at one side of the goal post, and our defense is on the other end, and we're playing volleyball with a football over the goal post (laughter). But that's Bobby Layne...that's how he bonded everybody. And they're (the Pennsylvania team) yelling, 'Oh man, we're gonna kick y'all's rear end!' and this and that. Blah blah blah. And we got tired of (hearing) it, and so I yelled down there 'Let me tell you something...boy we've got a lot of speed! To all of you coal crackers down there...we're gonna kick y'all's rear end too!'"[20]

The term "coal crackers" that Bradley used was a derogatory expression which poked fun at the profession of Pennsylvania's anthracite coal miners. One must realize that the era of butt hurt sensitivities was still several decades in the future. Bradley certainly did not mean anything malicious by his comments to his opponents. But talking "smack" was a pastime that has been handed down among young men for many generations, and few in those days took such good-natured ribbing seriously. Bradley felt right at home in expressing his humorous opinions toward his football foes, accepting the insults that were returned his way, and knowing that it was all part of the fun of the game. It was a practice that Bradley has reveled in throughout his days and years on a football field, regardless of the level of competition. Creativity often determined the winner of an insult-trading session. Once again, Bradley was usually able to hold his own when it came to coming up with imaginative slurs. But he was also able to realize that teenagers playing football in 1965 was not the overly serious business that it seems to be today.

"It was a good, clean rivalry, but nevertheless, it was a lot of bantering back and forth," remembered Bradley. "It was good clean stuff. There were no fights or anything like that."[21]

A fight of another kind, however, was being waged throughout the nation at that time. As both teams practiced in their own ways, an interesting side story to the 1965 tournament games (the North-South game in Texas, the Big-33 Game in Pennsylvania, and the Oil Bowl in Wichita) involved the societal norms of the time in Texas. One of Bradley's teammates was wide receiver Jerry LeVias, a young man who happened to be one of only three African American players on the Texas team, and who would eventually go on to an NFL career himself as a wide receiver with the Houston Oilers and the San Diego Chargers. Discrimination and the separation of the races was still a distasteful remnant of that era in several states, and such segregation practices reached into the realms of sports. No Caucasian member of the team explicitly wanted to have LeVias as a roommate, because for whatever reasons, they felt that it was still to be considered beneath their status as white players. But Bill Bradley was a free spirit, and a kid with a mindset years ahead of his time. He stood up and declared that LeVias would be his roommate on the road, a solemn moment of clarity to his friends, and a public example of how African Americans should be treated by all of their teammates—simply as teammates, without any connotations about one's race. That is how Bradley viewed the two races back then, and it is how he views the two races to this very day.

"We were still segregated in my hometown," recalled Bradley. "We had separate drinking fountains. The African Americans had to sit up in the balcony at the movies. They had their different bathrooms. But my dad told us that we couldn't use the "N" word in our house. And like I tell everybody, we didn't live across the tracks, which was usually a black neighborhood. We lived right next to the black families. We weren't racist or anything like that. A lot of people in Palestine weren't.

"As a matter of fact, at Palestine we played football on Friday nights, and the black teams played on Saturday nights. So, we had our black friends who we ran around with come by and stand down by the fence at our games, and we would go on Saturdays and watch their games. Mind you now, we had an old dilapidated house for a high school in Palestine, and they (the African American students) had a brand-new facility...a school, a football field...and everything. So, they actually had better facilities than we did."[22]

Pennsylvania at that time also had better facilities as a whole than what could be found in Texas, from buildings in the cities and the suburbs, to shopping areas (including the increased *number* of shopping areas), to the overall infrastructure of better roads and bridges. Perhaps on a cerebral level, and thanks to the result of the Civil War a century before, the people of Pennsylvania and of the other Northern states as well, may have felt themselves better—or at least more advanced—than the people of the vanquished and often scorned Southern states. Despite this, the specter of racism could still be found up in the Keystone State. Bradley found out for himself that everyone's opinions on the black-white issue did not necessarily change when one travelled up to the Northern environs.

"When we went to get our room keys at the hotel (in Hershey, Pennsylvania) the night before the Big-33 Game, I went to sign in," described Bradley. "The lady (behind the front desk) pulled me back three times and said, 'Are you sure you want to room with Mr. LeVias?' Well, we had four or five people to a room, and we had single beds. After the third time that she asked me, I said 'Well why?' She said, 'Well you know, he's a little colored boy.' I said, 'Excuse me?' Because I didn't grow up that way. And I said to her 'He's a football player, isn't he? Yeah of course I want to share a room with him! I only see colors in uniforms. I don't know about you.'"[23]

Bradley's opinions on race relations did not just stem from how he addressed the prejudicial opinions of others, or the black-white situations on the gridiron, however. He also took advantage of playing in baseball games with African Americans, even when many youngsters in the nearby Texas neighborhoods would not. Those games turned out to be idyllic in some measure, at least as far as what could be observed when the races got together to enjoy a summer day at the ballpark.

"At that time, nobody would schedule any white team to play the black teams, like it was in the old Negro Leagues," recalled Bradley. "But we (the Caucasian players that Bradley ran around with) had no prejudice. We would play those guys (African American teams) on Sundays. And you talk about a beautiful ballgame. Everybody comes from church, dressed up in their church outfits, their suits and coats, even in the hot weather. It was just like big-time major league baseball, only in a smaller stadium. It was just like in the movie *Field of Dreams*."[24]

In all honesty, it did not take the above examples of standing up for what was right for Texas teenagers like Bradley and LeVias to develop a bond with each other. They hit it off immediately. Bradley would consistently refer to LeVias not as "LeVias," but rather as "Roomie" or "His Roomie." It was a term of profound friendship that served as an expressive illustration as to how quickly Bradley could develop a bond of alliance with someone that he just met. Moreover, both young men came from the Lone Star State (LeVias was from Beaumont), and that home state pride stood amply strong between the two young men. The two scholastic football stars also had several other things in common, including their love of music.

"My sister Rosemay was four years older than me," said Bradley. "She got into Otis Redding, Wilson Pickett...all the soul music from Motown. So, I didn't really grow up listening to a whole lot of country music. I grew up listening to all of those Motown guys. That's one reason why Jerry liked me.

"And when we first double dated, he had an Anglo chick that was after him up in Pennsylvania with the Big-33 debutants. The Pennsylvania team had a curfew, and we didn't. So, we had 66 gals to pick from (chuckle). I double dated with Jerry one night, and all we did was walk out on a golf course, spread out a blanket, listened to some music on the radio, and all that kind of stuff. Later on, I beat everybody, whites and blacks, at pitching quarters up against a wall. I took home one of those white socks filled with quarters (laughter)."[25]

Nobody on the Texas team was doing very much laughing as the Big-33 Game started, however. The Pennsylvania team was getting the better of the Texas fellows in the first half, beating them by a score of 3-0 in the first two quarters. Football coaches have long been declared geniuses by their ability to make strategical adjustments and rejuvenate their players at halftime. Texas head coach Bobby Layne may not have been labeled as a genius by any football historian today, particularly if he is compared to recognized gridiron masterminds such as Tom Landry, Paul Brown, Bill Walsh, etc. But Layne was coaching young boys in this game, and he had the knowledge and the realization to know that very young football players run on emotion, adrenaline, and physicality, much more than they run on the strategical elements of the sport. As a result, Layne focused his attentions on getting his Texas team "fired up" to perform better in the second half. To accomplish that intention, he knew that he had to make a change in his lineup. Bill Bradley relates this telling memory of the scene:

"And so, we're sitting there in the locker room at halftime and we're down," said Bradley. "We had a couple of turnovers in the first half. Imagine these locker rooms were different than they are now. There's lockers on both sides of the room, and kind of a (narrow) walk through in the middle. So, they had benches and stuff like that, and basically, even back then in pro ball, to expand your locker, they gave you a hammer and a nail (laughter). Well anyway, Bobby is strutting up and down the middle aisle, and he is so pissed off, or mad, or disgusted, that we were behind (on the scoreboard).

"I'm sitting there with Norm Bulaich and Chris Gilbert, who was a really highly-touted high school running back from Houston. We (Bradley and Gilbert) had already committed to attend the University of Texas as blue-chip recruits. Bulaich went on to win a Super Bowl with the Baltimore Colts, and Gilbert turned down a contract with the Jets, and went and played in some Texas semi-pro league and made more money than we did (chuckle). So anyway, Bobby is marching up and down the dressing room and he yells out, 'Can anybody in here play effing quarterback?!?' I didn't raise my hand. I didn't even budge, because I didn't even know the offensive plays. I was playing in the game as a punter. I didn't get much reps in practice as a quarterback, because I went over there primarily as a punter/defensive back. So Gilbert, who is sitting next to me, raises his hand. Bobby says, 'Yeah Chris, what do you want?' And Gilbert, my buddy, says 'Bill just made the MVP as the quarterback of the North-South High School All-Star Game (in Texas).'"[26]

Bradley cast a glaring look at Gilbert as if to say, "Thanks a lot for screwing me!" Bradley apparently discussed this matter with Gilbert away from Coach Layne. "I said, 'Shut up Chris!' He said back to me, 'Well we want to win, don't we?'"[27]

There is a term for what Gilbert did at this moment that many young men throughout American history are familiar with. It denotes an abrupt, concise, and accurate way of describing the practice of volunteering someone else to do something perceived to be distasteful; a practice that no person who is being volunteered appreciates in any way, shape, or form. Members of the military are quite familiar with the expression, as are high school football players trying to lay low under the radar and stay out of trouble...in this case, at the 1965 Big-33 Game. That term is simply referred to as "buddy fucking."

"So Bobby Layne looked at me and said, 'You're playing quarterback this half!'" recalled Bradley. "And I just looked at him like I was dumfounded. And he said it again. 'You're playing quarterback! I'll teach you some plays real quick.' I said, 'Yes sir, yes sir...I'll try.' So I really didn't know the offense."[28]

Bradley was probably at this moment wondering several things. First, how in the world would he remember all of the information that Layne was force-feeding him in the space of just two or three minutes before the teams went back out on the field to begin the third quarter? Next, how would the other members of the Texas offense adjust to a brand-new quarterback calling the plays in the huddle, and the signals at the line of scrimmage? Finally, Bradley was probably wondering a most curious question: why did his so-called friend Chris Gilbert open his big mouth in the locker room?! As it turns out, possibly without even realizing it at the time, Bradley relied on his own athletic ability to make things happen. He also relied on the speed that his team possessed, particularly at the wide receiver position.

"So when I get in the huddle the first time, we're down (on the scoreboard)," remembered Bradley. "I don't know the plays, so I said, 'Everybody just run take-offs. Just run straight up the field.' We had a tight end and two wideouts. Jerry LeVias was going to line up on my right, and I told him, 'Hey Jerry, we're gonna run all go's, and I'm gonna throw it as far as I can.' I look out there, and I see Terry Hanratty. The Pennsylvania team had him playing defensive halfback, which is what a person playing cornerback is called today. So Hanratty is out there, trying to cover LeVias. I throw the ball deep, and Jerry had run by Hanratty. Jerry had to come back for the ball, but he catches it and he scores. And so now it's on."[29]

The Texas team got the jolt that they desperately needed from a pair of roommates to begin the second half. The quick touchdown was the kind of play that Bobby Layne obviously approved of, even if it was not the exact type of play that he had tried to explain to Bradley at halftime. It did not matter. Layne's trademarks all throughout his career were throwing the ball and winning games. Bradley's style of play catered to those trademarks quite nicely. The young signal caller knew that having his receivers run deep routes straight down the field might not succeed, but they would result in tiring out the Pennsylvania defensive backs, even if Bradley threw several consecutive incompletions. It was a good strategy, but Bradley and LeVias were just getting warmed up.

"So we hold them (the Pennsylvania offense), and the next series when we get the ball back, I get in the huddle and say, 'Same old, same old. Let's break,'"[30] related Bradley. One more long pass completion to LeVias, who caught six passes for 108 yards in the game, set up another Texas touchdown. Bobby Layne's boys rode their newly found momentum in the third quarter to cruise the rest of the way to a 26-10 victory. Redemption for Coach Layne, and a most joyful memory for his punter and his emergency quarterback. Following the game, Texas assistant coach Doak Walker saw Bradley and gave him a new nickname, one which has followed him to this very day. Walker simply called him "Super Bill," and a legend was born.

"He (Coach Walker) was the one who gave me that nickname," Bradley confirmed. "There's other people who tried to take credit for it at the University of Texas, but he's the one who gave it to me. I first heard it, and it kinda stuck, at the Big-33 High School All-Star Game. Doak Walker was coming down the aisle of lockers in the dressing room after our win, and he called me that."[31]

When a Heisman Trophy winner describes a young teenage football player as "Super," people are bound to take notice. And Bradley would certainly not be faulted for having his chest extend forward at least a few inches from that moment in time. But to his credit, the young man took it all in stride. In fact, he never really gave it too much thought. Bradley knew that football games were won by teams, not individuals. Even at such a young age, his modesty and his down-to-earth persona were not only very impressive, but they were evident for his friends and his teammates to see.

"Bill never, never got big-headed or conceited," said Bob Stephenson, one of Bradley's high school teammates. "We won the state championship, and he was just a part of the team. He never went on an ego trip or anything. I think that was one of the reasons that we were as successful as we were, because that didn't happen. And I don't think that, speaking for myself, but for most of those seniors (at Palestine High School), I don't think that we were jealous at all of his success."[32]

The incredible success and triumph of the Texas All-Star team over the Pennsylvania All-Star team in the 1965 Big-33 Game in Hershey, Pennsylvania, gave Bill Bradley—whether he was super or not—a feeling of euphoria and accomplishment the level of which he had never felt before. In all likelihood, Bradley believed that similar feelings of gridiron happiness could be found all throughout the next four years in his home state on the collegiate level of play. What he could not predict, however, was just how many unique twists, turns, potholes, and outright roadblocks he would encounter while as a student-athlete at the University of Texas, from 1965-1969. As we shall see, it was truly an eye-opening group of years for this Texas Twister from Palestine.

2

THE LONGHORN AUTUMNS

Bill Bradley's trip from Palestine to Austin was roughly only 175 miles, but symbolically, it was a much farther distance. It traced the time from Bill Bradley's youth to his adulthood, and that span of time produced memories aplenty for him that have lasted to this very day. Bradley looked upon his years at the University of Texas (UT) as an opportunity to expand upon his previous noteworthy accomplishments in high school, particularly in athletics. He was all-state in several different sports. Now he was going to get a chance to prove that the press clippings that he received at Palestine High School were not bluster, but rather, the natural base layer of an athletic career that would soon make him famous.

Many college freshmen go through a culture shock of sorts when they leave home, some for the very first time, to attend college. The adjustment to a new town is often a challenge, as is meeting new people and making new friends in an academic setting. But Bill Bradley's college experiences were different than most. That is because he spent a couple of summers in 1964 and 1965 at Tyler Junior College and Austin Community College while working on a ranch. It was that involvement which gave him a taste of college life and college classes, and which prepared him for the more regimented schedules at the University of Texas. Perhaps the greatest alteration for Bill Bradley as a bonafide college freshman involved the requirements of organizing his time to balance the demands of his studies with his obligations to the University of Texas football team. He adapted to this new world of his about as well as any new student could. Whether fortunately or unfortunately, Bradley was not thrown to the wolves as it were as a freshman athlete. That was because during the mid-1960s, there was a freshman football team at UT, where all first-year players would play the sport against all the other freshmen of the teams comprising the Southwest Conference.

"Freshmen weren't allowed in that time and era to be on the varsity," declared Bradley. "That was a good thing for everybody. We had our own freshman schedule. The population at college was huge and it was just overwhelming. But I took to it. I found it to be a whole lot of fun. We knew what time we had slotted for things. A lot of the athletes got the times for the classes that you wanted. And most of us started our classes at eight in the morning, and we were done by one or two o'clock in the afternoon. The rest of the day was for football. I was a physical education major and a speech major in college. It was a double major. I enjoyed my classes. I got into it. I was a B or a B-plus average student in most of my grades."[1]

For Bradley, the term "average" seldom applied to him, but when it did, it typically did not involve the sports in which he participated. He wasted no time in having a prominent role on the UT freshman football, baseball, and track teams. Sometimes, his involvement on some of those teams happened by more of a matter of chance than choice.

"In my freshman year at UT, I didn't even think about track," recalled Bradley. "But I did start at shortstop on the baseball team. So I was going to baseball practice one day, and the track coach cornered me at the end of the tunnel going out to the stadium. He called to me and said 'Hey Bradley! What are you doing this weekend?' I said, 'Well, I'm probably going to study, or just take it easy at the dormitory.' He said, 'No you're not. You're going to Rice University (in Houston). We're having a freshman Southwest Conference track meet.' I said, 'Well Coach, I haven't done anything (involving track) since high school.' He said, 'You're going to high jump, you're going to broad jump, you're going to pole vault, and you're going to throw the javelin.' I said, 'Excuse me? What the heck is a javelin?' He said, 'It's that spear...you know that they throw. You're going to throw that spear. You're going to get on that bus with us (the University of Texas freshman track team) this weekend. We're going to do it. I think you'll place in some of those events. If it's fifth or sixth, that's still going to help us win a freshman track meet.' So I did do it and I got three second places and I got the fifth place in the javelin. I had never thrown the javelin before.

"But anyway, I bettered my high school marks with the western roll in the high jump. The Fosbury Flop was not allowed. That was outlawed. So with a western role in high school, I got 6'4", and then I went down to the University of Texas, got another 6'4", and I finished second in the Southwest Conference track meet. And then on the pole vault, I got a mark of 12'6" in high school. That's with a metal pole. So when I had a fiberglass pole in college, I went up to 13'5". I finished second there, and second in the high jump. In the broad jump in high school, I had a record of 22'11". So when I did it at Rice University, I got a 23'5". So I bettered my own personal record on two of the four events. The javelin? I don't know how far I threw it, but it was far enough to finish fifth."[2]

Arm strength was important to Bradley in baseball and football as well. As a youngster growing up, he played several positions on the baseball diamond, and as we have already seen, he played a variety of positions on the gridiron, including quarterback. His freshman year at college saw more of the same. He continued to succeed at every sport at which he participated. Moreover, it certainly did not take the Palestine product long to endear himself with the other players on his team, regardless of which sport was being discussed. He was voted to be a captain at UT, just like he was when he participated in his high school sports. Like all good leaders, Bradley led by example.

"I got along with everybody, and I took my share of the blame," said Bradley. "That's how I grew up. I think that I tried to do everything right. I learned a lot of leadership qualities from my high school coaches, and during my years at the University of Texas. We all manned around together, and you were playing for your teammates.[3] But I was very, very confident in my abilities, because I had taken them all to the limit in all of my sports. I lettered in three sports as a freshman at Texas (football, baseball, and track), and that's hard to do."[4]

One of those sports was practically a birthright for Bradley, or at least he thought it was. Baseball was Bradley's first love, because it was a sport that his father would coach him every spring and summer in Palestine. It was also the first sport to offer Bradley a contract, which he turned down in favor of attending college. But while he was being recruited by football coaches at a number of different colleges, he kept one specific demand in the forefront of his mind, and in the minds of those who recruited him. He would accept a football scholarship, but only if he was also allowed to play baseball for that school. As it turned out, this particular episode in Bradley's life would end up being an important lesson for him. He decided to accept UT's offer for several reasons. First, it was an excellent Division I school with a reputation for outstanding undergraduate and graduate academic programs. Second, because it was less than a day's drive to his hometown of Palestine, should Bradley ever need or want to go home. Third and lastly, because UT's football coach Darrell Royal shook his hand while promising him that he could still play baseball for the college team in the springs and summers.

Everything was fine along the lines of those reasons during Bradley's freshman year at college. Nevertheless, a problem eventually emerged. The UT football team permitted around 100 players to participate in daily practices, but for some reason, the squad was deficient in the number of quarterbacks on their roster. That was primarily because of position substitutions. For example, several of the would-be quarterbacks would serve as tight ends, or running backs, or even offensive linemen on occasion at the practices. Coach Royal then had his work cut out for him, as he could have only 35 players suit up for the actual games, as per the rule in the 1960s.

Bill Bradley certainly planned on suiting up for UT's varsity football team in his sophomore year, but he also planned on playing on the school's baseball team in the spring of 1966. Unfortunately for him, he met with an abrupt change of plans. The Texas varsity football squad was hit with numerous injuries following the 1965 season, particularly among the quarterback position. The UT football team was preparing for their spring practices when a meeting occurred between Bradley and Coach Royal.

"Coach Royal said that they were light on quarterbacks, or they didn't have the quarterbacks that they thought they would have," Bradley said. "So I went to go to baseball practice one day, and he (Coach Royal) said to me, 'No Bill, you signed a contract.' I felt that I could still play baseball for UT, especially after we had a handshake to seal the deal."[5]

Where Bradley comes from in the Hill Country of East Texas, a man's handshake is his solemn promise. If you go against that, your trustworthiness goes down quite a bit. This is not to say that the young multi-sport athlete was naïve about the ways of contractual obligations. Far from it in fact. But this episode did open his eyes to how things can quickly change, despite what he felt was right.

"Of course, in recruiting they promise you a lot, as far as that's concerned," admitted Bradley. "But in my sophomore year, he (Coach Royal) said to me, 'You gotta play spring football.' It kinda upset me, and it got me off to a bad start with him a little bit. So I went into spring football training in my sophomore year, and I had a real good spring training, so I started as a sophomore on the varsity football team. I remember that my dad found out about me not being able to play baseball in college anymore, and he wasn't too happy, because he loved baseball as much as I did."[6]

Confirmation of Joe Bradley's displeasure with Coach Royal's decision comes from Bob Stephenson, a longtime friend of Bill's who went to high school with him.

"In my estimation, baseball was his sport," said Stephenson in a 2020 conversation. "He even says the same thing. But his parents wanted him to go to college, so he went to the University of Texas with the understanding that he could still play baseball. His daddy drove to Austin to confront Darrell Royal when Royal told him no, he (Bill) wasn't going to play baseball. And he didn't. But I know his dad made the trip to Austin. Coach Royal had basically told Bill previously that he could play baseball, but Royal backed up and changed his mind."[7]

Despite Bill Bradley's bitterness regarding his coach's decision, the extra football practice time during the spring of 1966 proved to be most beneficial to him. Royal inserted him into the UT varsity lineup as the team's starting quarterback, a position that required the athleticism that Bradley provided. But Bradley did more than just taking his stance under center, however. He was also the team's first-string punter, and his booming left-footed launches from punt formation regularly gave Royal's punt coverage team plenty of time to run downfield and make the tackle.

"Well, I did a better job of all of my positions as a punter," remembered Bradley. "Kicking to me was like passing a football. That's how I practiced. I had my friends run 25 or 30 yards down the field, and I would punt the ball to them. Kicking the ball with my left foot gives it a different spin. I did it so much, it was like playing golf with your foot instead of with a golf ball and a golf club. That foot was my club. I could extend my leg like a ballet dancer. You know, I just practiced it over and over. I could aim for a sideline and usually hit within a 10- to 15-yard target between the 20-yard line and the goal line. I worked on it every day. Why even growing up I would kick it straight up in the air as high as I could punt it, then run and catch it. Not for a long distance mind you, but just a little bit. And I did that all day long when I was by myself. You have to be an athlete to do that I would think. You have to have great coordination, and you have to have good body functions. I can punt with either foot, but I like to punt with my left foot. Once you get good at punting, you just welcome it. It's something that's in your blood."[8]

Speaking of blood, the sport of football is thoroughly injected into the blood of Texans. From the pee-wee kiddie level to the professionals and every level in between, football dominates the hearts and minds of practically every true Texan. And the intense following that the sport receives at the University of Texas at Austin is undisputable. Bill Bradley's first year as the school's starting quarterback in 1966 was successful by national standards, at least as far as achieving a winning record was concerned. The team started that season by winning only two of their first five games, however. The Longhorns would appear to have a mediocre year, at least until the final three contests of the season. It was then that they somehow managed to claim victories against Baylor, Texas Christian, and Texas A & M, which gave UT a final ranking of 40th in the nation and a berth in the Bluebonnet Bowl, held at Rice Stadium in Houston. Despite their winning streak at the end of the year, Bradley contributed only four scoring passes in 1966, while tossing nine interceptions.

Individual statistics notwithstanding, Coach Royal's charges could still salvage their season with a win in the Bluebonnet Bowl. This they did, as they played one of their finest games of the year in the meeting with the University of Mississippi, whom they easily defeated, 19-0. UT ended the 1966 season with a mark of 7-4. It was during this year, Bradley's first year as the team's quarterback, that he experienced his first collegiate injuries. While it was true that he sustained a knee injury in high school, the injuries that he weathered playing football at the college level were more pronounced and more numerous.

"I had a couple big-time concussions in college," recapped Bradley. "I also tore up my knee, and I had to have that operated on. I also had a separated shoulder and a hip pointer. So I played a whole season in college with tape from my ankles all the way up to my shoulder on one side of my body.

"At Texas, we had a great rehabilitation program. We had doctors on the staff, and we had two or three in-house rehab specialists in college. They were in there day in and day out, and they were there for every game. They got me back playing pretty good after having a big-time knee operation. They took off a part of my kneecap...about a quarter of it. So of course I hobbled for about a year and a half. We finished 7-4, and that's with a crippled quarterback. You couldn't let your buddies down. I was still able to perform and play. Not at the highest level, but close to it."[9]

Bradley's level of play was expected to improve the following year, as was that of the rest of his teammates. The 1967 season for the UT football team was unfortunately no better than the 1966 season. The team floundered on offense once again, as they were only able to score a total of 186 points all year long. They lost their first two games against the University of Southern California and against Texas Tech. Then, lo and behold, they went on a six-game winning streak. Included in those victories were wins against four Southwest Conference teams and two Big 8 teams, including the University of Oklahoma in what was (and still is) known as "The Red River Rivalry," honored as such because it is the river that separates Texas and Oklahoma. UT then ended 1967 with two more losses to finish the year with a 6-4 record.

In college football today, there are several dozen different bowl games to finish each season. When a Division IA team wins at least six games, they become what is referred to as "Bowl Eligible." In the years that Bill Bradley played college football, however, there were far fewer bowl games to go around. Just because you won six games in 1967 did not necessarily mean that you would be invited to play in a bowl contest. A team during those years might also discover that they did not provide adequate competition to play in a bowl game, regardless of their win-loss record. The UT squad found this out the hard way when Coach Royal offered them an opportunity to have a say in whether or not the team would accept an invitation to play in the Bluebonnet Bowl, just as they had in 1966.

"And so in my junior year we finish 6-4," recalled Bradley, "and Coach Royal does not accept a bowl bid. That was because he didn't think that we were good enough. If you did that today you would get fired. But that happened, and I'll go to my grave believing that Coach Royal put some plants (players who would agree with the coach's assessment of the team) in there. We voted on it. The team was in a room when he said that we were not that good to go to a bowl game. And we took a vote, and our vote to accept a bowl bid missed by about 10 people.

"Now Coach Royal and I became great friends, but I will always go to my grave saying that some of those guys voting were plants in there, and some of the players were told to vote no. He had some people in there, and the way that he was structuring his talk, was that we weren't good enough to play in a bowl game. Well hell! We weren't that good the year before when we annihilated Ole Miss in the Bluebonnet Bowl! That's what happened with all of that stuff."[10]

Life at the University of Texas proved to be more than just playing football and playing in a bowl game, however. Bradley, as the team's starting quarterback, was certainly going to get plenty of attention on campus. His list of friends kept growing, as did the activities in which he participated. He was a well-rounded young man, who saw college as a great opportunity to learn and to experience a more cerebral life. It is also a fact that Bradley heartily enjoyed the fun that he was having at college.

"They always wanted to have some athletes to be in their fraternities, so they recruited you for a fraternity," said Bradley. "So I got to go to all the big parties, and they were trying to get you to sign up for their fraternities, because it was a public relations deal if they could do it. I ended up joining the Lamda Ki Alpha fraternity, but I wasn't very active in it. I still went to the pledge bar because I had friends and all that stuff. And you know that fraternities and sororities were big at the University of Texas."[11]

Bradley really did not spend a lot of time partying, at least in the traditional definition of the term. In fact, many of his fun times at college involved something that many of us do at least once a week. Some of us even do it every day.

"My good times in college had nothing to do with drinking and parties," remembered Bradley. "My beautiful times came from just being around people. I had a cement bench where I'd go with James Street (Bradley's teammate) to people-watch. We'd watch folks go by and then comment on what kind of day they were having. (Sometimes), we'd fall off that bench laughing. It's amazing what you can learn about people by watching them."[12]

Another thing that was amazing at UT, or that Bradley at least thought was important, was making friends who had a different skill set than himself. Just as college educational advisors get students to enroll in as many different courses as possible to give him or her a more well-rounded outlook on a variety of subjects, so too did Bill Bradley look at other students as friends who he was interested in...or at least curious about. As it turned out, he really did not have to look far to observe what others around him were doing.

"I'm not an artist," announced Bradley. "I'm not a painter, but my roommate was. His name is Ragan Gennusa. He was my starting receiver on the football team when I was a little older. We roomed together in the dormitory. Ragan was the classical tale of the starving artist. He had to go to regular classes too, but a lot of times he had a tackle box full of paint brushes and paints to go to art school on the UT campus. We used to kid him all the time. You know we thought that (carrying a tackle box to class) was a sissy thing to do (chuckle). So when he needed money getting out of school...you know, paying off loans and different things...he had to take a job at a printing company. And back then, they didn't have the high-tech computerized stuff that they do today. And so that's how he existed as an individual artist, and so from that, he scratched out a living. He ended up working for the state, and he advanced real fast in the art world.

"But he was our receiver back then. We didn't have but one

receiver then. It wasn't like football today where they have five receivers in the game at one time, with three on one side and two on the other. Back then, he was the only starting wide receiver on the field, other than the guys in the backfield."[13]

In the same vein, Bill Bradley was Darrell Royal's only starting quarterback...at least going into his senior year (1968). Throughout his time on the team, Bradley learned a lot from Coach Royal, specifically in the realm of leadership. He observed the class and dignity that his coach possessed, and he did his best to imitate it. He learned how to present himself, how to deal with both success and failure, and how to always give his opponents credit. He had a vibrant personality, which was a prominent factor in his life that did not need any adjustment. Bradley was a very outgoing young man when he first stepped foot on the UT campus, and he was more than willing to express himself to others and communicate to others, regardless of who they were or their connection to him and to the college. Predictably, Bradley's popularity on campus soared during his college years. He was able to quickly and successfully ingratiate himself with his fellow students, his professors, and his coaches, and in the process, his adjustment to college life at UT was relatively smooth.

He was also willing to give all of his coaches some credit as well.

"I learned from the best," said Bradley. "I was very fortunate in playing college football at the University of Texas under some really great coaches. Men like Darrell Royal, Fred Akers, and Mike Campbell. You know the quarterback gets a lot of the credit, but he gets a lot of the blame too."[14]

Unfortunately for Bradley, the UT football team started the 1968 season with a mark of 0-1-1, which practically guaranteed him at least a portion of the blame. It was like a broken record. Coach Royal's players began each of the previous three years slowly, with a trend of defeat hanging around their necks. It was obvious that a change of some sort had to be made in Bradley's senior year.

The problem was not really the way Bradley was playing. Rather, it was the Wishbone offensive strategy that Coach Royal preferred to continue to employ. During the 1960s, the sport of football was first and foremost a running game, with extraordinarily little passing. The Wishbone offense addressed a team's ability to run with the ball. It often featured a full house backfield, with three running backs taking their stances behind the quarterback. As the team's quarterback, the Wishbone offense required Bradley to take the snap from center, then run parallel to the line of scrimmage. He then had the option to either pitch the ball to one of his running backs, or to turn up field and carry it himself. The quarterback had to be able to read what the opposing defenses were trying to do against the Wishbone. If they attempted to pursue Bradley, he would then pitch the ball to one of his runners. If the opposing defenses paid more attention to his runners, then Bradley would get a chance to display his own running abilities.

Regrettably for Bradley, his own talents as the team's quarterback did not adequately address the typical Wishbone attack. Bradley was more of a throwing quarterback, and even though he could run with the ball, the structure of the Wishbone offense stuck to a regimented carry and pitch system. It did not allow for much ad-libbing, something that Bradley was athletic enough to be able to do quite well. Moreover, the Wishbone offense required different skills than just dropping back into the pocket and tossing the ball downfield.

"You know in Austin, Coach Royal wanted three running backs," said Bradley. "You know, three yards and a cloud of dust was the MO (modus operandi) there, because he had three great running backs. As a matter of fact, in 1968, all three starting running backs at Texas had 1,000 yards rushing. So we ran the Wishbone. We didn't throw the ball much at all in college. When I ran the Wishbone, I didn't run it very well."[15]

Despite being unsuccessful in running the Wishbone, Bradley was nevertheless named as the team's captain. It was an honor that is bestowed on young men who display their actions over their words, a constant sense of unselfishness, and a loyalty to the rest of the players.

"I had a ball in college," Bradley admitted.[16] "I became the leader of that team. I was the captain of that team, and that was a great honor for me. It meant everything to me.[17] I was also voted in my senior year the Harry F. Byrd Leadership Award. Harry Byrd was an old UT guy, and he was instrumental in having the UT band back in the day. So that was a band and a school thing that was a trophy. And so I was winning those kinds of awards.[18] But my buddies all played college football. My best friends were football players because they knew what my life was like."[19]

Bradley's life took a turn of sorts after the second game of the 1968 football season, however. Texas head coach Darrell Royal had done a lot of soul searching after that game, a 31-22 loss at Texas Tech. He came to a choice that would alter both Bradley's life and the team's fortunes. In retrospect, it was a wise decision. At that time, however, Royal did not know how the scenario that he was about to enact would play out. Nevertheless, he knew that something had to be done. He could not take mediocrity any longer.

"I'm sure that the pressure and stuff had been rolling downhill on him," admitted Bradley, "and Coach Royal had a 7-4 season, then a 6-4 season, and not winning during the first two weeks of the 1968 season. He was about to be fired. I'm sure that the powers that be, namely the UT Alumni, were putting some pressure on him, and it flowed down to the quarterbacks."[20]

Royal was sharing some of that blame, but he was worried, and he had good reason to worry. He watched his star quarterback throw four interceptions in the final game of the 1967 season, a 10-7 loss at College Station to the Texas A & M Aggies. Had UT won that game, they would have been chosen to go to the Cotton Bowl as winners of the Southwest Conference title. Bradley correctly surmised that "... two of those interceptions weren't really my fault, they were some other people's faults, but I'll take the blame for all four of them. You know, if they had been touchdowns, I would have gotten the credit for them. So that was a low point."[21]

Then Coach Royal saw virtually no improvement by Bradley during the first two games of 1968. The moment was now at hand for the two men to discuss this forlorn situation and to come to an under-standing.

"Coach Royal had a Royalism that said, 'When you throw the ball, three things can happen, and two of them are bad,'" remembered Bradley. "Well I knew that we had just played Texas Tech in our second game of '68. I threw two interceptions in that game, and that didn't help matters. So it was 5:30 in the morning, and we had just gotten back to campus at 3 a.m. The football manager at UT, Joe Dungeous, was knocking on my dorm door. He said, 'Bill, are you in there?' I said, 'Yeah, I'm in here. I'm trying to sleep.' He said, 'Coach Royal wants to see you in his office.' I knew that when you go to Coach Royal's office at 5:30 in the morning, and the team is 7-4, then 6-4, then 0-1-1, three things can happen, and all of them are bad. So I go into his plush office, with about two hours of sleep, and I'm sore and beat up. So he leans across his desk in his plush office and says, 'Bill, we're gonna make some changes around here, and we're gonna start with you. I just don't like the way you're running the offense. Now if you want to keep your scholarship, you'll come back out to practice today, and we'll find a spot for you.'

"When I get out of his office, and it's daylight now, I go out and I call home. I called my dad, a hard-drinking railroad man and a base-ball coach. I said, 'Cephus (that's what I called my father), I was called into the coach's office. I think that my life is over with down here at the University of Texas. I'm gonna hitch-hike home.' Then there was a long silence, and I said, 'Cephus, Daddy...are you there?' And the next thing that comes out of his mouth after a long silence is, 'To hell you are!' I said, 'What?' He said, 'To hell you are! The Bradley's don't quit. Omar Bradley (American General) didn't quit. He's your sixth cousin.' And this is before they named a baseball field after my dad. He said, 'To hell you are. You're not living there to quit. The Bradley's don't quit. You don't have a home here...you're not welcome here...if you quit.'"[22]

The meeting with Coach Royal and the eye-opening discussion with his father could properly be defined for Bradley as a meet and greet with a solid dose of reality. Today, Bradley has the advantage of looking back at that time and knowing that his impending demotion out of the UT starting quarterback position was what was best for both him and the team. But back when he was ousted from his prized role in 1968, he knew that he would be void of hindsight. He would thus have to make a decision that would be more of a roll of the dice than anything else.

"It was my last year in college," said Bradley, "and it (the demotion) hit home. And so I went back out after that. My best friend on the team was James Street. Everybody thought that I hated him for taking my place at quarterback. James could run the Wishbone offense. He was like a riverboat gambler to be able to do that kind of stuff. Hell, James and I ran around together. I taught him how to drive a car. He didn't even have a driver's license when he came to the University of Texas. He didn't have to say he was sorry for taking my job. Hell, losing that quarterback job to him was one of the best things that ever happened to me. Because I made it man. I was relieved. It felt like the pressure was off of me. My dad pretty much talked me into staying at the University of Texas. So I go back out there at the next practice. Every media outlet from Dallas, Houston, *Sports Illustrated*, and *Time Magazine* was there, because I just got demoted. And they were going to see what would happen. They didn't have any local television stations there...no cellphones or nothing like that.

"So I lined up at the wide receiver position running a pattern, just to get loose. And before the play, I told James, 'James, I don't care what I do...throw the ball where I can catch it.' So we're in our sweats and our t-shirts. I decided to loosen the ties on my sweatpants. About halfway down the field they started running down to my knees, then my pants went down to my ankles, and then down to the ground. All you saw was a jockstrap and a butt. That's where I caught the ball. So when I caught the ball and I was on the ground, I looked back at Coach Royal, and he was laughing his ass off. And as a team captain, that's the day that I became the leader of that team. That loosened up the whole team. That's the day that I got demoted. And at the end of that practice, I said, 'Hey look…screw all of this media stuff…whatever they print, don't pay any attention to it. Let's go out and win some football games!'"[23]

Bradley and his teammates did exactly that. In fact, they never lost another game that season. Bradley was switched by Coach Royal to the defense, specifically as a member of the defensive backfield. The position of cornerback was one where his athleticism and speed could be used and were, in fact, required. Moreover, he continued to use his speed returning punts and kickoffs, and he also continued his punting duties for the team. He finished the 1968 season with an average of 42 yards per punt (on 85 punts), which was good enough for the sixth best average in the nation. Furthermore, with his coach's decision, Bradley would no longer be in a position where he might run the risk of turning the ball over to his opponents. And most important of all, Bradley would continue in his role of team captain, and he continued to represent the team during the opening coin tosses. It was during one of those coin tosses in his senior year where he took the opportunity to distribute a savory sprinkling of Bradley "flair."

"I'm on defense now, and we're playing Texas A & M," said Bradley. "They are one of our rivals that we need to beat in the Southwest Conference. If we beat them, we would go to play the University of Tennessee in the Cotton Bowl (in Dallas). Me, Corby Robinson, and Chris Gilbert were our captains. And I did all the talking, as you can tell (laughter). So we go out for the opening coin toss, and we're playing at Kyle Field at the Texas A & M campus. So at the coin toss, we shake hands with the captains at A & M, and the referee flips the coin, and we win the coin toss. He says to me, 'Bradley, you make the call. It's your decision. What would you like to do?' And I looked at the referee after we shook hands with the captains, and I said, 'We don't give a fuck.' So he (the referee) turns around and looks at me, and he looks at the audience because the stadium is packed, and he says to me, "You can't say that! You've got to make a decision.'

The second time I said, 'We don't give a shit.' Then he said, 'Yeah well you've got to make a decision or we're going to flag you.' Then I said, 'We'll take the ball.' And I come over to the sideline, and Coach Royal says to me, 'Bill, what the hell are you doing out there?' And that was the first and only time that I saw Coach Royal smile."[24]

The smiles would be dispersed all along the UT sideline by the end of this game. Bill Bradley would go on to have arguably the greatest game that he ever had on a college football field. In this game, which ended with a 35-14 victory for UT, Bradley would get a chance to make good use of all of the previous training and time that he spent in the quarterback position, and that preparation benefitted him greatly while he played his new position of cornerback. Finally, good fortune was paying him a visit. It was as if the specter of Murphy's Law did an about face. Everything that could go right for Bradley in this game, did go right for him.

"I'm playing right cornerback in the game," recalled Bradley, "and A & M's quarterback was Ed Hargett. He had thrown 108 or more passes without an interception. But their offense used the same sprint out system that I had run in high school and in my first three years at Texas. I knew what Hargett was going to do, because I had just been learning it for the past five years. Before the game, Gene Stallings, the head coach of A & M, goes up to Hargett and pulls him over to the side and says to him, 'Hey Ed, that Bradley is just new over there at weakside cornerback. I want you to pick on his butt all day long.' So they did. And I knew what they were going to do. I wasn't even looking at the quarterback. So I get four interceptions in the game. We had played pass rush and all that kind of stuff, and that helped. But I knew what their quarterback was going to do, and when he threw the ball, I knew where he was going to throw the ball.

"So anyway, after I got the fourth interception, Ed Hargett the quarterback goes over to his head coach, Gene Stallings, on the sideline. I heard that he asked Stallings, 'Do you think that we ought to still pick on that Bradley guy?' That's the story that I heard from reliable sources."[25]

It did not take too long before Bill Bradley was more thought of as a defensive back than as a former quarterback. That one game at Texas A & M certainly stood out as a highlight, but those four interceptions versus the Aggies was only possible because he studied opposing offenses. Additionally, his overall insight into a passer's tendencies on any one play, formed the foundation of his future film studies. He began learning how a cornerback views the game, and how a cornerback can become successful. When he had questions, the Longhorn coaches were more than happy to help him dissect the strategy. "It served me well," said Bradley concerning his film education and the repetition gleaned from the team's practices. "I studied the cornerback position, and I had good coaches."[26]

One of those coaches was Mike Campbell, a stern, hard-nosed defensive coach for UT. He was the type of coach who tried to imitate the mannerisms of a demanding and tough coach, like a Vince Lombardi of the Green Bay Packers or a Knute Rockne of Notre Dame University. You might think that Bradley, being the free spirit that he was (and still is) would have had difficulty adjusting and dealing with Coach Campbell, but rather surprisingly, that was not the case.

"I know one time we were playing Rice University," recalled Bradley. "Of course, everybody played off coverage back then. You didn't see much press coverage...or bump and run as they called it. So in that game I noticed the Rice receivers got down in a three-point stance. When they did that, if they were on the right side of the offense, they put their right hand down, and leaned their shoulder up and looked in at the ball. They were not standing up. They were in a sprinter's stance, really. Then it just dawned on me. I kinda knew what they were going to do by watching their receivers, and by previously playing quarterback. I ran up and timed it up and knocked the receiver back on his back. The quarterback sprinted out the other way, then stopped with the intention of throwing the ball back to that receiver on a go route. But that receiver was lying down on the ground behind the line of scrimmage after being knocked down by me. The quarterback then pulled the ball down, and one of our defensive linemen sacked him and caused a fumble which we recovered. That play helped us to win the Rice game.

"So I came off to the sideline. Coach Campbell grabbed me by the shoulder pads, turned my right shoulder to his face, and with his left hand motioning to the field, he said, 'Bradley! What in the *hell* are you doing out there?' I looked at him and I said, 'Coach, I was just taking advantage of the situation.' I thought that he was fixing to jump my rear end. Instead, he just said, 'Well just do it again (chuckle)!'"[27]

Bradley's anecdote would illustrate just one insightful example of his success during a great senior year for him at UT. He proved to his coaches and his teammates that besides punting and punt and kickoff returning, he was also adept at playing the cornerback position. Moreover, the way that he accepted the demotion was vital to both him and to his team. It showed how unselfish he was...that he put the team before himself. Even more so than before, he was looked upon as a team leader.

The Palestine cornerback also continued to enjoy his time at UT, simply by having fun. College students throughout history have gone out of their way for a laugh. Lasting friendships are typically born and solidified during this time of their lives, and Bradley was no different in this regard, even when some of the examples to illustrate this fact involved the President of the United States and some of his Secret Service agents.

"I had a buddy who was also one of my fraternity brothers in college named Joe Batson," said Bradley. "Joe was dating Linda Bird Johnson, the daughter of President Lyndon Baines Johnson. And so me and James Street went over to Joe's apartment one night when he had a date with Linda Bird. He was living in the Amarillo area of Texas. Joe said, 'Come on over, I want you to meet Linda Bird.' So James and I go over to Joe's apartment, and when we walk in, there's Joe and Linda Bird, me and James, and about four other guys dressed up like the Blues Brothers. They were the secret service, but they looked like the Blues Brothers (laughing). Linda Bird meets us, then goes into the bathroom. She had to fix herself up. And so they come out and they leave! With a couple of those Blues Brothers!

"Now there's two of them (Secret Service agents) that stayed in the apartment. And so James says, 'Aww man, it's great to meet you, but we've got to leave.' And they stood up and said, 'You cannot leave.' We said, 'Excuse us? What do you mean we can't leave? It's a free country, isn't it?' They said, 'No, you have to stay here with us until they get through with their date.' That was because they didn't want anyone to get out. It was a pretty well guarded building. And so we're in there with the other two Blues Brothers, both of whom also played college football. And so we got to talking to them about football, and this, that, and the other thing. And they figured that we were really just a couple of good guys."[28]

Bradley and James Street had certainly never met any Secret Service personnel before this evening. Both of them realized that these two men who worked for the federal government were officially in charge, and neither UT athlete wanted to do anything that would get them in any kind of trouble. So they played it cool and figured that they would make the most out of the situation. Regardless of how their state of affairs played itself out, both Bradley and Street knew that they should just take it easy and enjoy their new "friends."

"They said that we couldn't leave, so we didn't leave," asserted Bradley. "You know we didn't want to break any rules. So we got to know them (the two Secret Service agents) during the next couple of hours. And so we got to talking to them. 'What are those big briefcases that you guys got? What's in there? Paperwork?' They said, 'No, we can't let you see it.' We said, 'Aww, c'mon. We ain't telling nobody.' And I'm sure it's okay to say this now. We say, 'So let's see what's in there.' So one of them opened it up. It was almost like a small Samsonite luggage, but it was a briefcase. They opened it up and it had a Glock in there, two hand grenades...it had tasers...it had all kinds of stuff. And we got to see that talking to these guys. And when Joe, Linda Bird, and the other two Blues Brothers got back to the apartment, we got to go home."[29]

Shortly after this episode, both Bradley and Street got a chance to experience another unusual and unexpected situation. But in this circumstance, both young men actually had a say in what they would do. They had to make an immediate choice as to their actions, and they almost paid a high price for their decision.

"We got a phone call early one morning from Coach Royal," remembered Bradley. "He was having breakfast at President Lyndon Baines Johnson's ranch, which is not that far from Austin. Coach Royal said, 'We (the President and Coach Royal) want you both to come out here,' because we were the two quarterbacks. The President wanted to meet us, and he wanted to hang out with us. But James and I had dates with a couple of girls that morning. Coach Royal was out there waiting for us to come, but we never went (chuckle). We stood him up. Boy Coach Royal got hot at us. He almost took our scholarships away for that.

"So whenever we were questioned about it over the years, James and I always admitted that we stood LBJ up for breakfast one time. It happened. Coach Royal was *hot*. You don't ever stand Coach Royal up. It doesn't matter if he was having breakfast with a janitor. But later on in his life, when Coach Royal still had his faculties, he would laugh about it. Because we would take him out to lunch when he was in a facility. He'd say, 'These two guys (Bradley and Street) almost got me fired! They stood up the President of the United States!' He would start laughing about it afterwards...long afterwards."[30]

It is a bit of a stretch to presume that Bradley pulled this no-show stunt on Coach Royal and President Johnson as a form of payback for Royal taking away his opportunity to play college baseball. In reality, Bradley probably was not even thinking about that at the time. The simplest explanation is usually the most accurate and the most plausible. Bradley and Street just wanted to date a couple of college co-eds. Nothing more to it than that. As time wore on, and as Coach Royal's anger had settled down, he would later claim that Bill Bradley was the best athlete that he ever coached at the University of Texas. He also admitted in 1973 that "...there was a magic about him (Bradley). He is the kindest, sweetest, most loyal man I've ever met, and if I ever get into trouble, he'll be one of the first persons I'll call on for help."[31]

It was a statement of friendship between the generations of these two men who were on the same team, and who had one specific aim... to be successful. Both men—despite their age difference—ended up helping each other throughout their lives.

Sadly, Bradley's time at college also included witnessing the tragic action of another young man who could not be helped. Charles Whitman was a student at UT in the summer of 1966 when he climbed up to the Texas Tower building, and at a height of almost 300 feet above the ground, he began shooting at people with a high-powered rifle with a scope attached to it. He managed to kill 14 innocent bystanders and wounded 31 others before he was finally stopped by a shotgun blast from the police. It was indeed a harrowing event which garnered national headlines. Whitman had difficulty coping with the demands of college, and he allowed his anger and mental and/or emotional distresses to get the best of him. He also suffered from terminal cancer, and that certainly must have weighed heavily on his mind.

"He was going to die," Bradley recalled, "and that tower just blew his mind. He snuck up there with a chest filled with a big-time shooting rifle, and lots of ammunition. There was a ledge with a wall all the way around it, with little square holes in it for drainage. He ended up killing the people who were running the elevator, then he locked the elevator door behind him. When he got up to the top, he started shooting people below, and nobody could get to him because he had all of those little slits to shoot through. I was on the edge of campus when the shooting started. I saw a lot of people hiding behind trees. Whitman shot a guy sitting on a chair along the stores of the main drag. He also shot a guy getting a haircut right in his temple. The police and some citizens finally got up there and stormed him. They got to within 10 feet of him. When he turned around, they just blew his head off. You couldn't recognize him after that.

"It was an event that was really dark and sad. He was dying from cancer, and he really hated that clock tower, based on his writings that the detectives discovered later. He was just out of his mind."[32]

Bill Bradley's experiences at the University of Texas were nowhere near as catastrophic as Whitman's. But unfortunately for Bradley, his final days at UT included one major mistake that has haunted him for many years. Most college football players today never stay in school long enough to get their degree. Some even leave before their senior year for the opportunity to play pro football. Bradley certainly attended UT in his senior year, but he was guilty of leaving the university before he was supposed to graduate in the spring of 1969.

"As soon as I got drafted in the NFL, I dropped out of school," admitted Bradley. "At that time, I had taken a lot of the prerequisite courses and a lot of the electives. But I still had some of the prerequisites that I needed to complete. But once I got drafted, I did something stupid. It was the most stupid thing that I've ever done, because I probably would have graduated. I dropped all of my classes. But I didn't drop them properly...I just left. If you do that, and you don't drop them the way that you're supposed to...legally in writing to the President of the college, you're in the wrong. If you do it right, you won't get challenged. If you don't do it right, you get five F's. If you don't drop your classes right, it's just like you're going to score and making no scores on any test."[33]

Another choice by Bradley also proved to be a mistake, albeit a smaller one than his improper method of dropping out of college. Unfortunately for Bradley, this particular error was one that he repeated often enough to cause him some physical consternation. Cutting classes has been a time-honored practice of high school and college pupils for generations. Bradley was certainly guilty of it on occasions, and Coach Royal had a remedy for such actions which would teach his student-athletes a lesson.

"I took a lot of classes where sometimes you were looked down upon if you were a jock," said Bradley. "I took speech classes and physical education classes, and they were easy. They called them crib courses, and I was good at them. But as far as Coach Royal was concerned, if you cut class, you had to report it, and then you had to run up and down the stands in the stadium and do some extra work on the field. *A lot* of extra work. I mean I've seen guys puking, so we went through that. Oh God, I did it (cut class) a lot, so I was running every day. You know, I had things to do, so I cut class, which was stupid. But I was getting pulled in different directions."[34]

Bill Bradley would certainly be pulled away from Texas after his college days, to go in a direction he had never been in before. Well, sort of.

3

A FISH OUT OF WATER

The annual pro football selection meeting is typically held in the last week of every April, and it has become a growing and colorful extravaganza over the past couple of decades. But in 1969, the event known to most fans as the NFL Draft occurred in February, shortly after the previous season ended. Bill Bradley did not know for certain if he was going to be drafted by any team, but he was not really worried all that much. If he was not drafted, or if he was not signed by a team as a free agent, he had some other plans waiting in the wings.

"If I didn't make it in sports, I probably would have been a physical education teacher or a coach in high school or in college," admitted Bradley. "We didn't think about making the pros too much when I was in school. That never entered my mind. Making pro football wasn't my motive. If I didn't make it, I could do other things. I thought about going out and trying to play baseball again for some team."[1]

The fact that Bill Bradley could play so many different positions in college was quite appealing to many pro football scouts. Versatility would be the common term highlighted in every scouting notebook when team front office personnel were discussing Bradley. Almost as appealing was the fact that he played for the University of Texas, a Division I college that regularly played against some pretty stiff competition in the Southwest Conference. Pro rosters in 1969 stated that you could only have 40 men on a roster, so anytime a team could obtain a player who could play well at more than one position, that performer instantly became more marketable. This fact still rings true today, even with the current larger roster numbers. That is because every team suffers multiple injuries during the course of a given year, so substitute players will always be needed. Bill Bradley was destined to find a place for himself on one pro team or another.

"Every once in a while, you see some diversity," said Bradley. "The teams that are able to do that are typically real productive. I saved three roster spots because I could do more than one job. I was able to do four, sometimes five different things on the field."[2]

Naturally, Bradley would have preferred to play for a pro football team that was close to his home. Both the Dallas Cowboys and the Houston Oilers were likeable to him in that regard. His family members would be able to see him play more often if he stayed in Texas. But Bradley was wise enough to realize that just because you want something to happen, that does not necessarily mean that it will happen.

"Dallas had scouted me *a lot*," remembered Bradley. "(Scouting Director) Gil Brandt and (General Manager) Tex Schramm promised me that when the draft came in, they were going to draft me in the late second round. Well the second round came and went, and I don't even remember who they took. But then again, he (Brandt) was supposed to be the guru of Dallas' talent."[3]

Regardless of what team would eventually draft Bradley, he knew that he was not going to make a lot of money as a rookie. The American Football League and the National Football League would be merging into one league—the new NFL—in 1970. But from 1967 on, both leagues agreed to using one common draft, which ended the bidding wars between the two leagues up to that time. Now, one AFL team would make a draft selection, to be followed by an NFL team, then back to another AFL team, and so forth. It was deemed a fair and equitable way to share the college talent, and the team owners were certainly happy for it. Player salaries dropped exponentially after 1967.

"Before the merger, the players made a lot of money," asserted Bradley. "They were making $300,000, $400,000, or $500,000 per contract. But the merger meant that you had to take what you were offered, because there was no longer competition for the two leagues to pay you a lot of money."[4]

Bill Bradley finally got selected in the third round of the 1969 NFL Draft. Today, every ounce of the draft is televised, and every draftee is investigated by the media pundits to the 10th degree. Such was not the case back in 1969.

"I was sitting at home," remembered Bradley. "We weren't watching the draft. There wasn't any draft on television at that time. The Philadelphia Eagles' head scout called and told me that they wanted to draft me in the third round, but you didn't follow each round back then, like they do now. After the third round was over the Eagles called me again and told me, 'We selected you.'

"The head coach of the Eagles at that time, Joe Kuharich, talked to me on the phone. He said, 'Mr. Jackie Graves and Mr. Herman Ball (who were two Eagles scouts) really liked your punting, and we want to set you up as a punter/player.' We were happy in the household...just really happy. We celebrated by hugging and kissing. It was all worth it...all those years of practicing and playing the game. But I still had to make the team."[5]

As Bradley alluded to, just because a player got drafted, it did not necessarily mean that he would make the team's final roster. He still had to go through training camp and impress his new coaching staff enough to make them want to keep him on the team. He had already impressed the pro scouts, especially after the way his final college season ended. When you intercept four passes in one game against a tough opponent like Texas A & M, you are bound to make people take notice of your talents and abilities.

"Those interceptions did affect the pro scouts," said Bradley. "I got some in another game too, and I got some in the Cotton Bowl game versus Tennessee. So now I'm on their list. They're thinking this guy is a punter, but he can also play defensive back, he can do special teams, he can be an emergency quarterback, and he can be really good. He's got great ball skills. I'm sure that's how those scouting reports went."[6]

Bradley's ace in the hole when it came to his multiplicity on the gridiron was not so much that he could play several positions, but that he could do so many different things really well on a football field. That included running with the ball, employing a good deal of closing speed in order to make a tackle, reading what a quarterback plans on doing, leaping high in the air to deflect or intercept a pass, setting up his blockers on punt returns, busting a wedge on kickoffs, etc. Many players can do some of those things, but few were the number of men who could perform all those duties exceedingly well like Bradley could. He had the confidence to know that his was a success story waiting to happen, as he fulfilled numerous roles for the Eagles. For their part, the Philadelphia coaches knew that they would be able to find a spot for him on their team. The money question now took center stage for Bradley to think about. How much would his new team pay him? As a rookie in the NFL, there was a generally accepted minimum wage, and Bradley ended up being offered just above that mark.

"I signed my first contract for $15,500 a year for my rookie year, and $17,500 a year for my second year," remembered Bradley. "That is not a lot of money, especially when compared with what pro football players are making today. And I think that every player should make what they can get, because the owners are certainly making a lot of money."[7]

Bradley would eventually have to address the money question several times during the course of his NFL career. But for now, he had some other things to consider. Because he was an All-American at the University of Texas, Bradley was selected to play in several All-

Star games before he joined the Eagles in training camp. They included the Hula Bowl in Hawaii, the Coaches All-America Game in Lubbock, Texas, and the College All-Star Game in Chicago, where the previous year's Super Bowl champions would play a team of the best college players in the nation. The Eagles management conferred with him prior to those games and suggested that he join the team afterwards.

"They didn't have a combine back then," expressed Bradley, "but they did have these All-Star games. They gave the rookies a taste of pro ball. The Eagles management called me on the phone and determined in order to save time and traveling back and forth, that I should play in those All-Star games before I went up north to Pennsylvania to participate in the Eagles training camp."[8]

The three aforementioned All-Star games are not held anymore. That is primarily because players were getting injured in these exhibitions, none of which counted in any standings whatsoever. That is also true regarding the situation in today's NFL preseason games. Most of the veteran players on each team rarely play much at all during the preseason, especially if they are star players. Rookies are chosen to play most of the time in those games, primarily to give them an opportunity to show to their coaching staff what they can do. That is the situation that Bradley found himself in during the summer of 1969. Two of the three All-Star games that he participated in were rather nondescript affairs, where he played well, but he did not really accomplish anything spectacular. Such was not the case in the College All-Star game in Chicago, where he came face to face with a pro football legend, and somehow got the best of him.

"Well back then a lot of times, they taught the quarterbacks to look to see if the middle area downfield was closed, like if you had a free safety in the deep middle, or if the middle was open," explained Bradley. "So that's how I would bait some of the quarterbacks into throwing where they thought I wouldn't be. You would have to talk to Joe Namath. I baited him into an interception in the College All-Star Game, when we played the New York Jets (the winners of Super

Bowl III) in 1969. That's an interception that I've always talked about. They (the Jets) had to come from behind in the last two minutes to beat us with Namath.

"I would disguise my coverage, like it looked open in the middle, and then I would wind up intercepting passes over the middle of the field. And that's how I used to do it. I studied the quarterback's eyes. I taught all of my players, whenever I was coaching, to take a certain amount of time, and just watch the eyes of a quarterback as he's dropping back to pass. For example, there's a quarterback who I'm not going to mention, but there's a quarterback who gave me clues. I just studied him and all the other quarterbacks. Their first look, and how they set up to throw the ball, and the positioning of their hands on the ball. I mean really technically watching the quarterback. So that's what I did when I played. I would watch the end zone copy of the game films on my own, and I would watch nothing but the quarterback's head...his eyes, his mannerisms...it helped me. I wouldn't let him look one way and get me out of where I was supposed to be. And a lot of times when they would look at me, I would be in a specific area, and then get back to the right area, and then I'd see the ball thrown, and I would go get it."[9]

Strategically minded and athletically sound, Bradley would now have to go and get up to Pennsylvania following the three All-Star games in which he played. The Keystone State was not completely new to him, as several years before, he would venture up there to play in the Big-33 Game. Even some of the Philadelphia Eagles' practice facilities were familiar to him.

"Well for the Big-33 Game, the Eagles' training camp was in Hershey when we were practicing for our game against the Pennsylvania team," recalled Bradley. "And I'm sure that maybe those scouts who eventually scouted me were hanging out at that Big-33 Game. I had no prejudice against playing for Philadelphia. At that time (in the summer of 1965), we dressed in the same dressing room as the Eagles players did for their practices. And they had a practice or two while we were going toward the end of our game preparations, because they were just coming into their summer training camp.

"They were professionals, and they had jobs in the offseason. They had six months on and six months off. And heck I saw pro football players smoking in the dressing room! I couldn't believe it! You know back then it (pro athletes smoking) was common though. And there wasn't a whole lot of players smoking cigarettes, but a few guys did. Because I had such a good time at the Big-33 Game, I remembered it four years later when I got to the pros."[10]

Few are the players who have a good time at any kind of a sports training camp, but Bradley was a different type of character. He knew that he would have to apply himself in order to make the team. He also wanted to prove to his new coaches and to his new teammates that his exploits described in his previous press clippings while he was in college were not exaggerated. He ultimately wanted the Eagles community to know that they did the right thing in drafting him, regardless of which position he would play.

Because he was drafted as a punter first and foremost, he knew that he was going to get his first opportunities at summer training camp by punting the ball. So Bradley punted the ball...a lot. Repetition after repetition. Kicking it high and kicking it deep. All of the hard work that he had previously done punting the ball from his childhood on up started to pay off. He consistently booted the ball 65 yards in practice, and his impressive kicks were often extremely high. No one really measured the height of his kicks, but most of them are timed to see how long they stay in the air. Eagles beat writer Gordon Forbes described quite a few of his punts as "practically non-returnable moon shots."[11]

"They stayed up over six seconds," admitted Bradley. "The average lineman in college can run the 40-yard dash in 5.5 seconds, so you can guess the coverage on them. I try to keep the ball in the air 4.5 to 5 seconds. The average is somewhere between 4.1 to 4.3 seconds. It seemed that I always had a natural rhythm for punting."[12]

One Eagles assistant coach instantly noticed Bradley's punting rhythms at the practices. "I believe that I never would have made the Eagles if it hadn't been for Marv Levy helping me with my punting," Bradley modestly said. "Marv was the very first fulltime special teams coach in the NFL, along with Dick Vermeil. Coach Levy was just a good guy. Basically, about the third practice, when we were at two-a-days (two practices held on the same day; one in the morning, and one in the afternoon), he (Levy) came out and said, 'Bradley, you're going to be my punter, so take care of your body.' And that's when I kinda said to myself, 'Hey, I might make this team.' And that's how I did it. I made the team by punting."[13]

The trauma that is experienced by a rookie prospect in the NFL awaiting word on whether he has made the team is nerve-wracking, to say the least. Some players try to put it out of their minds, while others worry incessantly. Some of those worriers pace back and forth along their dorm rooms. Others put some headsets on and listen to music. Still others bury their heads in their playbooks, hoping to continue the process of memorizing their plays. Playbooks are the most important commodity for a young player to possess. As long as you have it in your grasp, you are still a member of the team. But as soon as you have to relinquish it, you are generally noticed by your teammates as a casualty...as a "former" player who was just cut from the squad.

"Back then, they (the coaches) pretty much found you around the facilities when you were at the dormitory or at the practice field," Bradley explained. "They would send somebody over to your dorm room. And they always had this saying...it's an old saying: 'Bring your playbook...Coach Williams wants to see you.' So that meant that you were probably cut. Mostly the head coach usually does it. Some of them have different coaches do it, but they've just got to get the word out (to the player). And that's how it was done then. You could get cut anytime. So if they told you to bring your playbook, you usually knew that you were out of there."[14]

But hope was not lost for some of those players who found themselves severed from the team's active roster. There were often a few men who found favor with the coaches, and who managed to show enough skills, abilities, and talents for the team to really want to keep them around.

"And then sometimes it may be, 'Hey we're going to release you, and if nobody (another NFL team) picks you up, then we're going to put you back on the practice squad,'"said Bradley.[15]

The rookies who make an active NFL roster rarely take the league by storm, however, and neither did Bradley. But he was not fazed by the enormity of the professional ranks. He was certainly a free spirit, but he had a calmness to him that belied his young age. He was the subject of plenty of attention while playing for UT, so he was fairly used to capacity crowds in the stands and being interviewed by many different members of the media in Philadelphia. Most of the practices at training camp were scrimmages, where the Eagles offense would go up against the Eagles defense. The preseason games (which did not count in the actual league standings) however, were completely different. That was a time when all rookies got a chance to play the sport against an opposing team in an actual game, not just in a scrimmage. There would be anywhere from five to six preseason games in 1969 for every NFL team, except for those who played in the Pro Football Hall of Fame Game in Canton, Ohio. The teams playing in that contest would play a seventh preseason game.

Philadelphia's preseason slate in 1969 began all the way across the country in Portland, Oregon. That city did not have a pro team of its own, but during the 1960s and 1970s, the NFL regularly experimented with playing several preseason games in different cities, if for no other reason than just to gauge fan support in those cities for the game. The Eagles' first opponent would be the Atlanta Falcons, a team filled with a multitude of young players, just as they were. Philadelphia gave Atlanta a tough time before falling to the Falcons, 13-10. When Bill Bradley stepped onto the field at Portland's Multnomah Stadium on August 9, 1969, it would mark his very first pro football game.

Philadelphia's new head coach, Jerry Williams, was similarly enjoying his very first pro football game as a head coach. Well, sort of. Williams had a distinguished career as a head coach for the Calgary Stampeders in the Canadian Football League prior to 1969. But he was nevertheless familiar with the city of Philadelphia, having served as an assistant coach for the Eagles from 1957 to 1963.

Bill Bradley was busy getting more and more familiar with the city also, especially after he officially made the Eagles roster. There was a lot to see in Philadelphia, from Independence Hall, to the Liberty Bell, to the Art Museum, etc. And you can bet that he enjoyed indulging in the city's famous cheesesteaks. He would often be seen riding his bicycle up to 40 miles round-trip through Philadelphia's distinct and scenic neighborhoods, from Germantown to Fairmount Park, through Center City, and then through the Italian market section of South Philadelphia. He moved into an apartment with fellow Texan and fellow special teams player Billy Hobbs, a place where Bradley admitted to "having some fun."[16]

"We have a good time up here," Bradley acknowledged when discussing his off hours with roommate Hobbs. "There's a lot of history here (in Philadelphia). We like to travel around and see it."[17]

Bradley would also be having fun playing the game. Team-wise, he would be the Eagles' first-string punter, and he would also return punts and kickoffs for Philadelphia. He also performed a necessary service for the team during practices, as he would play quarterback for the scout team, which was comprised of a group of Eagles players who would run plays similar to what their upcoming opponent typically ran, in an effort to help Philly's first-string defense prepare for what they would see from their foes in the upcoming game. It was a duty which Bradley executed for several years. If for nothing else, it helped to keep his quarterbacking skills intact while he played other positions.

Speaking of skills, Bradley's defensive skills were enhanced by the tutelage that he received from veterans such as Joe Scarpati, Ron Medved, and Nate Ramsey, each of whom were starting defensive backs on the team in 1969, and each of whom had at least three years of experience at pro level.

"I was learning at that time," Bradley said. "And I got to work behind some really savvy veterans. We had some really good secondary people. Guys like Scarpati, Medved, and Ramsey had all played either safety or cornerback. I saw them as some of the best defensive backs in the league. I picked their brains whenever I could as to what they were seeing on the field, what clues they were looking for, and what they did to answer the offense. I picked Scarpati's brain as we walked out to practice every day. He knew football and he was very smart. And Ron and I did all the scout teams for the offense, so I learned a lot of stuff that way too.

"You have to learn how to anticipate and really read the quarterback. I studied a lot of film from the end zone, instead of the wide angle from the sideline. I would look at it, but when I studied film, I would study nothing but the quarterback, to see what his tendencies were...to see how he tipped on plays. If you're playing a lot of zone defense, the films show the safeties how to break on the ball, how to stay in their position, and how to get an advantage on the quarterback...just by studying the little hints and stuff. But you gotta be right on it. You can't start making things up and say to your coaches, 'Well the quarterback looked over here.' You've gotta understand the whole body language of the quarterback, the receivers, and the whole picture. So that helped me."[18]

The learning would continue for the Eagles as they finished their 1969 preseason with a record of 3-2, with wins over the Miami Dolphins, the New York Giants, and the Washington Redskins. Bradley not only did a lot of punting during the preseason games, but he also saw some action in the punt returner and defensive back positions. All in all, it was a good set of exhibition games for a young team and a brand-new head coach. Philadelphia's first regular season game of 1969 would be at home at Franklin Field, an old edifice next to the Schuylkill River, which had a capacity of just over 60,000.

The stadium was named after Philadelphia's most historical citizen, Ben Franklin. It was also the home field for the University of Pennsylvania Quakers, an Ivy league team. The Eagles opponent on opening day would be the Cleveland Browns, a solid team that had made it to the NFL Championship Game the previous year. The Browns had some injuries to key personnel going into this game, but they nevertheless had plenty of talent on their active roster, and they would give Philadelphia a good test to begin the 1969 season.

Cleveland built up a 27-7 lead through the first three quarters, then hung on in the fourth quarter to post a 27-20 victory. Bill Bradley punted the ball seven times in the game for an average of 35.9 yards per punt. He also returned one punt for eight yards. It was a rather ho-hum beginning for a guy who would rarely—if ever—be referred to as ho-hum in anything. As time and the 1969 season would go on, Bradley would improve his punting statistics, and he would see more action on the field.

The Eagles would win their first game of the season the following week, as they easily humbled the Pittsburgh Steelers, 41-27. Bradley would only have to punt twice in this onslaught for an average of 44 yards per punt. But the win over the Steelers did not really reflect on the Eagles' talents as much as it focused on Pittsburgh's lack of talent. In a few short years, the Steelers would become extremely competitive, but in 1969, they were anything but. The Philadelphia team were also not too tough of a foe, especially considering the results of their next three games. The Eagles would drop out of contention in their division standings with consecutive losses to the Dallas Cowboys (twice) and the Baltimore Colts.

The second loss to the Cowboys on October 19, 1969, was important to note regarding Bill Bradley, however. He was making a trip back to his home state, and there would be a lot of local curiosity among his fans from his University of Texas days. They all wanted to see him succeed at the professional level, so many of them got tickets and filled up the Cotton Bowl (a stadium where Bradley had played many times before while he was in college) on this day. As usual, Bradley did a good job punting for the Eagles, averaging 44.7 yards per punt on seven punts. He also returned two kickoffs and four punts in the game. But what set this game apart for the Palestine product was that he was finally able to play a portion of the game in the second half as a defensive safety. During the fourth quarter of that game, he would foreshadow some of his future gridiron exploits.

The Cowboys were pummeling the Eagles by a score of 42-7 on the way to a 49-14 romp, but before the final gun, Bradley gave his fans a moment to cheer. He intercepted a pass and returned it 56 yards for a touchdown. The story behind the interception is best told by Bradley himself, and it shows just how intelligent he was at being able to understand what an opposing offense was trying to do, then acting on it for the betterment of his team.

"In '69, I got to come in whenever somebody was beating us up so bad," Bradley related. "They would put some of us rookies in then because I would hound the coaches. I'd say, 'Hey Coach, there's no way we're probably going to win this game. Why don't you let some of us rookies go in to see what we can do, and so the veterans won't get hurt?' So I talked to Coach Jimmy "Gummy" Carr (Bradley's defensive backs coach in 1969). I talked him into putting me in that game against Dallas. They were our big rival, and they were beating us so bad...they were up by 35 points at that time. I hounded the coach until he threw me in the lineup. 'Get in there damn Bradley!' he yelled.

"So I go in, and Dallas had the ball near midfield. They were giving (Dallas quarterback) Roger Staubach some time and experience. He had just come back from the service (the U.S. Navy), and their other quarterback (Craig Morton) had done a good job and was on the bench in the fourth quarter. So Staubach was in the game when they called a play for a tight end named Mike Ditka. And so I was in the game, and we're blitzing everybody. And when we blitzed everybody, that meant that the safety (Bradley) had to come over and cover the tight end. So you try to lay on the blitz to get the ball back with a sack or a fumble or whatever. And so, I had to come over and cover Ditka. Well back then I was studying and studying, and I played quarterback in junior high, high school, and in college, so I kinda knew what they were doing.

"So I ran over there to cover a quick slant or a quick hitch by the tight end. When you have an all-out blitz called, the quarterback will try to get rid of the ball quickly. When Ditka saw me running to his slant from way over the other side of the field, he straightened up and ran a straight up pattern, which wasn't what Staubach expected him to do. I ran to the spot where Staubach threw it. I caught the ball about four yards past the line of scrimmage, ran down the field, and scored. It was the first time that I had ever touched the ball on a non-punting down, and as a backup guy...a practice team guy. And the funny thing about it was that (Dallas wide receiver) Bob Hayes was on the other side of the field, and he ran to try to catch me at the other end zone. He *did* catch me, but I scored, and he hit me right at the goal line a little late, and he got a 15-yard penalty for unnecessary roughing. After seeing the film, he (Hayes) was just flying, and my heart was pounding. We had little battles going on...a lot of mouthing and all that kind of stuff."[19]

Bradley may have precipitated Hayes' reaction when he (Bradley) was run out of bounds a few minutes earlier by Dallas reserve running back Craig Baynham on a punt return. Bradley took umbrage at the way that Baynham had shoved him out of bounds, so he threw the ball at Baynham in a not-so-gentle way. The referee then threw his yellow flag at Bradley and gave the Eagles a 15-yard penalty for unsportsmanlike conduct. For the first time in his life, Bradley received a smattering of boos in the Cotton Bowl for the incident. Later in the fourth quarter, Bradley took aim at Dallas running back Les Shy, and delivered a clothesline tackle to bring Shy down. Such tackles were legal back in those days. Bradley just took advantage of the situation.

"We were just getting hammered by Dallas, and we were getting pissed off," remembered Bradley. "Then one thing starts another. They might hit somebody late, or block somebody below the knee. It was just our rivalry. Regarding my interception, they didn't know that I ran the show team for our offense in practice. And I learned. I watched a lot of film. I watched so much film that I ended up living for a time with Steve Sabol of NFL Films (laughing)."[20]

Bradley's touchdown in the loss at Dallas may have provided a boost of momentum for his team. The Eagles went on a modest two-game winning streak following their big loss to the Cowboys. They defeated the New Orleans Saints, 13-10. Then they went to Yankee Stadium and pulled out a 23-10 win over the New York Giants. Philadelphia would have made it three wins in a row were it not for a 28-28 tie at Washington. Those three games proved that the Eagles were improving at least a little bit, but the good feelings would unfortunately not last. Bradley and his teammates lost five of their final six games to finish the 1969 season with a 4-9-1 record, good enough for last place in the NFL's Capitol Division.

No team ever enjoys finishing dead last at the end of a season. Looking back and looking for silver linings, however, only one of those five losses to finish the year was a blowout, a 27-3 loss to the Atlanta Falcons. One particular loss was indicative of the typical growing pains that rookies across the league experience. Bradley and his teammates were beating the NFL Coastal Division's leading team, the Los Angeles Rams, in the first half. A couple of Bradley's punts in that game were some of the longest and highest arching gems that had ever been seen in Franklin Field. One in particular was so deep, that Los Angeles punt returner Alvin Haymond had to retreat a full 10 yards from his stationary position in order to field the booming kick. It just seemed to stay up in the sunny Philadelphia sky forever. But later in the third quarter, Bradley fumbled one of his kickoff returns, and that miscue led to a Rams field goal in Los Angeles' 23-17 win. Such were the travails of a rookie in the NFL...you take the good with the bad.

The other defeats that Philadelphia weathered were by an average of only 4.2 points per game. And some of their close losses came at the hands of some pretty competitive teams, such as the Cleveland Browns and the Baltimore Colts (who won the NFL

Championship in 1968). So at least there was a token of positive feelings in barely losing to very good teams to sum up the 1969 season for Bradley and the Eagles.

"If I were to give a grade to our team in '69, as far as standings and record-wise, we would be a D or an F," said a judicious but realistic Bradley. "But I would say playing-wise, I'd say that we were probably graded about a C. In every one of our games we were competitive you know, for the most part. So we would win one out of every two or three or four, and that would give us enough hope. But we always practiced well, and we always played as hard as we could."
21

Playing the game hard was a prerequisite for all pro players in the 1960s and 1970s, but there had to be more on their minds during those years. Pro football in 1969 and during that whole era was not a full-time occupation. Most players had to get a second job during the offseason, because most of them did not make a large sum of money playing football in those days. Bill Bradley was no different, at least not when discussing finances. But he certainly was different when discussing his lifestyle and his choices in life. He was a free spirit after all, and that mindset has never left him. Moreover, he was a curious sort...a guy who wanted to see new things and do new things. He was quite frugal with his money, and now he wanted to get a taste of what life in all its splendor had to offer. So in the spring and summer of 1970, he had some free time for the first time in his life. Six months of free time where he really had no entity requiring him to be at some particular place and complete some kind of chore. He was experiencing the beauty of freedom at this time, and he did what most young people do with a lot of free time. He went on a road trip.

Bradley's home state of Texas certainly possessed miles and miles of beautiful scenery, but he wanted to see what elements of nature's splendor and God's handiwork were waiting for him to explore and experience in the western states, like Wyoming and California.

"I bought a van and checked it out," said Bradley. "It wasn't fancy. It was a Jeep janitor's van. And before that I had a '62 Volkswagen bus. It was a big bus. It's probably worth a lot of money if I had kept it. So I decided that I could live in it and travel around the United States and get close to nature. So I decided that I could live in National Parks, and one of the first big ones that I stayed at was Yellowstone. I wanted to see America...the good side of it, not the hard side. So I did, and I stayed in National Parks, and I was a steward of the land. I kept my food up in the trees. I had a cook stove, a bed, and all that kind of stuff. And so I stopped at Yellowstone, and for $2, you could stay there for two weeks. And so I'd get in there, and I parked and I took care of the campground, and made people clean up their trash before they left. Well, I went to leave after two weeks, and as I was leaving, the game warden or the park ranger said to me, 'Hey Bradley, where are you going?' And I said, 'Well, my two weeks are up.' And he said, 'No, we like you. You're a good person for the parks and for recreation. Just pull out of here, turn around, give us another $2, and stay here another two weeks.' So I basically gave them $6 and stayed a month and a half at Yellowstone. And I migrated up to Yosemite, then over to Red Rocks, and several other different places."[22]

Despite what you might think, the sight of an NFL player visiting a National Park or two was not that uncommon in the 1960s and 1970s, especially if that player was not really that famous. A player with a household name such as Joe Namath or O.J. Simpson would probably have been noticed out in the public, even if they wore sunglasses and a hat. A young man like Bill Bradley, who, outside of Texas, had really not accomplished a whole lot in the public eye, would seldom get recognized in an outdoor setting. Bradley said as much when discussing his road trips.

"No, the other campers didn't really notice me or know that I played pro football," admitted Bradley. "I was mostly enjoying the wildlife. I did find out during that time that you don't pet buffaloes. They appear docile, but even as docile as they look, they can jump six feet in the air. I think that every year back in those days, a person or two would get killed in National Parks. So I stayed at National Parks, and I visited some state parks here in Texas. They are pretty neat too."[23]

Traveling around the country and seeing a bunch of new and beautiful sites proved to be a worthwhile activity for Bradley. While many of his teammates were working at one kind of job or another, he was getting a rare opportunity to travel and observe some sites that overall, not many Americans really get a chance to see during their lives. As far as Bradley was concerned, that offseason went fast, but it was fun, and it was time well spent.

"I knew that I didn't want to work as a used car salesman or as an insurance salesman or something like that," Bradley stated. "Those kinds of jobs just didn't interest me. I just liked to travel and see new things."[24]

What was of interest to Bill Bradley, at least upon his return from his trip out west, was to help his team to become winners. He got back up to Philadelphia with that very goal in mind. On an individual level, however, he was aware that there has always been a thing called a "sophomore jinx" in sports, and he was determined to make sure that his second year with the Eagles would be a natural improvement from his accomplishments during his rookie year. Unfortunately for him, a roadblock would stand in his way, and it was a roadblock that most players sooner or later must deal with.

4

SKIN IN THE GAME

Bill Bradley had made it through his first season in the NFL with a mixture of good times and bad times. He had succeeded as a punter, but he was a member of a team that had failed to offer any real competition to most of the rest of the teams in the league in 1969. Bradley and his teammates were all hoping that the 1970 season would be better for the Eagles, at least in the category of wins and losses. They were looking to build on whatever momentum that they could muster, even from a small two-game winning streak that they experienced during the prior season. Bradley certainly wanted to see more action on Sundays during 1970, most notably more action beyond just punting and returning punts and kickoffs. He wanted to get some more playing time in the defensive secondary, and not just when games were already out of hand and unwinnable.

But the young Eagles punter/defensive back was honest enough to realize that he would have to make his own breaks. He was also smart enough to grasp that football is as much a mental game as it is a physical game. He therefore wanted to continue studying defensive strategy by sitting down with a notebook, his playbook, and a 16 mm film projector. The tedious and sometimes mind-numbing chore of watching numerous game films...minus the popcorn...was often the key to understanding the various nuances of the game's strategy. Bradley recognized this, and to him, it was a small price to pay to achieve the improvement that he sought in his pro career. He also wanted to keep working hard at the physical demands of the game, namely making good tackles, using his speed to knock down opposing passes, and covering receivers and tight ends as closely as possible. To accomplish these important elements of his position, he therefore kept in top physical shape. His offseason regime included running, lifting weights, muscular stretching...and more running. He was determined to become one of the fastest defensive players in the NFL.

Thus, the 1970 season would be a year of introspection for Bill Bradley. It would be a year where he was going to have to stay focused on making inroads toward his individual development and his advancement in the game.

When Bradley came back to Philadelphia following his trip through portions of the National Parks in the western states, he returned sporting a different appearance. He was an iconoclastic individual through and through, but in this "Age of Aquarius," Bradley decided to copy the hair style of so many young men during the 1960s and 1970s. He elected to not only grow his hair long like they did, however, but it also appeared to many that he chose to perm his hair (which he did not). It looked to be one of the largest tumble-weeds ever perched on a man's head. Combine that with the requisite curly moustache that he displayed, and one would probably consider or believe Bradley to be a star in a Western movie, in addition to being a pro football player.

"My dad's hair was curly, but not curly-curly," explained Bradley. "When my hair grew longer, it was wavy is what it was. The people of color on the team taught me how to fluff it out. And back then, they didn't have a whole lot of those little small combs. (But) what they did, they took a cake rake back in the day. They had cake rakes that had a handle on them, and little metal deals that go down for the hair. And they called them cake rakes. Well I found a really nice one and I let my hair grow long. Sometimes I would put it in a ponytail. I just never got any pictures of it. Ponytails weren't really a neat thing to wear back then, because they were odd.

"(But) having long hair was a sign of the times, you know. It was the movement back in the 60s and 70s. It was a new style coming in... free thinking and all that kind of stuff. There was long hair on a lot of people that came through (the NFL). Mine was just one of the earlier ones in football. And I ran around with Tim Rossovich...three or four of us (had long hair). So my hair was long, and I fluffed it up. And on top of that, it was pretty good padding for the helmet. It was like having rubber foam under the actual padding."[1]

Like Bradley, the 1970 NFL landscape had a new look too. For the first time ever, the old AFL merged with the old NFL to form the new NFL, with a total of 26 teams in one league. New divisions were formed, new alignments of the teams were unveiled, and two new conferences, the American Football Conference (AFC), and the National Football Conference (NFC), were born. The game exhibited more competition than ever before, and as it turned out, the 1970 season was probably the most exciting in pro football history up to that time. Many teams stayed within reach of making the playoffs all the way until the final week of the regular season.

The Philadelphia Eagles as time would tell would not be one of those teams. Nevertheless, they followed suit with this big sweeping change across the new league's appearance by employing a shakeup of their own in the team's lineup. It was a roster move that caught Bill Bradley by surprise. Joe Scarpati, one of the best mentors that Bradley had during his rookie year, was unexpectedly traded by the team to the New Orleans Saints. Obtaining knowledge and experience was—and still is—especially important in a player's longevity in the game. Bradley gleaned that experience from Scarpati, and he was indeed a benefactor of Scarpati's knowledge. "I spent my rookie year picking his brain," admitted Bradley.[2] Now he would have to rely on fellow defensive backs like Ron

Medved, Nate Ramsey, and Al Nelson to share their experience with him.

Unfortunately for Bradley, however, he fell victim to a fate that seems to attack 99 percent of all football players sooner or later. Bradley sustained a knee injury in the opening preseason game of the year versus the Oakland Raiders at Franklin Field.

"It was the first play of the second half," Bradley recalled. "The guy (Oakland running back Charlie Smith) cut back on me before I could react. I went to tackle him, but he juked me out of position. He veered in real fast and I took him too high. I was standing there, waiting for him to come to me, and when I went down, my knee buckled.[3] My left knee kinda went sideways on me, and it screwed up my cartilage."[4]

Bradley knew that he was hurt, but he did not know the extent of his injury. He managed to jog off the field and back to the bench, but in retrospect, he probably should have accepted help from his teammates to leave the game, rather than potentially injuring his knee any further. It was a moment such as that which displays the macho image of the sport, where a player wants to send a message to his fans that he was tough...a manly warrior if you will. Jogging off the field on your own power also sends a message to your opponents.

"You don't want to give the other team the satisfaction of seeing you carried off," Bradley admitted. "I don't want to be carried off any field. If a team sees a guy (an opposing player) carried off, right away they feel superior."[5]

The verdict was damage to Bradley's knee cartilage, but the team physicians were not sure if the cartilage was torn or just strained. To know what type of repair was required, the doctors would have to operate on his knee. During the early 1970s, microscopic surgery was not available to NFL players. Only after a full-scale operation would a determination be made on how much time Bradley would be out of action, and what type of rehabilitation efforts would be needed. Dr. James Nixon performed the operation, and he discovered that the cartilage was intact. There was no rupture of any kind. Bradley had dodged a bullet and would be back punting in less than two months. As it turned out, however, punting would be the name of his game for the remainder of the 1970 season.

"All I did was punt the rest of the season," confirmed Bradley. "I didn't run down on kicks. I didn't return kicks or do anything else. All I did was punt. They repaired me in my mind well enough to where I could come back and punt. I was gimpy, mind you. I think that year (1970) brought my average down below 40 yards per punt for a career (Author's Note: it did. Bradley's career average for yards per punt was 39 yards).[6]

"I just had to do everything that they (the team's medical staff) said to be able to play again. So I was out for about six weeks (throughout the preseason). They put a cast on my leg, and I came back and rehabbed it. The one thing I didn't want to do was rush it. I wanted to come back soon, but not until I was really ready. In the middle of the season or so, I started punting again. It hurt, but I learned to tolerate that. It felt for a time like I was walking around on a wooden leg. Pain is part of football, as the saying goes."[7]

The pain of dealing with a knee injury is also shared with the pain of dealing with the various stages of the rehabilitation process. Bradley had been through that before at the University of Texas. Now he would have to go through all of those maneuvers again. All the stretches, whirlpool and analgesic balm treatments, and daily knee exercises would be repeated on an ad nauseam basis to improve the strength and the flexibility of the joint and the cartilage. The rehabilitation process requires time and patience, and it is tough for every athlete to deal with. Bradley would look depressed throughout this time, and that was to be expected. He wanted to be out on the field, playing the game with his teammates, and contributing to the betterment of the Eagles. For the meantime, however, all he could do was just offer his support and encouragement to his teammates. He knew that he had to be patient.

"It's just frustrating to think about all the work that I'll have to go through to rehabilitate it," said Bradley immediately after the operation.[8]

But there were other issues regarding the aesthetics of the game for Bradley and his teammates to address. The actions of modern science added to the players' frustrations in rehabilitation, and certainly not in a way that most of them appreciated. Someone during those years decided that replacing natural grass football fields with fake grass called AstroTurf, or Poly Turf, or Tartan Turf, would make the game look more photogenic and visually appealing for fans to watch, both in the stadiums and at home on television. The artificial surfaces also made life easier for the stadium ground crews, who would no longer have to deal with muddy fields, the time spent growing natural grass, chalking the yard lines, etc. To the players, however, virtually everyone—except for the placekickers—abhorred the artificial surfaces. The injuries were the main reason for this distaste. AstroTurf was credited with thousands of skin abrasions every year, and numerous ankle and knee injuries (like Bradley's), where a player's joints would pound against the unforgiving hardened surface. Many veteran players today are still feeling the effects throughout their aging bodies of playing football on artificial surfaces during their younger years.

Bill Bradley was pragmatic and realistic enough, however, to know that such surfaces were growing in number and were around the league to stay. He also knew that some were better than others.

"It depends on how they build it," explained Bradley. "And so what they did at the Vet (Author's Note: Bradley would play his home games from 1971 to 1976 for the Eagles at Philadelphia's Veterans Stadium, known as 'The Vet.' Prior to that, in 1969 and in 1970, he played his home games at Philadelphia's Franklin Field. Both of those fields had an artificial surface during those years), the way I understood, was that they put some form of a pad between the asphalt and the turf, and this was early on. It was brand new stuff. And it worked good for a while, but in Philly you know, they have all kinds of hard weather, and pretty soon that pad breaks down, and then you're just playing on AstroTurf on top of asphalt.

"And it (Veterans Stadium) was also a baseball field, so things moved a little bit. They would border the dirt part, and they would cover it up with AstroTurf on first, second, third, and home and the pitcher's mound. And those things never fit, especially the pitcher's mound. That's the kind of turf that we practiced on. Now we did practice at (nearby) JFK Stadium some, and at a little lot that was close to Vet Stadium. I liked Franklin Field better than the Vet. Franklin Field was a good stadium. It was an old Ivy League stadium, and even though it didn't draw as many people, I thought that it was really neat. But then they built the Vet, and it held a lot more people. But the Vet was a dual stadium, and it got worn out, but we stayed on it for a long time."[9]

Bradley and the rest of his teammates came to the pros with the plan of staying in the NFL for a long time. But the players knew that the possibility of injuries would have at least some say in how long they would play the sport. While it was true that the injuries that were caused by artificial surfaces could have been avoided on natural grass and dirt fields, it was also true that injuries were as prevalent for the veterans as for the younger players in the league. The teams, however, typically have a say in how injuries and the aftermath of such are handled. Most teams have exceptionally good trainers and team doctors, and no expense is spared to keep the players as healthy as possible. In the end, it is every team's goal to try to get all injured players rehabilitated as quickly as possible, regardless of the severity of the damage to his body. The hope is to get athletes back on the field to continue their productivity for the team.

In some instances, however, it was actually preferable to sustain an injury and be placed on the "Injured Reserve" list, rather than to be cut by the team, or to be placed on waivers, or to be "sentenced" to the practice squad, which back then was labeled the taxi squad for the numerous times that released players returned to the team via crosstown taxis. The "Injured Reserve" list was a designation where an injured player could not play or even wear a uniform for the games, but they were still members of the team, and they would continue to participate in the team meetings. They would also continue to get a paycheck. The Eagles, however, had another option available in the late 1960s and the early 1970s for some of their taxi squad players.

"We had a bunch of guys that were just close enough to make it, to make our practice squad," recalled Bradley. "They went up to Pottstown and played for the minor league Pottstown Firebirds (Author's Note: Pottstown is a small town about an hour's drive northwest of Philadelphia. During the early 1970s, the town's population numbered roughly 25,000 citizens). Wade Key, one of our offensive linemen, ended up starting for us. But he went up to Pottstown (for a time), but he always came back to the Eagles. He was the Eagles' property. But he and some others were on our practice squad.

"So they went up there, and actually, they made a little (extra) money. Some of them made more money than we were actually making! Well, a couple of hundred dollars more, which was a lot of money back then. I think that between every game that they played up there, they made between $300 and $500. A bunch of our guys that we allotted up there—who were allowed to go—they'd come back and ended up being starters for us a little later, or even that year."[10]

Bradley avoided being waived in 1970 and sent to Pottstown, primarily because he was needed to perform an important role for Philadelphia, namely as a punter. Fortunately for Bradley, however, he still owned enough natural ability—despite his knee injury—to punt at an adequate pro level for the coaching staff to keep him on Philadelphia's active roster. Moreover, after conferring with the team's training staff, Eagles head coach Jerry Williams was convinced beyond any doubt that Bradley would be back performing full-time punting chores for the team sooner rather than later. Bradley would also continue to rehabilitate his injured knee throughout the season.

The Eagles players like Bill Bradley who survived the summer training camp and who were on active duty, were looking to help their team rehabilitate their win-loss record from the previous year. Their preseason games in 1970, however, featured nothing but defeat. Five of them in fact. Philadelphia's offense was not clicking, as the team managed to score only one touchdown in each of their final three preseason games. Such poor results continued in the opening day of the regular season, as Dallas managed to defeat the Eagles 17-7. It was a depressing beginning to a season that saw the Eagles collect only 3 victories against 10 losses and one tie.

But Bradley eventually got the green light to punt for the team in the third week of the regular season, a 33-21 loss versus Washington. Despite the loss, it was a game where Bradley desperately wanted to prove to his coaches that they had made the right decision by keeping him on the team's active roster. He boomed six punts for a total of 256 yards, an average of 42.7 yards per-punt, which is considered excellent, even by today's standards. It was his best punting performance of the season, and it was proof positive that his rehabilitation efforts demonstrated at least some measure of success.

He followed that up the next week at Yankee Stadium. Philadelphia lost to the New York Giants by a score of 30-23, but Bradley still punted serviceably well, as he booted the ball seven times for a 36.3 yards-per-punt average. He improved on his average in the fifth week of the 1970 season with a 39.6 yards-per-punt average against the visiting St. Louis Cardinals. For the remainder of the year, Bradley would hover close to that magical 40 yards-per-punt average, but he was never able to equal it or eclipse it for the rest of the season. He certainly got plenty of chances, however. The Philadelphia offense had trouble all throughout 1970 sustaining drives, and as a result, Bradley was called upon quite often to punt the team out of trouble. He finished the 1970 season with a grand total of 61 punts for a 36.8 yards-per-punt average. That was not too bad of a statistic, especially when you consider that Bradley's injured knee was still bothering him all throughout the year.

Bradley even risked further injury when, against the Baltimore

Colts on December 6, he fumbled a snap from center while in punt formation. His natural instincts immediately took over, and he ran for 14 yards and a first down. It was the longest run of the game for the Eagles. Bradley could not have been outwardly blamed for fumbling the ball. The 22 mile-per-hour wind gusts that blew through the dirt of Baltimore's Memorial Stadium all game long led to several fumbles and dropped passes from both teams. Fortunately for Bradley, he made it to the safety of the sidelines without getting hit. It marked his only ball-carrying activity of 1970.

"Trust me, I was running scared on that play," Bradley declared. "That was one of the deals where they (the Colts) had a return on, and they all turned their backs and started running to set up the wall. But normally, there is usually somebody who is designed to rush (the punter). But after the punter catches the ball, normally the guys all go to their assignment. So I caught it and the wind blew it off my hands as I was going to drop it (to kick it). It went sideways and fell out of my hands. I'm sure people are on red alert when you're playing in those kinds of climates (and weather conditions) in the outdoors...you know that they probably assign a couple of people to watch the punter."[11]

The Eagles faced an old rival in their final game of the 1970 season, when they defeated the cross-state Pittsburgh Steelers at Franklin Field, 30-20, on December 20. The game versus Pittsburgh marked the final Eagles regular season game ever played at Franklin Field, as the team was due to move into a brand-new edifice in South Philadelphia the following year, a home called Veterans Stadium. The contest versus the Steelers also marked the only time all season that Bradley actually got to see some playing time on defense. He was naturally a little rusty, and it showed, particularly when fleet Steelers wide receiver Dave Smith broke one of his tackles for a big gain, and when Pittsburgh running back John "Frenchy" Fuqua broke another of Bradley's attempted tackles for a 72-yard touchdown jaunt. Nevertheless, the Eagles pulled out a much-needed victory, to give them at least a somewhat savory taste in their mouths as they headed into the offseason. Moreover, Bradley survived his experience against the Steelers without agitating his knee too much or enduring any further injuries.

"I don't remember too much about that game," Bradley said. "I didn't hardly do any defensive stuff until toward the end of the (1970) season."[12]

It was obvious to the team that their punter would need another operation, however, if for nothing else than to gauge how much more damage was done to his knee by his punting activities throughout the 1970 season. Dr. Vincent DiStefano performed the next knee surgery for Bradley immediately following the end of the 1970 season. It was called a "Cleanout" operation, and it was exactly that. The plan was to clean out anything from his knee that was causing pain in and around the joints and the muscles surrounding Bradley's bony kneecap. It proved to be a successful surgery with no complications, but there was a lot to it that Bradley was not totally aware of or informed about.

"They put me under the knife once that (Pittsburgh) game was over with," Bradley recalled. "They (Doctor Nixon or Doctor DiStefano) didn't explain the operation to me before they did it, to be honest with you. Doctor DiStefano had done some really good stuff with ligaments and things like that. So I had strained some ligaments, and one of them was going to have to be cut all along and repaired with the other side of cartilage.

"I kind of have a conspiracy theory to the point where I think they just repaired it so I could punt (in 1970), but they didn't do microscopic surgery. I had to keep it in a cast for (several) weeks (during the preseason). So after the season was over, Dr. DiStefano had found some really neat new procedures for ligaments. They took cadaver tendons and transplanted them in my knee. Then they took the damaged cartilage out. Dr. DiStefano had previously visited Italy and discovered this new surgery while he was there, and he believed in it."[13]

The Texas product now had the whole offseason to rehabilitate his healing knee. This he would do, minus the perceived pressure to build up the strength in his knee in a short amount of time. Bill Bradley now needed a break from the game at this time, even for just a short respite of a couple of weeks or so. He needed something to take his mind off punting and recuperating from his injury. In previous off seasons, he would go on a vacation of sorts, and he would do so again following the 1970 pro football season. Bradley at this time desired some entertainment, and the biggest name in entertainment in America during the late 1960s and early 1970s was none other than Elvis Presley, "The King." What does Elvis Presley have to do with this story? Quite a bit, as you shall read. There are several segments to the following saga, but the tale is quite true.

The story goes like this: During most of his time away from football, Bradley enjoyed the camaraderie that he received from his University of Texas buddies, especially James Street. The two young men had been friends for years all the way back to college, and Bradley was proud of his friends, and they of him. According to Bradley, they were always "...a tight-knit group, telling stories, and laughing their butts off. I've got friends from high school, to college, to the pros, and we'd always stay in touch with each other. They were all good people."[14]

One day, several years prior to 1970, Street—who was still in high school at this particular time—got word that Elvis Presley was going to do a show in his hometown of Longview, Texas. That show changed everything for Street.

"When Elvis came through Longview to a farm or some county fair or something driving a pink Cadillac, and that's when James, as a junior in high school, fell in love with Elvis' character," Bradley said. "And from that point on, he was an Elvis freak."[15]

Street's endearment with Elvis, or at least of Elvis' persona, would eventually be taken to higher levels when he, Bradley, and several other friends from their University of Texas days, got together to take a few road trips to Las Vegas. It would be several connections that Bradley and his friends had that would allow this story to become just one more unique episode in Bradley's life. Those connections had an indirect link to gambling, and to fate in some degree. While it was true that the only "real" gambling that Bradley ever really did was on deciding which selected pass coverage to employ on a football field, it was also true that he just enjoyed the heck out of the camaraderie that he experienced with his buddies while they were gambling in Vegas.

"Bobby Layne was friends with a rich oil man from Kilgore, Texas who knew all about Las Vegas," Bradley explained. "So Bobby Layne, Doak Walker, James Street, and I, forged a big-time connection in Las Vegas. Not for money, not for anything like that, not for gambling...although we played a lot of Booray, which is a little bit of a gambling game. You know, you could lose $5 or $10 a night, or maybe $50. But I never played it. I was just there sweating it. I was just sweating the games...you know watching it and having fun. We were all tight man.

"So we end up having a connection at Caesar's casino. We also had a big connection at the Frontier casino. And we had a connection at the Dunes casino. And these are all Bobby Layne's buddies. Bobby Layne loved to play dice. As a matter of fact, right outside of Lubbock, Texas, we went out there one time, and we'd go out in the middle of *nowhere*. And this big wooden gate opens up, and there's some restaurants. One side is surf and turf, and the other side is dice tables and blackjack. I'm talking about something that looked like a lounge in Vegas. Oh God, yes it was illegal! I'm sure that the county sheriff was involved. He was getting a cut (of the profits), knowing Bobby. But it never got raided or anything. Even (University of Texas Head) Coach (Darrell) Royal didn't want to know anything about it (chuckle)!"[16]

Like Bill Bradley, Elvis Presley was not much of a Vegas gambler. But Elvis was an incredibly talented young man who naturally drew a lot of people all across the nation—and indeed all across the world—to become interested in him, in his music, and in his movies. He was indeed a legend in his own time, and his legendary status has not diminished one bit in the years since his death in 1977. James Street certainly was among the multitude of fans who went crazy for Elvis. So much so, in fact, that Bradley swears that Street tried to resemble him.

"As an Elvis freak, James would sometimes slick his hair back and dye it from brown to black," Bradley recalled. "He became the spitting image of Elvis Presley. I mean better than Elvis. He could have gone to Vegas and been an impersonator of Elvis. He knew every line to every one of his songs. He knew every line to every one of his movies. And he could sound just like him and he could act just like him.

"Now we've got all of these connections out in Vegas, and every time that we'd go out there, they'd just start featuring Elvis at the hotels and casinos. Elvis stayed at the Hilton and performed there. He put it on the map. So we would go to Vegas to see everyone's act at that time. The Rat Pack (Dean Martin, Sammy Davis Jr., Frank Sinatra), Nat King Cole, Neil Diamond, Tom Jones, and many others. And we went out there quite a bit, especially in the offseason. But we could never get James to go with us to see all of those other acts. As soon as we got to Vegas, he would take off and go see Elvis!"[17]

There is an old saying which paraphrased here states that if you ever meet your idol, you will probably come away disappointed. This is primarily true because we are all human, and few are the people who can portray a perfect persona every day. The relationship that James Street would have with Elvis Presley, however, was an obvious exception to that saying. As it turned out, Street's fandom of his idol turned into a lasting friendship.

"Some of the people at the Hilton got a chance to actually meet Elvis after one of his shows," Bradley recalled. "James was one of those who did. He went over there, and he made friends with Elvis. He started to talk to him. Someone would say, 'Hey James, do a little tune by this guy (Elvis),' and he did it. Elvis said, 'Man, you ought to be in Vegas imitating me.' So he (James) didn't just meet Elvis. Almost instantly, Elvis falls in love with James! So James forged a friendship with Elvis, and he (James) could go up to his suite! So he would go up to Elvis' suite, and there were celebrities and women everywhere. Elvis could have his pick of those beautiful women out in Vegas. So James became friends with Elvis! And he hung out with him!"[18]

It was getting so that Bradley and the rest of his buddies were in awe of Street. Just think of it...one of your best friends is a good friend with a bonafide entertainment icon. It kind of blows your mind to some degree. But the story does not stop there. Street was a down to earth guy, and it was that mindset that Elvis yearned for, amid all of his celebrity status. A phone call one particular evening illustrated that point.

"As a matter of fact, right before we went out there (Las Vegas) one time, we're sitting in our room playing Booray, and the phone rings," remembered Bradley. "There's about six or eight guys in there, betting on this little game. James was playing Booray, and Tommy Asaff answers the phone. The guy on the other end of the phone says, 'Who is this?' Tommy tells the person who he is. Then the voice on the line says, 'Tommy, tell James I want to talk to him.' Then James tells Tommy to tell the person on the other end of the telephone line that he (James) '...will get back to him in a minute.' Okay, so James comes over there, and they're right in the middle of a big (betting) pot, and Elvis says something to James on the phone for a few minutes, and then they hang up.

"Now we didn't know who was on the other end of the phone asking to talk to James. We said, 'James, who the hell was that?' He said, 'That was Elvis.' We asked him, 'Why didn't you talk to him some more?' James said, 'Well, I'm busy...I've got to win this pot of money.' That's Elvis. That's why Elvis *loved* him. Because he (James) treated him (Elvis) like one of the guys. Elvis fell in love with James! You know, in a manly way. That's it right there! I get chill bumps just talking about it. Elvis loved him! He loved him!"[19]

Later that offseason, Bradley himself would have a brief encounter with Elvis Presley. It was another unique moment in time where "The King" once again displayed how down to earth he really was.

"One time we went over to Graceland (Author's Note: Graceland was the name of Elvis' mansion in Memphis, Tennessee)," said Bradley. "We got a private tour, and it was beautiful. We went down into the basement. He had about six or seven televisions in his basement, and it was all dolled up like a Vegas show down there. Then Elvis came in and said, 'Hi.' I briefly met Elvis. Of course, James was with us at the time. Elvis looked at his TVs, which had boxing matches being televised. He said, 'Man, I love this boxing. I want to watch this match.' Elvis was a boxing freak. That's how he came to do all of that judo crap. But he left a little later with James to go do something else. I stayed a little longer to watch his TVs. It was great.

"James treated Elvis like one of the guys...like one of his teammates. And that's the main reason why he liked James so much. James was cordial to him, you know, and he (Elvis) kind of ran together with James. But when Elvis got involved with that group of men called 'The Memphis Mafia,' his life changed for the worse. The Memphis Mafia gave Elvis everything he wanted, and they got Elvis all messed up on drugs...on drugs. That's what eventually killed him. That and a fast life, and that's how Elvis died...he overdosed on his commode. But he loved James, and James loved him. James took it really hard when Elvis died. I'm not embellishing this stuff. This stuff really happened. I've got other teammates who can verify this story." [20]

Bradley's teammates in the Philadelphia Eagles were hoping at this point to prove to the rest of the NFL that they were a better team than their win-loss record from 1969 and 1970 indicated. Bradley knew that the team was counting on him to help with that verification process, and to be fully recovered from his knee injury from the 1970 preseason. And for certain, he wanted to contribute more to the team than just punting. He had been actively rehabilitating his knee for many months, all the while sticking to the workout schedule that the

Eagles' doctors laid out for him. He wanted to come back from his injury better than ever.

Part of his rehabilitation did not even happen in the United States, however. Following the 1970 season, Bradley decided to take advantage of what Europe had to offer to do some running. While such a drastic move for a couple of months might be strange to most of us, to Bradley, it was just par for his free-spirited course. He was the type of individual who was always eager to try new things, and to travel to new places. He ended up hitchhiking around noteworthy places such as Paris, France, and the Berlin Wall. He was running around two miles a day in Spain to strengthen his knee. By the time that he got to Valencia, he was running three miles a day without a problem.

"I wanted to rehabilitate my knee the right way," Bradley explained. "Because it had been operated on during the (1970) preseason, I rehabbed it, but I still punted. And I was still hurting that knee every time I would punt a ball or plant a foot. They repaired my knee just enough for me to punt. And I think they knew at the end of the (1970) season that they were going to have to do another operation. And so, they went in right after that season and operated on it to repair the cartilage. And so really, I shouldn't have punted that year (1970), but I did. They got the use out of me that they wanted. And so at the end of the year, I decided that I wasn't going to have any pressure from anybody. I wanted to get *away*. I wanted to do my own rehab. The only way that I could do that was to disappear."[21]

And disappear he certainly did. Bradley was by this time used to exploring the United States every offseason. In Europe, he expected to see even more unique scenery, towns, cities, buildings, and people. He was an unknown wanderer in this new continent, but he was still the same man. He went to Europe as a person who was being true to his nature, that of an iconoclast who did things his way. That was the mindset wherein he was the most comfortable and the most familiar. And that was the mindset which had often guided him from his earliest days to the present day. However, as far as this overseas trip was concerned, Bradley was on a mission, more so than on any of his other previous trips and junkets. In the back of his mind, he knew that he had to heal up. If he were able to do so, it would possibly point the way toward a more rewarding and successful NFL future. But he would have to keep doing things his way.

"I wanted to go to Europe where nobody could get a hold of me, including (Eagles general manager) Pete Retzlaff," admitted Bradley. "If he got a hold of me, he would make me stay up there (in Philadelphia), but I'm not a proponent of doing all of that work on an injured knee. So I took a backpack—which weighed 25 pounds—and every day (in Europe) I would walk between five and ten miles. I let my knee heal naturally, rather than going to a place, and getting on an apparatus where you've got to extend your leg out, which puts a lot of pressure on your joints. And then you've got to turn around and do your hamstrings, and then you've got to use the weights, and all of that. Well, I've never been a great weightlifter, because I didn't want to start injuring that knee joint again, and I didn't want to shorten up my athletic muscles."[22]

Bradley's knee muscles did not take too long before they started to heal while in Europe, which proved that his decision to go foreign was a good move in the right direction. Another benefit of his decision derived from his initial desire to avoid the Eagles brass. He was right...Retzlaff was never able to contact him while he was trapsing across Europe. In retrospect, Bradley's move makes sense to anyone who has ever had to answer to a nagging boss.

"What are they (the Eagles management) going to do?" questioned Bradley. "They ain't going to fly anybody over there (to Europe) to pick you up or holler at you every day. They had no cellphones back then. And so I wanted to do my rehab *my* way, which was a little bit selfish. But it worked out the best for me. I came back totally healthy. True, I also did it (went to Europe) because I wanted to get a little education about those foreign countries. Heck, I was single, and I wanted to explore. I made some great friends over there and I'm still pen pals with some of those folks today! But the main reason why I did it was because nobody could get a hold of me. When I came back (to Philadelphia), I was just naturally in good shape. My knee was in great, great shape. The knee was sound, and that's when I felt that I could get on a (weight) machine to build my quad and hamstring to function right. You know, that's just the way it was."[23]

The way it was for Philadelphia head coach Jerry Williams involved designating Bradley to step into the first-string free safety position that had been vacated when Joe Scarpati was traded to New Orleans the previous year. The free safety position relies on speed and quickness, and fortunately for Bradley, he still retained those two traits, even after enduring his 1970 knee injury. But the position also required a good amount of intelligence and football sense. Bradley had spent his first two years in the NFL learning and dissecting the methods and practices of the veteran defensive backs on his team. Moreover, he also continued to watch game films, make notes, and study different opposing offenses. Such efforts on his part contributed to his football wisdom, which would be tested like never before in 1971. It would be his first year as a starter in what would soon be recognized as his most natural position.

The most natural hope for Philadelphia would be overall improvement on the field and in the standings. Coach Williams, his assistant coaches, and every Eagles player, were all hoping for a better start to the 1971 season than what they experienced to begin 1970, when they endured a woeful seven straight losses to commence that year. Unfortunately for Philadelphia, the beginning of 1971 appeared to offer nothing more than a repeat of the start of 1970.

5

IT CAME OUT OF NOWHERE

Paying your dues is a prerequisite to success in virtually any walk of life. The dues that one pays can be offered in various forms. They can be mental as well as physical. They can also involve other people, other unexpected elements, and other plans or ideas that can sometimes change in the wink of an eye. Most commonly, they come in the form of hard work, and the supposed payment of one's dues can often be required without any type of warning or advanced notice.

For Bill Bradley, the dues paying time—at least for the moment— was now behind him, although he did not know it at the time. The years that he spent at the University of Texas, and his first two seasons in the NFL, adequately served as a measuring stick of his sacrifices toward becoming a professional athlete. Now keep in mind, Bradley was an optimist, and as he prepared for his third season in the rock 'em, sock 'em world of pro football, he knew full well that injuries and time spent in rehabilitation were as much a part of the grid game as the goalposts and the yardage markers. He also could not predict what his future would hold. He did not know if he would still have to make more sacrifices or endure still more hardships or injuries.

But he certainly hoped that he would soon reap the harvest of his sacrifices and dues paying. You see, Bill Bradley—like all of us—wanted to finally achieve at least some appraisal of success. In 1971, he would receive that evaluation, and it would turn out to be one of the most satisfying years of his life.

The words success and satisfaction, however, had no part in the early weeks of the 1971 Eagles season. As in their recent previous years, Philadelphia started off slowly in '71, but in a most debilitating way. They were getting destroyed on the field, to the tune of a 37-14 loss in the opener at Cincinnati, a 42-7 thrashing from Dallas in week two, and a 31-3 felling at the hands of the San Francisco 49ers in the third week of the season. It was indeed a time of forlorn bitterness for Bradley and for the team as a whole.

But the Eagles coaches had placed their faith and confidence in Bradley. With Joe Scarpati traded to New Orleans, Philadelphia was banking on Bradley to fill the free safety void, and somehow deliver well enough to help the defense. The only factor lacking in Bradley when he was compared to Scarpati was experience. Practically every other category, such as speed, leaping ability, good hands...Bradley possessed those important ingredients in abundance. Despite this, football was and is still a team game, and the Eagles team was still not clicking on all cylinders. They were simply not competitive in any phase of the sport during the first month of the 1971 season.

You could see this acrimony fester by observing the expressions on the players' faces. You could also see it by watching the overt actions of Bill Bradley. In the home opener versus Dallas at Veterans Stadium on September 26, Bradley intercepted his first two passes of the year. But even that was no cause for celebration, as the Eagles were losing the game by several touchdowns. On one of his thefts, as soon as he reached the Philadelphia bench area, he took off his helmet and slammed it to the hardened artificial turf. He then did something which he had never done before or since.

"I was so pissed off," Bradley remembered. "We were working our asses off. We were trying to win football games, but not everybody was on board. You know what I mean? So essentially, I took my helmet and slammed it. There happened to be a trainer underneath a table reaching for a tape box. I kneed the table on one side, and the other side hits him right in the jaw. He looked up at me, and I just...I just lost it. Well it (the kneeing of the table) was stupid. I wish that episode wasn't out there, because it was stupid."[1]

Many teams made stupid mistakes against the Cowboys that year, as Dallas would later go on to win 10 straight games en route to victory in Super Bowl VI to end the 1971 season. But in the same game where Bradley assaulted a defenseless table alongside his team's bench, he also managed to draw one of his opponents into making a mistake as well. Mike Ditka was a veteran tight end who would go on to one day earn a Hall of Fame bust, but when he went up against Bradley...well, he had his share of difficulties. Bradley took the opportunity to pile on top of Ditka in the first quarter after a couple of his teammates made a tackle on the burly pass catcher. The play drew the ire of Ditka all game long, until in the fourth quarter, Ditka "got even" by hitting Bradley out of bounds. That hit cost Dallas 15 yards. Even in the midst of an unwinnable game, it showed acknowledged proof that Philadelphia's free safety knew how to get under the skin of his opponents.

"Mike (Ditka) was always good for a retaliation," admitted Bradley. "Every time we played against him, I could milk him out of a 15-yard (unnecessary roughness) penalty, because the second guy (in a fight) always gets caught. So, in most of the games that we played against Ditka, I would just lean against him and slap him, and he would always swing and hit you. He was a highly tempered, competitive guy, and I have gotten a couple of 15-yarders against him."[2]

For his part, Ditka acknowledged that there were simply more similarities between himself and Bradley than there were differences. Well, sort of.

"The reason we clashed is because we're similar type players," admitted Ditka. "We're both great competitors. I thought Billy was flaky and he thought I was nuts. You might call that an understanding."[3]

Whether or not Ditka "understood" the strategy of infuriating an opponent, he also undoubtedly knew that it could work against some. But professional players are schooled by their coaches to keep their emotions in check during a game. No player wants to cost his team penalty yardage, as Ditka was guilty of at Philadelphia. But even Bradley would have to admit, however, that he had a lot more in common with a player like Mike Ditka than what meets the eye. Bradley wanted to win football games as much as anybody, and as a member of the Eagles, he was unable to acquire many victories.

"But I get fired up for football games, especially on a team that can't win," Bradley explained. "Because that (the constant losing) wasn't in my DNA. All the way through college, I play on a winning team, or at least a good, competitive team. We won a state championship in high school, and it took some work in getting everybody together for that. And then we started a nine-game winning streak at (the University of) Texas. So I was used to winning...and losing was unnatural for me."[4]

While Bradley was unaccustomed to constant defeats in the pro ranks, he discovered that he was not alone. Eagles owner Leonard Tose bought the team in 1969, and by 1971, he was also tired of enduring loss after loss. The last straw came after his team's big disaster at home to San Francisco. Tose decided to blame head coach Jerry Williams for Philadelphia's failures, which was not unexpected. The head coach is the man who usually gets the majority of the blame if the team is mired in a perpetual losing pattern. Tose abruptly fired Williams three games into the 1971 season and promoted assistant coach Ed Khayat to take over the helm of the Eagles.

"Jerry Williams was a heck of a coach," admitted Khayat. "I had played for him and coached for him, and then they (the Eagles management and ownership) asked me to finish the year as the team's head coach."[5]

Khayat was wise enough to realize that he had to be his own man if he were to succeed. He knew that he could not and should not try to emulate the patterns and methods of coaching that he had learned from Williams. So he expressed his own personality to the team and decided to lead them with a strong and disciplinary approach.

"They elevated Eddie Khayat, who was a great guy," Bradley said. "Khayat came in and he was going to change the culture, as they say today. He said, 'No hair can be over the top of your ears. No moustaches. No beards. We're going to start to have some inner discipline around here.' Well people *hated* that. I remember at our first team meeting, Nate Ramsey, a safety, had worn a moustache since he was a teenager. I guess in a way in Eddie's mind, he thought that he was going to bring some discipline, you know. But the length of your hair doesn't matter. I've never heard of long hair winning or losing a game. It's all on the football field and in prepping (to play the game). Hell, Jesus' hair was down to his shoulders."[6]

The Almighty aside for a moment, Khayat's new methodology to the game did not result in victory...at least not right away. Philadelphia was still trying to shore up their defense, a unit that had permitted a woeful 110 points and 1,411 total yards throughout the first three weeks of the 1971 season. But luck was on the Eagles' side, at least to some degree. Their opponent in their fourth game was the Minnesota Vikings, a team that was not scoring a bunch of points in '71, and a team that did not focus their offensive attention on throwing the ball. Philadelphia played Minnesota tough, but they lost to the Vikings, 13-0. Despite their fourth straight defeat, surrendering only 13 points to a perennial playoff team was certainly a reassuring sign that the defense at least showed some modicum of improvement.

The goal of improvement appeared to be unobtainable the following week, as Philadelphia traveled to Oakland to take on the defending AFC Western Division Champion Raiders. The Eagles, however, operated as if they were a brand-new team at the beginning of the game. They erupted for an early 10-0 lead, something that rarely happened during any game in the past few years. Bill Bradley picked off his third pass of the season when he leaped high in the air to snare a long bomb intended for Oakland tight end Raymond Chester. Bradley then instantly jumped to his feet and showed off some of his sparkling open-field moves in a 27-yard interception return. The play could have been correctly credited to Bradley's success at running track, pole vaulting, and high jumping in high school and college, not to mention his knowledge of playing the quarterback position at those levels, and realizing where Oakland quarterback Ken Stabler had planned on throwing the ball.

"I had a lot of experience from junior high to high school, and at UT," expressed Bradley. "I had some moves. I ran a 9.8 100-yard dash. I was also the first leg of our 440-yard sprint relay team in high school. They say your first leg and your last leg are the two fastest, categorically."[7]

Unfortunately for Bradley and his teammates, their overall speed was unable to keep pace with the team speed of the Raiders. One could also state that the strategy of Oakland's offense proved too strong, as Stabler found his open receivers often enough to complete 11 of his 15 passing attempts. The Raiders racked up 34 points and held the Eagles scoreless for the entire second half of the game.

Philadelphia's fifth loss of the year was not without its moment of pathos, however. Bradley had been the target of Oakland head coach John Madden, who spent most of the contest verbally berating the young Eagles safety. Later in the game, after one play near the Raiders sideline, Bradley had listened to enough of Madden's spoken discourse.

"I got a couple of head coaches mad at me on the sidelines," Bradley recalled. "John Madden bitched at me. Finally, I got tired of it and I went over there and I said, 'Hey Madden! You know what you look like? You look like a damn full-grown Cheshire cat!' And he did! He did! And boy I turned around and walked off. He went crazy as I walked off (laughter)."[8]

Philadelphia's 0-5 record was no laughing matter, however. To their credit, the Eagles had been playing with more intensity since Ed

Khayat became their head coach, but they were still unable to notch their first win. That fact would be rectified the following week, when the division rival New York Giants paid a visit to Veterans Stadium. Philadelphia's offense finally put together a full game of outstanding individual efforts from several vital positions, as the Eagles triumphed, 23-7. As the final score indicated, the defense also had a good outing, as they limited veteran Giants quarterback Fran Tarkenton to a meager 71 passing yards. This was the type of result that Bill Bradley was accustomed to. He and his teammates finally got their first taste of victory in 1971, and they salivated at the possibility of developing a trend of winning.

The Eagles got that chance in week seven, when the American Football Conference's Denver Broncos made their first visit to Philadelphia. The Broncos were like the Eagles, in as much as they were comprised of mostly younger players. It was in this game where the innate skills of Bill Bradley were on display for all to see. Both teams were in a competitive struggle as Denver quarterback Don Horn tested Bradley's range with a couple of deep throws. Bradley proved equal to the task, however, as he intercepted both passes to preserve Philadelphia's 17-16 victory. On one of his thefts, Bradley outraced Broncos receiver Jack Gehrke to the ball. Then with Gehrke draped all over him, Bradley somehow managed to snare the ball in one of the best examples of hand-eye coordination in the league.

"I had really good peripheral vision," admitted Bradley. "I could be looking outside and staring at a tree, and still I could see stuff along the right side of my eye. I sit on the porch all the time and watch the sparrows off to my right, almost even with my ear. And, I'll look just to locate the bird. And I had hands now. I was blessed with good hand-eye coordination. Plus, some really good defensive back coaches used hard balls and tossed them to their players in drills, where they have to change directions. Your eyesight has to really focus.

"I studied quarterbacks on film even back then from the end zone. I'd watch the wide angles. And so what I would do was after everybody would leave, I would stay in the film room and put the end zone copy of the film on. I would watch that, and all I would do is watch the quarterback's head when he took the snap. Then I would watch his steps. I would get clues as to what the play was going to be based on what the quarterback was doing. That's how I watched football. Plus, being a former quarterback didn't hurt."[9]

The final score of their next game would hurt, however. To begin the second half of their 1971 season, the Eagles got in busses and traveled three hours down Interstate I-95 to visit Washington, a division rival that was having their best year since 1955, when they went 8-4. The Redskins had a bunch of older and knowledgeable veterans dotting their roster, and that experience would equate to their first playoff season in decades in 1971. Few pundits predicted that Philadelphia would give Washington much of a challenge in this contest, but that is exactly what happened. In a pitted defensive struggle, each team could only manage to score one touchdown apiece. Bradley and the other members of the Eagles defense exhibited one of their best efforts all season long. The Redskins could account for only 61 rushing yards, despite having a pair of young, solid, and often dynamic running backs in halfback Larry Brown and fullback Charlie Harraway. Those two ball carriers were miserably frustrated at the treatment that they were receiving from Philly's defense, which seemed to have tacklers stopping them on many plays almost as soon as they took the handoff. Then when Washington tried to throw the ball, Bradley made his presence felt all over the field. "Super Bill" was seemingly everywhere and anywhere, as he covered Redskin receivers well enough to cause plenty of confusion for Billy Kilmer. Besides breaking up numerous passes, Bradley would also pick off two of Kilmer's tosses on this day, giving him a total of seven corralled interceptions, with almost a half of a season still yet to play. On both of those thefts, Bradley would give Kilmer the disguise that the intended receiver was open. But such was not the case, as the third-year free safety jettisoned across the previously concealed area of the field to pilfer Kilmer's attempts.

It was becoming apparent that 1971 was playing out to be quite a special season for Bradley. All of his studying of opposing quarter-backs was reaping dividends. Moreover, there were some signal callers—like Billy Kilmer—that Bradley could read rather easily all throughout his career.

"I became real good friends with Billy Kilmer," acknowledged Bradley following both of their retirements. "After football, I was married and living in Fort Lauderdale, and I had a sailing company. And his wife was a stewardess, and he lived about three blocks away from me. And I would go to his house, and he liked to have happy hour. And I did too. So we would meet, and he'd come up to my place, and I'd go down to his place.

"So anyway, one day I went down to his place, and we were sitting out on the beach, and I said, 'Golly Billy...I just want to thank you.' And he looked at me, and we could banter back and forth with each other you know. And he said, 'What are you talking about Bradley?' And I said 'Eagles, Redskins...we played twice a year. I got two interceptions off of you every game. That's four interceptions. I really want to express my appreciation to you for putting me in the Pro Bowl.' Then he turns red and says, 'Aw Bradley, yak, yak, yak. You didn't intercept two off of me every time we played.' And back and forth it would go. Truthfully, he was one of the best quarterbacks to never throw a really tight spiral."[10]

The two wobbly Kilmer passes that Bradley did account for in his team's meeting with the Redskins on November 7 were not enough to produce a victory, however. The Eagles ruined numerous scoring opportunities with four missed field goal attempts, any one of which would have resulted in a win for Philadelphia. Despite this, a 7-7 tie versus the Redskins, the Eagles' 2-5-1 record was not a true indica-tion of how much they had improved since the beginning of the year when they were being wiped out on the field by their first three oppo-nents. Their upcoming foe, however, was one of those rival teams that obliterated the Eagles the first time that they met early in the 1971 season. The Dallas Cowboys were in the early stages of the best winning streak in the entire NFL in 1971. No one expected that

Bradley and his teammates would offer Dallas much of a challenge in their second meeting on November 14. But Philadelphia did so, and even though they lost by a score of 20-7, they still acquitted themselves quite well in dealing with a team that had the highest scoring offense in the league.

Bill Bradley held a special feeling of inspiration anytime he played against the Cowboys, being from Texas himself. It was not anger or bitterness, mind you. It was just his desire to play well in his home state, and to do everything that he could to obtain a win against a division adversary. Early in the game, Bradley made his presence felt in Texas Stadium by dishing out a pugnacious hit against future Hall of Fame wide receiver Lance Alworth, on a pass over the middle from future Hall of Fame quarterback, Roger Staubach.

Then later in the contest, Bradley fielded a punt and began weaving his way toward the Cowboys end zone. He made it deep into Dallas territory when he realized that he sped past the pursuing Cowboys. Then as an act that was probably more of an instinctive afterthought than anything else, Bradley reached the Dallas 15-yard line, then whirled around and trotted those remaining 15 yards backwards. After he crossed the goal line, he lobbed the ball at the closest Cowboy player, reserve running back Claxton Welch. Bradley's toss plunked Welch in the head. Unfortunately for the swaggering Bradley, a roughing the kicker penalty on the Eagles wiped out his touchdown. It was part humiliation, part frustration, and part overkill.

"That was a little bit of showboating," Bradley remembered. "Coach Royal sent me a letter after that. He said (in the letter), 'Bill, what the heck were you doing?' Because it was a joke. He (Royal) always said, 'Act like you've been there (in the opposing team's end zone) before.' And that's what everybody used to say. Now they throw it out the window. The players scoring touchdowns in today's game choreograph everything. If you didn't toss the ball back to the referee (during my era), you might not play the next week.

"'Act like you've been there before' was Royal's mantra. There's still a whole game left, in most cases. Is this a game-winning interception? Or are you just celebrating yourself? But there are three or four more quarters going on, and they're acting like 'I'm the king. I'm the best.' And well, you didn't win a football game yet."[11]

Winning football games seemed to be exceedingly difficult for the Eagles in 1971, just as it had been in the previous two years that Bradley was on the Philadelphia roster. Their two wins were against struggling teams, the New York Giants and the Denver Broncos. That fact notwithstanding, Philadelphia would travel to St. Louis in week 10 to take on the Cardinals, a team that, on paper, would present a good match for the Eagles. Bradley and his teammates knew that they were slight underdogs going into this game, but they also knew that a team like St. Louis might be apt to not give a lot of credence to a young and inexperienced team like the Eagles. That possibility appeared to be realistic, especially throughout the early portions of the game, as Philadelphia built a 23-20 lead entering the fourth quarter.

At this time, the Eagles managed to provide those in attendance at Busch Memorial Stadium a display of character. Many players and coaches believe that games are won or lost more in the fourth quarter than in the first three quarters. That certainly was true in this game. Philadelphia's offense finally kicked into high gear, controlled the ball, scored two touchdowns, and ultimately prevailed over St. Louis, 37-20. Bill Bradley picked off two passes in this much needed victory and ran his second interception back 28 yards to end the game. It was a showing of vibrant team strength. The Eagles had finally displayed that they were now becoming a cohesive unit of men who were not going to lay down for anyone. They were going to fight as hard in the closing moments of a game as they did in the early minutes of a game.

"We're no longer an easy Sunday's work for anyone," surmised Philadelphia defensive end Mel Tom after the game. "This is the first time we've put it together offensively and defensively," proclaimed Eagles middle linebacker Tim Rossovich. "Other times we've played pretty well on defense but couldn't move the ball. This time we had it all put together."[12]

Philadelphia was indeed putting things together. They were building momentum, step by step. And Bill Bradley was playing the best football of his career. He now had a total of nine interceptions on the year, which was good enough to tie the Eagles team record for interceptions in a season. It was quite a long time since a Philly player had garnered so many positive headlines. This was truly an achievement that Bradley himself did not plan on or expect. On a team with a losing record, it was difficult to lead the league in any important category. But Bradley to his credit was setting a new standard for Philadelphia defensive backs. And probably most importantly, he was not finished, and neither were his teammates. They now had an opportunity to derail another division rival, the Washington Redskins. Recall that they had managed to tie the Redskins a few weeks prior, in a game that Philadelphia should realistically have won. Now they had a chance to prove that they truly belonged on the same field with some of the other competitive teams in the league.

The rematch would be held at Veterans Stadium on November 28. And just as in the first meeting, the Eagles defense once again offered a showing of stinginess to the conglomerate of Redskin running backs. Both eventual league's Most Valuable Player, Larry Brown, and his stalwart backfield companion, Charlie Harraway, were limited by the Eagles defense to a subpar total of only 102 ground yards. Philadelphia's offense also chipped in with a strong effort, as they contributed 280 total yards against one of the best and most experienced defenses in the NFL. That total was 23 more yards than Washington's total amount of yardage. Unfortunately for the Eagles, however, one big mistake by quarterback Pete Liske ended Philadelphia's hope for a win. Liske threw a pass toward the sideline that was intercepted by Redskin defensive back Mike Bass, who returned the ball 38 yards for the game-winning score. Such an error proved the principle that a team can play extremely well all game long but can still lose if they make just one key error.

Making mistakes was something that the Detroit Lions did not do too much of during the 1970 season, as they won five straight games to enter the NFL playoffs. But in 1971, however, the Lions were ripe for a possible upset. They were sporting a 7-3-1 record at this point of the season. But they also may have been overlooking the Eagles to some degree as they met them, amid some overcast and blustery weather, on December 5 at Tiger Stadium. By this time in the year, it was evident that Philadelphia was going to give their opponents a solid effort throughout most of the 60 minutes of each game. They managed to come from behind late in the struggle to post an impressive 23-20 victory over the Lions.

This game was filled with several big plays from both teams. One of the biggest was a crucial interception by Bill Bradley, who disguised his coverage well enough in the Philadelphia end zone to baffle Detroit quarterback Greg Landry. Bradley's primary responsibility on the play was to cover Lions wide receiver Ron Jessie. But Bradley proved his worth as a supreme multi-tasker on this play, as he managed to stay out of the sightline of the Detroit backfield.

"I didn't expect Bradley to be there," admitted Landry. "We had the play designed to occupy him somewhere else. He must have just sensed something."[13]

The interception was not a fluke, and nor was it just a lucky break. Rather, it was the result of the application of Bradley's own skills and knowledge of what was happening on the play. The ball was slightly tipped near the line of scrimmage by Philadelphia defensive tackle Ernie Calloway. But Bradley's quick adjustment to the flight of the ball was at least in small measure due to the result of his willingness to deceive Landry on the play.

"Yes, I remember that I would bait the quarterbacks," said Bradley. "I would find out their tendencies. And Greg Landry would take the snap and look you off to the right or the left, but then once he set up and focused his eyes, he never looked at you again. He looked at the free safety (Bradley) to see if I was dropping to the middle, or if I was dropping to the hashmark, for a Cover Two coverage. So that's what he would do. So what I would do after the ball was snapped, I would open up. Let's say that the sideline is to your right. I would open up and cross oversteps until he took his eyes off of me, and then I would square up and get ready to run the other way. So he's either going to throw down the middle, or he's going to hit the seams or a fade route. I didn't hesitate. I did it (run toward the ball) on purpose. I think that I even turned around backwards to get to the middle of the field."[14]

Bradley's key interception and his 50-yard return set up place-kicker Tom Dempsey's 52-yard field goal, which was a team record at that time. Speaking of records, Bill Bradley now owned the Eagles team record for interceptions in a season with 10. He was the Pride of Palestine well before his most recent accomplishment in the ranks of pro football, however. After hearing of his interception feat, his old friends beamed with enjoyment for their long-time buddy. To a man, none of them were the least bit surprised when they heard the news that he broke a team record in the NFL.

"Bill was a natural, and he has always been a leader," reflected Mickey "Mule" Hubert on his youthful connection to Bradley. "He excelled at every sport that he ever took part in. He just stepped onto the field, and he was a natural. I wasn't surprised at all when I heard of his interception record. I have always been proud to call Bill Bradley my friend."[15]

"I wasn't surprised that he did that (broke the Eagles record for interceptions in a season)," admitted Bradley's high school football coach, Marion Turner. "You know that he just sometimes had a sense...a natural knack, of making plays, and anticipating plays."[16]

Bradley's own modesty combined with his team-oriented mindset to admit that he rarely kept up with records was on display. "We were just trying to win a football game," Bradley stated. "I had no clue what people did before us. I think that maybe Chuck Bednarik was the only former Eagles player that I knew about."[17]

The 1971 Eagles were inconspicuously becoming a team that prior players from the organization's illustrious past could take pride in. Previous Eagles teams of the past possessed the reputation of never giving up despite the score, and of always striving to do their best, regardless of their win and loss records. The '71 Eagles now appeared to also own those traits, as they had won their fourth game of the year against a very good Detroit team. Philadelphia's next game —their final home game of the season—would be a rematch of one of their best victories of the season, as they would once again face the St. Louis Cardinals. It was a contest that the Eagles felt assured that they could win, if they just stayed focused and made a big play or two. As it turned out, the team—and Bill Bradley—made several big plays.

Philadelphia's defense provided one of its best performances of the year in this meeting with the Cardinals. They limited St. Louis to just 10 first downs and forced them to commit five turnovers. The Eagles offense, in contrast, built what was an insurmountable 16-0 lead in the third quarter. Philadelphia wide receiver Harold Jackson caught a 69-yard touchdown bomb from quarterback Pete Liske, and placekicker Tom Dempsey booted a 54-yard field goal, which bested by two yards the team record that he set the week before at Detroit. Bill Bradley contributed what would be his final interception of the year when he snared an overthrown pass by Cardinals quarterback Jim Hart, and returned it 28 yards to set up one of Dempsey's four field goals in the game. The Eagles triumphed, 19-7.

"This is some kind of defense we've got here," said Bradley in a celebratory mood after the game. "I'm just glad to be a part of it. All I ever wanted was a chance to play the game up here (in the NFL), and now I've got it. I couldn't be happier. This is the greatest feeling in the world."[18]

The great feelings continued in the final week of the 1971 season, which saw Philadelphia travel to Yankee Stadium to take on another division rival, the New York Giants. As a replication of their situation with St. Louis, the Eagles had previously defeated the Giants earlier in the year. They would sweep them in the finale, as they took an impressive 41-14 lead into the fourth quarter, en route to a 41-28 victory. Liske threw three touchdown passes in the game, and Jackson caught seven passes for 145 yards and one score. Defensive back Al Nelson managed to intercept one Randy Johnson pass in the game, which he returned 19 yards for a touchdown. Philadelphia ended the year with a 6-7-1 record, which was their best mark since 1967, when they put up an identical 6-7-1 record. But what was really a great statistic that pointed to a hopeful future was their 6-2-1 record during the final nine games of 1971. To top things off, the newly anointed leader of their defense, Bill Bradley, finished the 1971 season with 11 interceptions, a new Eagles record.

"Sometimes I feel I get all the glory for it (the team interception record), but the defense plays as a unit and the interceptions show how far the defense has progressed," said a magnanimous Bradley. "To me it means we're getting good pressure from the front four, (and) great linebacking.[19] I don't do anything special. I'm just me. I do what comes naturally."[20]

Bradley's humility notwithstanding, his ability to do what "came naturally" most likely was a God-given gift. Even his friends from long ago have remarked on that subject. Many of them have described how some individuals like Bradley are able to excel at some sports, even without expending all that much effort, or without spending a whole lot of time practicing the sport in question. And that type of talent does not necessarily end when a guy like Bill Bradley was done playing pro football. In fact, that type of talent does not necessarily just involve the sport that he played professionally. It can—as in Bradley's case—involve a sport that he may have rarely spent much time ever playing.

"I know about two years ago, we played golf at Frankston, Texas, at a real nice course, and we invited Bill to come play with us," recalled Bob Stephenson, one of Bradley's long-time friends. "Well, he (Bradley) doesn't play golf. Once in a blue moon maybe, he would play in those golf scrambles, and he'd just go kinda hole to hole, and meeting and talking to people. But he got out there, and the first two or three holes, he was hitting the ball really well. And the fourth hole is a dog leg to the left. For the average driver, it's almost impossible to get on it too, because you have to draw the ball around that dog leg to even have a chance. And he hit a shot that had a perfect draw to it, and he was about 140 yards out. And I looked at him and told him, 'If you hit one more shot like that, we're gonna send your ass back to Palestine!' That just shows you the athlete that he was, that he could just come out there and hit a golf ball so pure, and never (really) play golf."[21]

To be sure, Bill Bradley was certainly becoming a "pure" free safety, especially in the aftermath of his 1971 season. His moniker of "Super Bill" now took on additional credibility with the fact that his 11 interceptions that year were good enough to lead the entire NFL. Bradley made the National Football Conference's Pro Bowl team, which was an absolute certainty. It is indeed difficult for a player who leads the league in interceptions not to make the Pro Bowl roster. He was also named as a unanimous first team member of the All-Pro squad, a designation and honor that is symbolic and representative of a player's acknowledged greatness in the NFL. But despite his enlarged fame throughout the world of professional sports, Bradley remained humble and modest to a fault, as was—and still is—his nature. He also continued to exhibit his own unique brand of deadpan humor. For instance, when he was confronted by some of his teammates regarding his "Super Bill" nickname, Bradley took it all in stride as he *reasoned* with his friends.

"I sat down with my teammates and we talked about it," clarified Bradley. "I was afraid they'd resent it. But I said to them, 'Heck, you guys are my friends. You can just call me Soup.' They laughed and that broke the pressure."[22]

The pressure of finally putting together a winning season escaped the Eagles by only one game in 1971. But their overall improvement in many phases of the game at least was as pronounced as ever during Bradley's three-year pro career. They were on the right track, and to a man, they could not help but believe that they were going to achieve even more greater things the next year.

"Oh gosh, yes, we felt optimistic after the '71 season," Bradley admitted. "We ended up just one game shy of .500 (the break-even percentage). We were optimistic."[23]

The past offseason, Bradley spent most of his time mending from his previous knee injury that he sustained early in a 1970 exhibition game. Following the 1971 season, however, he could finally enjoy the satisfaction of achieving a remarkable team record. He could enjoy the fruits of his labor...at least to some degree. You see, he also had a lot on his mind, most notably, his desire to get paid more money with a new contract. A cloud of doubt seemed to hover over his head regarding that. Practically anytime that a pro football player has a truly remarkable season, as Bradley had achieved in 1971, he would often try to discuss with team management the possibility of obtaining a renegotiated contract. And that discussion would certainly occur between the player and management if the player in question had completed the requirements and stipulations agreed to in his previous contract. Bradley was due to sign a new contract in the summer of 1972, and he would most certainly try his best to obtain more robust monetary payments in his upcoming deal.

Finally, Bradley also had the team on his mind. He spent some time wondering if the Eagles could improve on their best showings in years as the next season approached. He was certainly hoping that a winning record would finally be their lot, as he worked out and stayed in shape for the numerous challenges that 1972 would bring to both himself and to the team.

6

CARVING A NICHE

Pro football is a business. Yes, it is still primarily a game, a sports spectacle filled with excitement, drama, action...indeed all the visible superlatives, if you will. But to play this game on the professional level, teams need to reach agreements with their players and sign them to individual contracts, which are based on what the teams feel their players are worth. How much does each player add in his benefit to the team? Similarly, each player will—with conviction—feel that he is worth something positive to the team. The two sides will then agree or disagree with each other's assessment, discuss in closer details their points of view, and ultimately, if things work out well enough for both parties, put pen to paper. That give and take between management and the athlete is what helps to make the sport a business.

Bill Bradley got another chance to sign another pro contract following his super season of 1971. He was a young man who came back spectacularly from a knee injury, and his efforts and successes were due to be acknowledged by the team's upper management in the form of more money. Bradley went into his contract negotiations with Eagles General Manager Pete Retzlaff with a foundation of knowledge about finances, which he learned as a youngster. Bradley knew the value of a buck, having observed how hard both of his parents worked to provide the necessities for their family. He also knew that no good thing came easy, especially when monetary wealth was concerned. But in his mind and in the minds of many Eagles fans, he had proven his worth to the team. He now was saddled with the challenge of trying to convince Retzlaff that a record-breaking free safety was worth the investment for the team.

This was not going to be an easy task for Bradley, however. The early 1970s were certainly not a promising time for a good player to obtain a better contract, especially after a debilitating knee injury. As a result, he was forced to accept a one-year deal from the team at the beginning of the 1971 season, because his 1970 season consisted of punting, and little else. Punting certainly did not strengthen Bradley's bargaining platform.

"You see I got my knee hurt in '70, so I had to take whatever contract they offered," admitted Bradley. "I didn't hardly play any downs (in 1970), other than punting. I had no clout to go in (to the contract negotiations with the general manager), so I had to take what they offered me."[1]

Back in those years, a knee injury could often end a player's career. But Bill Bradley had already displayed to his coaches that he could still punt while recuperating after his surgery, so they kept him on the active roster. He would not make much money on his 1971 contract, but he could not worry about that. He had a much more pressing problem to claim his concern. The business side of football once again struck just before the start of the '71 season. The Philadelphia management determined that their ace free safety, Joe Scarpati, was now expendable, and they sent him in a trade to New Orleans. Gone for good was the tutelage that the veteran offered to the youngster. Thus, as fast as one could say starting defensive back, Bradley became just that for the Eagles.

"Well after they ended up trading Scarpati, who was our starting free safety, and then after they inserted me in that position, I led the league in interceptions," said Bradley. "But as luck would have it, my contract was up. My contract ended as soon as '71 ended. Then I was under negotiations. I was going to have to get a new contract anyway to play pro football in '72. But going into '72, I finally had some clout (his 11 interceptions to lead the NFL in 1971). And even in that, I had some clauses in my contract in '70 that I couldn't exercise, but they went over to my next contract.

"I think it's real important to know. Of course, they didn't pay us like they pay today's players. My first contract in 1969 was worth $15,500. The second year, it was $17,500. But I still had some of these clauses in there, like if I led the team in interceptions, I got an additional $5,000. If I led the league in interceptions, I would get (an additional) $10,000. And if I punted for 40 or more yards for my punting average, I would get (an additional) $2,000. There were all kinds of little incentive clauses in there."[2]

Bradley was indeed looking forward to getting a bigger pay day with all those incentives, and that bulge in his wallet was just around the corner, as soon as he would sign on again in Philadelphia. But a funny thing happened on the way to Bradley's contractual discussions with the Eagles management in the spring of 1972. There were no salary cap issues in the NFL during the 1970s, so teams could afford to pay their players whatever they thought their services were worth without affecting the other members of the squad. A front office's opinion of a player in question could certainly become a cause for debate, especially with that player and that player's agent. Opinions mattered, and the feelings held by each party could certainly be opposed to each other. As far as Bill Bradley's case for more money was concerned, it had some obvious validity streaming from it.

"So, I led the league in interceptions in '71, and the first thing I did was confirm to the Eagles that I wanted to be paid what I was worth," explained Bradley. "I was starting at four positions, if you call it starting. It would have taken four guys to do what I did. I was holding (on kick placements), and they don't get contracts for doing that, but that's what I was doing. I was playing safety and intercepting footballs. I was punting, so if I wasn't there, they would have to go out and get a punter. And I was punt returning, so (if I wasn't doing that) they would have to get a receiver or someone like that (to do that job). But I was really starting at four positions, and by then I was making $17,500."[3]

The Eagles brass was certainly appreciative to Bradley for his record-breaking performance in 1971. But would their mere words of gratitude be all that Bradley could reasonably expect from them? As any pro football player from the era of the 1970s will tell you, the team owners were extremely thrifty, or tighter than a drum if you will, with the money that they paid most of their players. Some teams were more generous than others, but overall, most teams undervalued their athletes, hoping to save some money. That sentiment was expressed in the salaries that they were willing to offer to their players.

"So, I went to (General Manager) Pete Retzlaff and I said, 'I want to keep all of my bonus clauses in there, but I want to be paid for four people,'" said Bradley. "And then I added, 'I'll even go down to three people, because holding...I can see a quarterback doing that. But I want to be paid three times the $17,500 that I made in 1971.'"[4]

There was generally an established science when it came to contract negotiations, especially within the realm of pro football players, agents, and general managers in the 1970s. When it came to the give and take between parties, each side often did their best to display stoic poker faces, and yet one or both of the parties in question occasionally were predisposed to fidget in their chairs. Sometimes, an adamant refusal of terms by the player in question was met with an equally bold stance and sentiment from the front office. The time-honored response of "take it or leave it" was usually a phrase that most players in the 1970s heard from the team's general manager at least once or twice. The situation would sometimes get heated, judging by some of the dialog. If Bill Bradley did not already know what type of a confrontation, he would have with Retzlaff, it would certainly not take him long to find out.

"Once I told Retzlaff what I wanted," Bradley recalled. "He said, 'We're not going to do it.' I said, 'Well then, I'm not coming to training camp.'"[5]

Retzlaff undoubtedly entertained several thoughts in his mind at this point. One, he probably felt that his All-Pro free safety was bluffing. I mean, would Bradley actually go through with his distempered claim of skipping training camp? Such a drastic move was difficult for Retzlaff to believe. Two, Retzlaff knew that the Eagles *needed* Bradley. He was one of the best free safeties in the league, as proven by his extraordinary showing in 1971. His appearance in Philadelphia's defensive lineup was vital if the team had *any* hope of improving their win-loss record. Third, Retzlaff certainly did not want to willingly upset Bradley or become the cause for Bradley's departure from the team offices without a signed contract in his hand. Such a happening would not look good in the eyes of the public.

But that is exactly what happened. Bradley walked out of the team offices in Veterans Stadium minus a contract. The ball was now in his court. He would now have to decide what his next move would be. Would he swallow his pride and show up to the team's summer training camp anyway, even though he told Pete Retzlaff that he would not be there? Or rather, would Bradley choose to hold strong to his word, that being to stay out of summer training camp? He chose the latter. Soon after he did, however, another wildcard in the deck showed up and sided with Bradley.

"So that's when, all of a sudden, Timmy Rossovich's contract was up, and he jumped in there with me," Bradley stated. "He was going to hold out and get a better contract for himself. We ran around together, and he came to me at this time. I told him, 'I don't mind if you jump in with me (in holding out). I'm not helping you (with your contract), but you can hold out if you want to.' And so he did.[6] He wanted to get out of Philly, so he kinda buddied up with me, which was not a good thing for me to do, but he was a friend, and I thought it would help him get his (new) contract."[7]

The idea of getting a new contract would take some time for sure.

And it would take some high wire risks, as both Bradley and Rosso-vich had already taken by holding out of training camp. The summer of 1972 was indeed a circus of sorts in Philadelphia. Both men were young veterans who were both entering their prime. Eagles fans became quite apprehensive at the thought of the team not having two of its best defensive players practicing with the rest of the squad. The media was also scratching their collective heads, wondering when these two players would come to their senses and come back to the team. The media was also asking an even more basic question: where in the world did Bill Bradley and Tim Rossovich go? Practically no one could find them. It was almost as if these two noticeable Eagles players (both men sported similar hair styles and moustaches) had disappeared off the face of the earth. Or at least, away from the surroundings of South Philadelphia.

"So, let me tell you how this stuff happened," said a chuckling Bradley. "The *Philadelphia Daily News* and the *Philadelphia Bulletin* could not get pictures of us, because we did not go to camp. I went down to the (New Jersey) shore, to work out in the sand on the beach where I could stay in shape. Timmy (Rossovich) didn't go with me. I went, (but) I don't know what he did. But when we did hang out together in town (Philadelphia) during our hold out, we drank some beers at some little nondescript place, and we continued working out, running, doing this and that.

"But they (the media) couldn't get a picture of us. We kept dodging the publicity. All they wanted to do was get articles and pictures. One day, we went down to South Philly to stay at a girl's apartment, and before you knew it, the media was out front snooping around! So, we snuck out the back door and went to another place (chuckle). We had all of these little places to hide. We were playing cops and robbers at that time with the *Philadelphia Bulletin* and the *Philadelphia Daily News*, the two main sports papers in town, and they could not find us (laughter)."[8]

The "crimes" committed by Bradley and Rossovich were not a laughing matter to Pete Retzlaff, however. While it was true that the two players were playing the press for fools, Retzlaff knew that the disappearing act of Bradley and Rossovich might go on for much longer than the team management could tolerate. Retzlaff had a few options left to his disposal at this time, however. The most common action taken by general managers of every team when a player refuses to attend training camp is to fine the player a monetary amount. In 1972, any fine would typically do some major damage to most players' cash flow, mainly because players of that era were not making anywhere near what they are making today. The natural consequences of this dilemma for Bradley and Rossovich was that the longer they held out, the more money they would be charged by the team.

"We were fined," explained Bradley, "...and I don't exactly remember how much it was. I think it was $200 or $400 a day for missing camp (Author's Note: Bradley was fined $200 per every day that he held out of training camp). We held out for 16 days, times $200 or $400 a day, I can't remember for sure. That's a lot of money! You add that much money...hell, it was as much as a regular player's contract!"9

Retzlaff's first move in fining Bradley and Rossovich did not have the desired results. In fact, it may have strengthened the resolve of the two Eagles defenders. In his own case, Bradley knew that his cause was just. Players throughout the league who had not achieved what Bradley had accomplished were in some cases getting paid more than he. Furthermore, most of those players only played one position on the field, or maybe two at the most. Bradley was on the field so much in 1971, that he barely had enough time to drink a cup of Gatorade before he was summoned back onto the field.

Retzlaff seemed not to care. His next move was to separate the two players by trading Tim Rossovich to the San Diego Chargers. Rossovich played for the University of Southern California before being drafted by the Eagles in 1968, so the trade was a good one for him in a familiar area of the country. He readily accepted the move back west. If Retzlaff had thought that the trade might result in a dose of worry for Bradley, however, he was quite mistaken. His free safety was not worried in the least about being the possible subject of a trade. He knew that as the league leader in interceptions, his value was pronounced all throughout the NFL.

As the days went by, time was not really on either party's side in this struggle of wills. Retzlaff figured that Bradley would be running short of money as his holdout persisted, but Bradley's dedication to holding out was getting increasingly stronger each day. And as luck would have it, his finances actually started improving—in a free enterprise sort of way—as the summer training camp continued.

"I was really into Volkswagen buses," admitted Bradley. "I even lived in them sometimes during the offseason when I would go and stay in them in National Parks or state parks. I got me an Econoline van later on and did the same thing. So, I had that Volkswagen van when the '72 training camp was being held in Reading, Pennsylvania. The first thing that I did that summer...I went and got a food vendor's license. Back then, you didn't have a whole lot of people (fans) going to the practices like they do now, but they had enough. They had 50, maybe 75 people around every practice. And at Albright College (in Reading, Pennsylvania, where the Eagles' summer training camp was held that year), there was a road that went all the way around the practice field. It was a public road, and our practice field was in the middle of a road that was the campus road.

"So, what I did was, I showed up (chuckle) with my van, and I had Cis Rhundel, who was a girl *friend* of mine, and all of her girl-friends as well. Cis eventually ended up going to Hollywood and became a cheerleader for the Los Angeles Rams. She also was Cheryl Ladd's double on the television show *Charlie's Angels*, and she ended up being a nanny to some of Jack Nicholson's kids. She was like a sister to me. You see, I had girl*friends*, not a specific *girl*friend. I ran around with them...they were all buddies, and they lived in those row homes, right by the Pagoda, which was nice."[10]

Reading was an industrial town in Berks County, Pennsylvania, and in 1972 it included roughly 50,000 inhabitants, numerous factories of one sort or another, and some unique architectural buildings to boot. One of those buildings was the Pagoda, a seven-story Japanese styled structure that was built circa 1908 near the top of Mount Penn. The Pagoda had (and still has, because it is still standing today) a distinctive Oriental appearance, with sloping awnings jutting out on the roof of every floor, and with each upward story narrowing in a square shape to increasingly smaller sizes. Along the north side of the building was its large and stretching parking lot. Visitors to this tourist attraction could always find a good parking space, look out over the span of the city of Reading, and in the evenings, marvel at the city's lights shining for miles. The sweeping metropolitan vistas were not the only thing that enticed people to pay a visit to the Pagoda, however...especially at night.

"The Pagoda is where we'd all go out," remembered Bradley, "...not necessarily to make love, when we had a special girlfriend, but that's where we would go. Maybe you know, if you weren't into actually consummating your love affair. You know, you would go to the Pagoda and get some other fringe benefits (laughter). Our fringe benefits included dry humping and shit like that (more laughter). Fringe benefits, you know (still more laughter).

"But anyway, I had this Volkswagen van at that time, and I painted the words *The Cottonmouth Blues Wagon* on the side of it (chuckle). I took it to the Pagoda now and then, and I put a lot of work into it. It was a van that had windows...it was nice. I lived in it for a time. I had a propane heater in there, a bed in there, carpeting...all that kind of stuff. It was a great damn vehicle, and it was plush. My mother made all of the curtains that went up on all of those windows."[11]

Windows into the world of Bill Bradley at this time of his life would include a peering look into how he viewed his profession, and how he viewed the rights and wrongs of what he had to deal with by taking a stand against the Eagles management. On some of those hot and humid days in July and August of 1972, the seal of approval of what Bradley was doing by not attending summer training camp came from many different people. Included in that list was someone whom the young free safety held dear to his heart.

"I feel that Bill is absolutely right (in holding out)," said Bill's father, Joseph H. Bradley. "He has proven his ability, and he should be worth more money. He will hold out forever (if he has to)."[12]

Pete Retzlaff, however, did not have forever in which to sign his free safety. He could only look out of his office window and try to observe what Bill Bradley was doing during the 1972 training camp. You could imagine how the team's general manager felt, knowing full well that one of the best defensive backs in the NFL—who happened to play for his team—needed to be on the practice field with his teammates, not chatting with the fans or eyeing a half dozen scantily clad females. To his credit, however, Bradley was certainly not a time waster. And as previously stated, he knew the value of a buck. Moreover, he was also an entrepreneur of sorts, in providing a beneficial service (sandwiches and soft drinks) for the football fans at Albright College. Added to that was the fact that Bradley was wise enough to anticipate what Retzlaff might do in each situation, in much the same way that he foresaw what a wide receiver might do on any particular pass pattern. In short, the unsigned free safety planned his moves, much like a champion chess player would do in a match against another champion chess player.

"So, I parked my van on the road next to the practice field," related Bradley. "Like I said, I got me a vendor's license, because I knew that it was going to be an issue. That's the only way that the Eagles management could run me off the property...if I didn't have a vendor's license. See, I was selling fried baloney sandwiches, some bananas, and some oranges. I (also) sold those two-liter bottles of soda...Cokes, 7Up, RC Cola, and some ice. I opened up my van doors and set up some card tables and put tablecloths on them. So, I went out there and I had my girl*friends* in short shorts and tank tops helping me sell that stuff (chuckling).

"So, I would have a line of people out there, all around my van after practice! It was around 50 to 75 fans that wandered around those open practices every day. So, shit! I figured out that the players were only making $12.50 or $13.50 a day per diem during training camp (Author's Note: Per Diem is a daily stipend, which was paid to the players to help defray any small expenses, such as food, cab fare, etc. It was usually a mere pittance of money, often under $15 a day). I decided to go out there and sell my sandwiches and sodas, in the midst of some good-looking chicks alongside of my van. As it turned out, I was making around $125 a day selling that stuff. In 1972, that was a lot of money, no shit about it."[13]

The issue of making money and saving money was also not far from Retzlaff's mind in the midst of Bradley's absence from training camp. One day, he noticed Bradley and the crowd mulling around his van next to the practice field. At this time, it was Bradley who was making the best of his situation. Furthermore, the University of Texas product was not working up a sweat chatting with the fans and making small talk with a number of his girl*friends*. He certainly enjoyed a much more relaxed physical state than his "profusely sweating in the summer sun" Eagles teammates. Retzlaff decided to walk over to the van and try to find out what Bradley was up to.

"So Retzlaff is watching every practice, and he saw me over there," conveyed Bradley. "He just came sauntering over to me. You could tell that he was pissed. He came up and said, 'Bradley, are you able to do this (sell sandwiches on a college campus)?' I said, 'What are you talking about Mr. Retzlaff?' And he said, 'Do you have a license to do this?' So, I pulled out my vendor's license and showed it to him. He just looked at my license, then he looked at me and shook his head, and he walked away. I never heard anything more from him about selling sandwiches again (laughter)."[14]

Bradley would next have to sell his teammates on what he was doing by holding out. Just like a precedence is set in a courtroom or in the halls of Congress, so too was Philadelphia's most famous free spirit trying to set a precedence on a practice field in contract negotiations with the Eagles' ownership. He knew that if he could win this battle of dueling opinions on how much money he was worth to the team, then his example of holding out would lay the foundation of future success for his teammates in their contract talks with the team. This indeed was an episode where Bradley was trying to show leadership.

"I met with most of the guys on the team down at the Eastern Bowling Alley," recalled Bradley. "It's where everybody went every night during training camp, have a couple of beers, and make bed check. We all hung out there. So, I got with all of the players and I said to them '...Hey look...I just want you guys to know...I'm not doing this (holding out) because I don't want to be here. I'm doing this for all of us. I'm doing it for me, yeah, because I want more money. And I'm doing this so eventually, *all* of us are going to make more money.

"You guys are making $13.50 a day, and at the end of the year, Mr. Tose (the Eagles owner) is writing a six-figure check to charities for every preseason game. We've got six preseason games. No wonder he can give $200,000 to his charity. And here we are making per diem. And he's filling the stadium with six preseason games?! I know that he's got a lot of positions, but to me, that just don't add up. So y'all just be patient. I'm doing this so eventually, all of us are going to make more money.' And so I did that for all of us. And Retzlaff...he was so pissed, but he couldn't do anything. And I was just over there standing by my van, having a ball."[15]

The time was now at hand for the two sides to come to a realization. It was in the best interest of both parties for Bill Bradley to play football again. But Bradley managed to hold out longer than Retzlaff had figured that he would. Neither Bradley nor Retzlaff disliked each other, mind you. Nor did the men involved disapprove of each other's strategy (or lack of such) during the hold out. Both sides could understand and sympathize with the how and why the other side was going about things, but Rossovich had been traded, and Retzlaff finally came to his senses. Bradley had not asked to be traded. He was willing and eager to play for Philadelphia. All he wanted was a salary that was commiserate with his skills and abilities. All Bill Bradley wanted was fairness in his new contract.

"Here's what happened on the contract," explained Bradley. "They needed me. I led the league (in 1971) with 11 interceptions. Plus, the fans in Philly loved me. If they (the Eagles management) had gotten rid of me, there would have been a war. So, they called me in to the office. They said, 'Here's what we're going to do. We're going to give you what you want. We'll give you a base salary of what three starters would make.'"[16]

That news certainly felt like a major relief was lifted off Bradley's shoulders. His new contract was worth $140,000 for the next three years of his service. But he was still not content with what else had happened during that summer. He knew that the Eagles management were positioned to reclaim much of that money through the imposition of the daily fines that he had accrued. But Bradley had a plan, and as it turned out, his plan was acceptable to Pete Retzlaff and to Leonard Tose.

"You just add up whatever my fines were...that's a large sum of money," said Bradley. "And so, I said to Retzlaff, 'Before I sign this contract, y'all got to waive all of the fines.' Because back then, the recipient of the fines was voted on by the players, and they'd take one to charity. So, we did Mother Teresa's charity one time, to help her down wherever she was...down in South America or someplace. But the team gets to vote on where all the fine money is going."[17]

The discussion between Retzlaff and Bradley continued, but it was for a good cause. Unbeknownst to the Eagles general manager at this time, Bradley had an idea to help a cause and a group of people who were dear to his heart. The first segment of Bradley's plan involved the chopping of his fines. The second segment sent him back to his hometown. Well, maybe not in person, but certainly over the telephone wire.

"I told Retzlaff that '...if you'll knock my fine money down to half of what it's worth, then I get to send it to my favorite charity,'" Bradley explained. "Well at that time, I had a brother who was a special needs student back in Palestine. We have a beautiful high school there...it's been there forever. But there were also some prefabricated buildings. One of them was for storage, and the other was for the special education classes. You know that there wasn't about 10 or 12 of those students, and my brother was one of them. And I know that sometimes during the summer, I'd go in there and say 'hi' to my brother, and they would all be sweating in those prefabricated buildings like they were stuffed pigs. I mean it was *hot* in there."[18]

Hot and due for an upgrade to the building. Specifically, Bradley knew that those kids and his brother all deserved to attend school in comfort. His family connection held weight in his mind. As it turned out, Bradley's family bond somewhat surprisingly also seemed important to Retzlaff. The Eagles general manager always loved to see the players show a relationship to those that they help with their time or money. Bradley's plan fit the bill about as well as a football fits on a kicking tee.

"I went back to Philly and thought that this would be a great idea," remembered Bradley. "And I didn't do it for notoriety. I said, 'Mr. Retzlaff, I want to take my fine money (which was up there quite a little bit) and I want to provide air conditioning for my charity.' He asked me, 'What charity do you belong to?' I told him that I would tell him about it the next day, after I spoke to the caretakers of it. So, I called the lady that night, and I found out that the real name of the charity was the Anderson County Mental Health and Retardation Association. And I knew this lady was friends of our family, so I said okay. So the next day I met with Retzlaff and I said, 'I want my fine money to go to the Anderson County Mental Health and Retardation Association for air conditioning for their pre-fab buildings.' And he said, 'Okay, that sounds pretty good.' So, I did all of that...got everything settled...and all these contracts, and the deals (clauses) stayed in the contract.

"Now in regard to my fines during training camp, they had to show something on the books," said Bradley. "I think that they fined me like $500 or $1,500 total, or something like that. I can't remember the actual amount. But the rest of it...I bought air conditioners, not to make publicity or anything like that. It was for my brother and for the kids in Palestine. Because we knew all their families."[19]

Bradley's unselfish act was indeed timely. As luck would have it, influential people on the team and in the league office started to notice what he was doing, in particular what he was doing off the field.

"Fast forward, there's a lot of stuff in between there," admitted Bradley. "But at the end of the year, I got voted third in the ballot for the NFL Man of the Year award. They put me on the ballot for the NFL Man of the Year for that reason (giving air conditioners to the kids in Palestine). And they still give out that award. So, what happened was I was on the list, and I didn't even hardly know this until after it happened...after it came out. I was the third person in the voting. I was third in line to be the Man of the Year. I felt really good about that. That was kinda cool. And I didn't do it for publicity. I did it because it helped my brother."[20]

Bradley's good deeds did not stop with that act, however. He also had a hand in one of the most successful and lasting charities throughout the city of Philadelphia, and indeed throughout the entire United States.

"On top of helping the kids out in Texas," said Bradley, "...during the time after I signed my (new) contract, do you know what we started in Philadelphia on Broad Street (the main thoroughfare through the heart of the city)? It's one of the biggest charities that has ever been developed."[21]

The Ronald McDonald House hosted sick children and their families. The charity pays all the expenses, so the kids can focus on getting well, and their parents can concentrate on providing their children the love that they need. It was a place where human beings are busy doing God's work, and it is spectacular to see. In speaking to Bill Bradley, one can easily tell that this cause still owns a special place in his heart.

"We stood on the steps of the house on Broad Street," Bradley recalled, "...and as a matter of fact, they sprung up all across the country. I went in and publicized the house. I rode a hook and ladder fire truck around the parking lot, and we stopped at one of those strip malls. On top of the ladder! Just to promote it! The hook and ladder was way up in the air, and I was riding around there, waving at people, throwing some confetti and candies out, and stuff like that, to bring attention to that particular Ronald McDonald House.

"That's how it all got started. Now there was a lot of people involved...it wasn't just because of me. But my son used it. After he got hurt, he had to stay at a Ronald McDonald House at one time in place of hospitalization. At no cost to the families, it is probably one of the best organizations going. But anyway, all of my teammates were behind me, because they knew that I was doing stuff (holding out of training camp, participating in various forms of charity work) to benefit more people than just myself."[22]

Bradley's teammates in the aftermath of his successful holdout resisted the urge to call him "Dollar" Bill Bradley as a replacement for "Super" Bill Bradley. Instead, those players proved their solidarity with their free-spirited free safety with a decision that they made leading into the beginning of the 1972 season. The Eagles players annually pick several team captains. As a result of his philanthropic gestures and his willingness to hold out to prove his worth to the fellows, Bradley became their natural choice as an Eagles team captain. It also helped that he led the entire NFL in interceptions, but that fact only adds more honor to the award. It was (and still is) a great tribute that all pro football players who ever receive such notoriety will attest to.

"My teammates took votes," said Bradley, "and that's what they did at (the University of) Texas too (when Bradley was chosen as a team captain in college). And I'm sure that the head coach (Ed Khayat) had some persuasion. He probably asked some leaders of the team...you know, some veterans, 'Do you think that Bradley is capable of being a team captain?' You know that when you have 11 interceptions, they really have no choice. But I was a team player. I did a lot of things. I held (for kicks), I punted, I returned punts, and I did play safety. We weren't having good teams then, but we were trying to build one."[23]

The building process of the 1972 Philadelphia Eagles, however, was not a good one. Right from the get-go, the team was a no-go. Bill Bradley's captainship began on an ominous note, and then repeated that note time and time again, all throughout 1972. The Eagles lost five of their six preseason games. True, those games did not actually count in the standings, but a team nevertheless feels a sense of accomplishment if they are able to win a few of those games.

"We were worried about losing those preseason games," admitted Bradley. "Well, it's a bit of a worry. You know once the regular season starts, all the preseason stuff is swept under the rug no matter what. You go forward, you know. I know that preseason (in 1972) wasn't much fun though."[24]

Neither was the regular season. Coach Khayat's charges lost their first five regular season games, which effectively ended any legitimate chance that they would have of making the playoffs. This was a major downer, because in each of Bradley's previous seasons, he had witnessed the team fight a losing battle, also having lost many of their early games.

The Eagles only won twice in 1972, a 21-20 victory at Kansas City in the sixth week of the season, and an 18-17 win at Houston three weeks later. They were decided underdogs in their game against the Chiefs, so winning that one was a huge upset that no one saw coming. Their win at Houston was achieved without scoring a single touchdown. Eagles placekicker Tom Dempsey did all the scoring, as he booted six field goals for the victory. Philadelphia ended the year by losing five straight games, which contributed even more demoralization to the team.

In addressing all the team's losses, Bradley was forced to look at it from several different viewpoints, none of which really made him feel any better about the results.

"About the only thing I can say is that maybe our concentration is lacking somewhere along the line," surmised Bradley during the 1972 season. "We're just not executing as a unit. (But) it's certainly not a hopeless cause from my standpoint. I always try to do the best I can. When we lose, even if I've had a good day, my mind only reviews the times I messed up...which coverages I missed. When you lose, the bad things always outweigh the good."[25]

Following one of the team's losses, the story has it that Bradley was so upset with the outcome, that upon his return to the locker room, he flung his helmet the entire length of a row of lockers.

"Well, I don't know if it went the length," said Bradley, "but it rattled around a couple of different lockers. Look, some of these guys were just out there. Well, all of them had good intentions. I played the game harder because I played to win. I got to be kind of a nuisance to some of the guys, because whenever they weren't doing their job, I would get a little ticked off at them. Not in a hateful way, you know. I just wanted to win. But we were in there fighting every game, even though at times it didn't look like it."[26]

One instance of a potential fight—or at least a mild disagreement —occurred in a loss at home later in the season versus the Chicago Bears. The Eagles took a small lead into halftime, only to watch the Bears come back to register a 21-12 victory. On one extra-point conversion play in particular, Bradley's anger at surrendering the lead in the game got the best of him. Future Chicago Hall of Fame middle linebacker Dick Butkus was on his team's field goal squad when a fumbled snap by holder Bobby Douglass led to a fire drill of sorts. When a play like this is botched, you must make the best of it, and that is exactly what the Bears did. Douglass found Butkus open in the end zone and hit him successfully. Butkus then gave Bradley a close look at the football.

"On that play," as Bradley recounts, "Butkus said to me, 'How do you like that, you son of a bitch? What do you think about that?' You know I wasn't covering him. I was covering somebody else. They fumbled the ball, and we should have tackled Douglass, but he got loose and threw it to Butkus, who was wide open in the end zone. I had my guy covered in the flat. It was a bungled play, and Douglass should have been tackled behind the line of scrimmage. So, when Butkus stuck the ball out to me, I didn't say too much to him. I just slapped the ball out of his hand and said, 'That's what I think about it.'"[27]

Another attempted slap by Bradley occurred in one of their more one-sided losses in 1972, on November 19 at Veterans Stadium against their division rivals and defending Super Bowl Champions, the Dallas Cowboys. Bradley tried to inspire his teammates by picking a fight with Dallas defensive end Pat Toomay, a player who stood 6-foot-5, and who weighed 250 pounds. It was a mismatch to say the least. Nevertheless, Bradley's effort was admirable for pugilists across the league.

"I couldn't reach his face," admitted Bradley. "I couldn't scratch him if I wanted to. The thing that (really) makes me mad is that I broke my fingernail off on his facemask."[28]

The Eagles had plenty of trouble reaching anything worthwhile as the season lingered on. Another one of their disturbing defeats was a 62-10 drubbing from the hands of the New York Giants, a division rival that improved every single one of their statistical categories in this destruction of the Eagles. It still stands as Philadelphia's worst loss of point disparity of all time. "I'm embarrassed," said a dejected Bradley after the debacle versus the Giants. "What else can I say? It's as disheartening as heck. It was a big-time loss. I felt like Chicken Little running around out there with the sky falling. Today, the ending was different. Today, the sky really fell."[29]

That rout was all anyone really needed to see, in the sky or on the ground. As soon as the 1972 season ended, head coach Ed Khayat and general manager Pete Retzlaff were unceremoniously fired by the team owner, Leonard Tose. Khayat's desire to have his players cut their hair and remain clean-shaven certainly had little to do with his team's bad fortunes in his final year as Philly's head coach. And to both men's credit, Bradley continued to admire his former head coach well after he was terminated.

"You've got to respect the man," said Bradley. "He's an honest man. He's consistent. You've got to respect him for that. We have one thing in common—football. We both enjoy it. He's a football nut and I am too.[30] I was against his firing because he was the only one who got us up near .500 (in 1971). The vets were real unhappy because we thought that with Eddie, we thought that we had turned things around. We thought we had some momentum going. And then the next thing you know, he's gone."[31]

The departed Coach Khayat understood that even though football was first and foremost a team game, individuals in the sport can nevertheless excel at one specific role or position on the team. Despite the team's losing 2-11-1 record in 1972, Bradley would nevertheless have another outstanding season. He had proven his worth to both Khayat and Retzlaff, as evidenced by their willingness to allow their free safety to roam around in the defensive secondary at his own discretion. True, many opposing quarterbacks started to throw the ball away from Bradley's usual area of coverage, but even so, the four-year veteran free safety still managed to make his share of interceptions. He picked off nine passes, good enough for the best mark in the entire NFL. It marked the very first time in history that a player has led the league in interceptions two years in a row.

Also occurring for the second straight year was an invitation that Bradley received to the Pro Bowl, which was pro football's version of an All-Star Game. The players with the best statistics are usually considered as shoo-ins to play in the game. Moreover, the honors coming Bradley's way after the 1972 season were also tangible in nature.

"We had these big banquets at the end of the year," remembered Bradley, "and everybody who led their department was there. For instance, running backs who had the most rushing yards would be there. They had a great big premiere. It was like an Oscar Awards premier. Every year in Chicago, they had a big premier and banquet. All the league leaders got awards. I got two trophies that look just like Oscars, except they are football awards. They're the best trophies that you could get. You're at the top of the game when they did that. Those are my treasured trophies. Those are my Oscars."[32]

The honors that Bradley earned came his way also because of his ability to adapt to a major change in the game. The league's playing fields were altered following the 1971 season, as seen with the change in hashmark placement. The hashmarks are the inbounds lines marking each yard in the middle of the field. In between those hashmarks is where the ball is placed at the beginning of each play. From there, the ball gets snapped by the center, and each new play begins. In 1972, the hashmarks were placed 18 feet and 6 inches apart from each other on every professional field, the same distance as the goal posts stands apart from each other. Pro football experts believed that the move would increase more passing attempts and more passing yardage in the game. Instead, the new hashmark placement gave rise to more 1,000-yard rushers than any previous year. Despite this fact, when the opposing offenses did throw the ball, Bradley was ready. His skills at being in the right place at the right time enabled him to curtail many opposing offensive game plans. The result? Bradley continued to pick off passes and was lauded all throughout the league.

"Bill Bradley is the only player in NFL history to lead the league in interceptions with two different fields, and this is *huge!*" acknowledged noted pro football historian and author T.J. Troup. Noting the wide side of the field from 1971 to the short side of the field in 1972, Troup declared that "Bradley's ability to adapt and adjust meant that he could handle any coverage. He could take the back coming out of the backfield, or he could play a deep centerfield. He was athletic, instinctive, and quick. And he led the league in interceptions as a result."[33]

Even though he lost his job after the 1972 season ended, Eagles general manager Pete Retzlaff must have felt at least some measure of satisfaction, and maybe even relief, by knowing that his decision to suck up his pride and give in to Bill Bradley's contract demands proved to be the right move. Bradley's league-leading interception statistics were confirmation enough of that. But Bradley was not satisfied. He intensely disliked losing football games, and he wanted desperately to amend that occurrence. Moreover, he knew that his talents were greatly needed if Philadelphia was ever going to have a winning season. But his talents were also just one part of an established group.

"I like to do whatever I can if it will help the team," acknowledged Bradley. "And I want to do them well. But when you have a 40-man squad (Author's Note: the roster limit for all NFL teams in 1972 was 40 active players), it takes all 40 men. Everybody has to have a part. All 40 have to play an important role."[34]

Bill Bradley had now—by the end of the 1972 season—officially established himself as a defensive back who was one of the best in the game. He had secured an important role on the team, and everyone on the Eagles looked up to him as an integral part of their defense. He now owned a title in the NFL record books, as the first man in the history of the game to lead the league in interceptions two years in a row. Other players have and will continue to tie that record as the years go by. But no one else will ever be the first to own that honor. That distinction belongs to a free-spirited guy from Palestine, Texas, by the name of Bill Bradley.

WATCHING THE TURNSTILES TURN

Numerous changes were in store for both Bill Bradley and for the Philadelphia Eagles as the 1973 season dawned. Leonard Tose began the year by trying to find a new head coach for his team to replace Ed Khayat. During the early 1970s, most NFL teams seeking a new mentor on the sidelines would usually look throughout the league for a promising assistant coach. That is exactly what Tose did when his search ended right in Philly's own division, the NFC East. Mike McCormack was a great offensive lineman for the Cleveland Browns from 1954-1962. During the early 1970s, he was also an assistant coach for George Allen and the Washington Redskins. Tose heard plenty of good comments about McCormack, so he offered him the job, which the future Hall of Famer eagerly accepted. It would be his first head coaching assignment in the pro ranks.

The Eagles of 1973 somehow held a measure of excitement in Philadelphia. For whatever reason—or group of reasons—the specter of hope permeated the team and the public. Obtaining a new head coach and a whole new coaching staff was getting to be a regular occurrence for the Eagles, at least once every few years. But there was more to this optimistic feeling than just a new group of teachers.

Another big reason involved obtaining a guy who played the most important position in the game, that of starting quarterback. But landing a superstar quarterback? That did not happen all too often, for most teams were extremely covetous of a quarterback who has proven his worth to them. Nevertheless, occasionally, such a quarterback can be found, especially if the most recent word on him involved his injuries. The subject of injuries can strike fear in the hearts and minds of even the bravest of general managers. No one wanted to take a chance on a quarterback who was injury prone.

The Eagles, however, were to find such a quarterback on the open market in 1973. McCormack worked out a deal with the Los Angeles Rams to obtain a proven passer, Roman Gabriel, in exchange for Eagles wide receiver Harold Jackson. It was a trade which immediately helped both teams, as Jackson ended the year by catching 40 passes, a total of 13 of which went for touchdowns. Gabriel, a 12-year veteran, would lead the league in passing attempts (460), passing completions (270), passing yardage (3,219), and touchdowns (23) for the Eagles in 1973. The knock on Gabriel from many onlookers was that he was over the hill, and that his throwing arm no longer possessed the needed strength, thanks to several recent surgeries. By the end of the year, however, he was being labeled, fairly or not, as "The Messiah." The hype surrounding Gabriel might have been justified, because the team's offense—especially its passing attack—unquestionably improved by leaps and bounds in McCormack's first year, thanks largely to Gabriel's throwing prowess.

The Eagles defense, however, was another story entirely. McCormack spent much of his time working on improving the offense at the expense of the defense, a unit which also had to deal with untimely injuries. Bill Bradley remained healthy and was affixed to the free safety position, but he had to get used to several different defenders sharing the field with him. In fact, by the time that 1973 rolled around, Bradley would notice a trend on the roster—both on offense and defense—that was occurring far too often. The whole team was changing again too quickly for the squad to develop any consistency or stability.

"One of the problems that we had throughout all of those years, was that the team wasn't patient," explained Bradley. "I had four different head coaches in Philadelphia. So, what the management would do...was that they weren't patient. We'd get everything starting to go in the right direction, and then they would fire the coach, because we couldn't get a winning season started. So they bring in a new coach, and mind you, he's coming in, and he looks to bring in some of his (trusted) people where he came from. Not just new assistant coaches, but new players too. I mean you're changing out sometimes upwards of 15 guys. And every coaching staff had a new agenda, and so we changed coaches like we changed underwear.

"It was hard to get continuity within a team if you're shifting people around. You know, six, eight, or more players that a coach swaps out for other players that were doing good from wherever they came from. So you're not going in the right direction, but they're changing head coaches all the time. Now I know the press will put pressure on the owner of the team. A lot of the owners don't really know much about football. But you know they're running a business, so sometimes a change in coaches is going to renew the interest in building up the team in the press. That's just my opinion."[1]

Bradley's opinion in retrospect was sound, especially if you look at the results of the changes about which he spoke. But Bradley was not just going to have to get used to a whole new coaching staff in 1973. He was also going to have to get used to a whole new defensive philosophy. His new defensive back coach was John Mazur, a former head coach for the New England Patriots. Mazur did not prefer to duplicate the coverages that the previous coaching staff selected to employ. You see, Bill Bradley was most effective when he could roam around the defensive secondary on his own in various zone coverages. He had by this time in his career the brains and the talent to successfully read both quarterbacks and receivers, and he was more than able to cause incompletions and interceptions to occur.

The position of free safety was tailor made for a guy like Bradley. The role required a man who possessed blazing speed to keep pace with wide receivers, who were typically the fastest players in the league. It also required the quickness to backpedal, stop on a dime, change directions, then sprint to the point of attack. He once even admitted that it seemed that he could run as quickly going backwards as he could going forwards. Bradley could excel at all of those important maneuvers, and he could perform them about as well as any free safety in the NFL. He could effectively thwart an opposing passing attack, all by being able to fool or confuse opposing quarterbacks. It was partly a chess match, partly a guessing game, and it required both strategy and skill. Judging simply by Bradley's 11 interceptions in 1971 and his nine interceptions in 1972, he was obviously one of the Eagles' greatest defenders during the decade of the 1970s.

"Some people have called it the free spirit position," said Bradley, "where you're free to create. I think that's so."[2]

Nevertheless, Bill Bradley could not afford to get too used to having free reign back there in the defensive secondary. He still had to acknowledge and address the common accepted elements of pass coverages...and of reading what the opposing quarterbacks were trying to do.

"The safety and the quarterback are playing games with each other's mind," explained Bradley. "Most pro quarterbacks are good thinkers, and the challenge is to get on their wavelength, to figure out what they are trying to do to you. The quarterback is moving his people, trying to distract me. So while he's going back to pass, I like to react to what the quarterback is doing. I try to piece everything together at a hurried pace. I can't just read in front of me. Maybe the quarterback sends his tight end across my face, but I have to have peripheral vision and see if a wide receiver is trying to get behind me, too. Then, when the quarterback sets to throw, I pick him up. Eventually, he has to telegraph where he's going to throw. Even if he's trying to look me off with his head and eyes, his body language may be tipping me off. I have to take him in as a whole person."[3]

But in 1973, the "whole" safety position would change dramatically for the Eagles. Mazur stifled the freedom that Bradley was familiar with when he retreated into his various coverages. Now, he would be required to stick to a predetermined area in a zone, and he would not have the autonomy to rove around the variety of passing lanes. The results of this new strategy were seen in the statistics. Bradley only intercepted four passes in 1973, five less than he picked off in the previous year. However, fairness dictates that there was more than one reason for Bradley's lesser amount of interceptions.

"I don't know for sure," surmised Bradley, "but I feel that if McCormack and Mazur would have left me alone in the secondary, I would have gotten more interceptions in 1973 (than what I did). But I do know the opponents, especially in our division (the NFC East)... they knew that I was apt to intercepting passes. So by '73, some of their game plans included not throwing deep balls or not throwing to where I could roam and go get to the ball. And that happened to me because of leading the league in interceptions for two years in a row." 4

Philadelphia's 1973 season began like all the previous seasons, at least since Bill Bradley was playing for them...by losing. Another losing streak to start the year, meaning that the team really did more than enough damage to its own potential playoff chances, all before mid-October. Broken record time again for the boys in South Philly. But there was one difference worth noting. The Eagles were not getting blown out by their opponents in 1973. They remained competitive in every game. They were not winners...but they were playing almost like they were. Ample proof of this occurred in their first game against the St. Louis Cardinals at Veterans Stadium. The Cardinals vaulted to a quick 24-6 halftime lead. Eagles teams from previous years might have packed it in and quit at this point, but to their credit, the 1973 Philadelphia squad ignored the scoreboard and fought back hard in the second half. They came to within one point of tying the game at 24-23, until St. Louis took advantage of a couple of big plays late in the fourth quarter to post a 34-23 win.

Even so, the mere sight of an Eagles comeback was pleasing to their loyal fans.

It was also quite pleasing to Bill Bradley. For years, he had yearned to see some signs of life in his team, some signs that showed that they were now on the right road. Up to 1973, such signs were few and far between, if visible at all. Bradley desired to observe a welcomed signal or two that there was hope for the team's future, and that there was hope that they could compete well, even after falling behind on the scoreboard. Bradley wanted the team to develop a new mindset, where they knew that they were not far from being winners.

"I think," said Bradley back in 1973, "that the biggest thing this team has to do is convince themselves that there's not that much difference between themselves and the (World Champion) Miami Dolphins. You HAVE to convince yourself. It's a state of mind."[5]

Both Bradley's and the Eagles' states of mind would once again be tested during the next several weeks, and the end results would not be too pleasing. They once again fought back in their second game to take a lead against the host New York Giants. But they allowed New York placekicker Pete Gogolak to kick a 14-yard field goal with no time remaining to produce a 23-23 tie. A couple of weeks later, Philadelphia placekicker Tom Dempsey missed a makeable field goal in a similar situation at Buffalo, which cost the Eagles a 27-26 decision.

Nevertheless, this 1973 season was a marathon, not a sprint. McCormack, Mazur, Bradley, and indeed everyone involved with the Eagles knew that to be the case. They also knew that just one big win might turn things around. They got that one big win in week five, when they came from behind to post a thrilling 27-24 victory over the St. Louis Cardinals at Busch Memorial Stadium. Roman Gabriel tossed two clutch touchdown passes late in the fourth quarter to secure the win—the team's first of the year. A couple of weeks later, they notched what was probably their biggest triumph in the past several years, a 30-16 rout over division rivals the Dallas Cowboys. This was probably one of the most important games of the year for the Eagles, because it proved that they could defeat a Super Bowl-caliber team like the Cowboys.

"The overall spirit, the attitude, was the difference," said Philadelphia head coach Mike McCormack, who knew that his free safety's spirit and emotion did a lot to inspire the defense, which was vital in causing four costly Dallas turnovers in the game. "We wanted the game and we weren't going to be denied. This is a game of emotion, and we were emotional. Our young people were hitting. We have improved each week and have become a solid football team. We have not been embarrassed, and (we) won't be embarrassed against some tough football teams."[6]

A week later, Philly proved Coach McCormack's words to be quite prophetic, as they came from behind again to post an impressive 24-23 win over the up-and-coming New England Patriots. This was starting to be an uplifting season after all for the Eagles. Their offense was making big plays, and their defense and special teams were as well. In the victory over the visiting Patriots, the Philadelphia special teams contributed two blocked kicks, and rookie defensive end Will Wynn scored a touchdown when he recovered a New England fumble on the snap back to the punter and sprinted 24 yards to the end zone for a score.

"We have a lot of pride in our specialty units," affirmed Eagles linebacker and special teams player Steve Zabel.[7]

By the middle of the 1973 season, these prideful Eagles had already bettered their record by one victory over what they accrued throughout all of 1972. Moreover, it was becoming evident that Bradley was adjusting well to his new defensive assignments. So much so, in fact, that even though his interception totals were way down from the previous two years (he only intercepted one pass in the first nine games of 1973), his new secondary coach, John Mazur, was quite pleased with what he was witnessing.

"They (opposing quarterbacks) are steering away from him (Bradley), which is fine," said Mazur. "Bill's doing a fine job pursuing and getting into the action, jarring balls loose. The fact that he was named a defensive co-captain by the coaching staff shows how highly we think of him as a player and a leader."[8]

Bradley's leadership would be tested in the next two weeks, however, as the Eagles dropped consecutive games to the Atlanta Falcons and to the revenge-minded Dallas Cowboys. In both of those contests, Philadelphia took early leads, only to have their opposition come back strong to obtain wins. These two losses eliminated any hope that the Eagles had to make the playoffs. Even so, the team did not give up. In fact, they did the opposite. Philadelphia won a game that they were expected to win by beating the New York Giants on November 25 by a score of 20-16. McCormack's bunch then had another difficult challenge on their hands in the following game. Once again, the Eagles had every reason to surrender their hope for victory when they traveled to San Francisco to take on the 49ers. That was because the Eagles gave their fans an unwelcomed flash-back view of the previous year, when they got behind San Francisco by a demoralizing score of 28-0 at halftime.

One of the 49ers touchdowns was scored when Bill Bradley made one of his few mistakes of the season. Bradley was no longer required to be the team's first-string punter, but he was still being required to return punts for the Eagles. As he attempted to do so in the first quarter at San Francisco, he was immediately hit by a torpedo, which appeared to most onlookers as 49ers offensive lineman and special teams performer, Forrest Blue. The resulting fumble was recovered by San Francisco defensive back Windlan Hall, who returned it 61 yards for a score.

"I just brushed it off," said Bradley, who would later intercept a pass in the game. "It was one of the only fumbles that I ever had on a punt return. My fumble wasn't a case of a lack of concentration. Blue's helmet hit the ball, and it went 20 yards up the field. They recovered it and went in and scored. I remembered that because it cost our team a touchdown, which ended up being a touchdown that won the game for them. But it was a legitimate hit, and a helmet right on the ball. It was a weird deal. I think that I returned 100 punts in my career (Author's Note: Bradley returned 122 punts throughout his nine-year pro career). I was good for 10 or 12 yards every time I caught a punt, but fielding it cleanly and holding on to it was the most important thing."[9]

The Eagles held on to the huge halftime deficit against the 49ers for only a moment, however. As soon as the third quarter began, they met their opposition with both fervor and determination. Philadelphia's frustration and embarrassment that was felt throughout the first half melded in the minds of McCormack's players in the final two stanzas of this game. They began hitting the 49ers players harder and with more intensity than they hit any team all season long. This battering display resulted in four San Francisco turnovers, which in turn led to some Philly scores. The Eagles offense registered 28 points of their own in the second half, but unfortunately, that was still not enough to obtain a win. The 49ers held on for a 38-28 victory, and the Eagles now held on to a 4-7-1 record, with two more games remaining in the 1973 season.

The second-to-last contest featured another game that the Eagles were expected to win. It was at home versus the New York Jets, a team that was in the midst of one of its worst seasons in years, thanks primarily to an injury sustained by their superstar starting quarterback, Joe Namath, who missed most of the year with a separated shoulder. But despite what the oddsmakers may have thought about who *should* win this contest, it was the Jets who embarked upon a 17-0 lead in the second quarter. Nothing new for the Eagles, who by now were quite accustomed to falling behind early in most of their games. But despite their deficit, this Philadelphia team was also accustomed to coming back and staying in contention, which is exactly what they did when they scored 17 points in the third quarter on their way to a clutch 24-23 triumph. It was the fifth victory of the season for the Eagles, which was three more wins than what they could accomplish in 1972.

"It wasn't an artistic victory, but we'll take it," said Philadelphia head coach Mike McCormack following his team's come from behind win over the Jets. "I'm real pleased with the defensive unit. They got together and saved me from going completely white-headed."[10]

No one at RFK Stadium the following week would be able to avoid sporting white hair, however. Philadelphia's final game of the 1973 season would be held in a blizzard in Washington, D.C. The host Redskins needed to win to make the playoffs, but the Eagles did everything in their power to keep them from doing so. Gabriel threw for 302 yards despite the falling snowflakes, but Washington's running game was too much for Philadelphia's defense to handle. The Redskins prevailed, 38-20, and the Eagles ended 1973 with a 5-8-1 record. The result of this match signified and displayed a common trend that was viewed during the year for the Eagles defense. Their opponents were wise enough to realize that the Philadelphia pass coverage, led by Bill Bradley, was their strongest element. As a result, opposing teams would simply spend more time running the ball against the Eagles than they did throwing it, for it was on the ground where they experienced most of their success. Philadelphia's defense—and Bradley in particular—would thus have to focus most of their efforts on stopping the run. The adjustment to this strategy often met with unsatisfactory results, as evidenced by the 2,423 total yards (4.7 yards per carry) that the Eagles defense gave up to their foes when the plays were of the ground variety.

"Other teams weren't throwing much (against us)," explained Bradley, who picked off his final pass of the year against the Redskins and returned it 18 yards. "And when they did, they didn't throw it to the deep middle (where Bradley was usually situated). I wound up playing the run like a middle linebacker."[11]

The 5-foot-11, 190-pound Bradley ended 1973 by doing the best that he could to tackle opposing runners, quite a few of whom outweighed him. He typically just did whatever he could to get in their way, then latch a hold of them and try to slow them down enough so that a teammate could catch up to the runner and help Bradley bring the man down. It was a strategy that he utilized all throughout his years playing on defense. His main asset was his speed, and if he could use that speed to catch up to the ball carrier to slow him down, then that strategy was deemed a success. No coach can criticize a defensive player who helps to make a tackle, regardless of how he does it.

And Bradley readily admitted that although 1973 was a rewarding season for him personally, it was still a season that his team failed to achieve a winning record. That was the most important goal for him, and in his five-year career, he had yet to see it happen. Nevertheless, as soon as the season ended, Bradley made a trip down south to Texas. He was invited to play in the annual Pro Bowl game, which in this particular year would be played in Dallas, at Texas Stadium. The Pro Bowl was the final NFL game of the season, and it featured the best players in the AFC versus the best players in the NFL. In the 1970s, it was considered an honor to play in it. Before that game, however, Bradley experienced one of the most incredible and humorous stories of his life. It is a story that has several different segments to it, and woven together, those segments all had a role in what eventually happened. It is an unforgettable story that, almost 50 years later, still gives Bradley a hearty laugh today.

"It's one of the funniest stories in the world," admitted a chuckling Bradley. "I was in my hometown of Palestine, Texas, and I had to drive 112 miles to Dallas. I had to take my dad's pickup truck, drive it up to Dallas, and check into a hotel. But I didn't go alone. It was me, (former Eagles teammates) Billy Walik and Tim Rossovich, and my girl*friend*, Cis Rhundel. We were joined by my parents, my aunt, my uncle, my brother Red, and my aunt Jackie, all of whom went in another vehicle. We went to this resort hotel on the Central Expressway, and we went to see a show. It was Wayne Cochrane, who promoted himself as the white James Brown. He was just like James Brown, but he was white. He had the wig, the cape, all that kind of stuff. He sang soul music really well, and he was a big hit in Florida and some other places. So anyway, we get shellacked (drunk)."[12]

Whenever alcoholic beverages get introduced into a Bill Bradley story, the outcome can sometimes be predicted. Even so, the drinks in this particular story played just a small role in all of the other elements that helped to make this anecdote one for the ages.

"So after the show, we left to do some other things," said Bradley, who was trying his best—but still in a failed effort—to slow down on his giggling all throughout the retelling of this gem of a tale. "My mother and them went back to their hotel where they were staying, but me, Billy, Cis, and Timmy...I think Timmy was with us. I can't swear that he was, and I'm pretty sure he was. Anyway, we go back to our hotel, and it was sometime after 10 (p.m.). The hotel bar was still open, and they had a jukebox and some pool tables. So we came in there, and it was pretty much empty, but we could still get a drink. So we get in there and these two old men were sitting and talking at a table behind a pool table, close to the jukebox. So keep in mind, we were shellacked. We walked over there, and we didn't know those two guys from Adam. It seemed like they were having fun."[13]

There is usually a feeling of shock and awe when we meet a famous person. It is almost as if it is hard to believe that a famous person is actually in the same room, right in the flesh, with us "normal" people, and whenever a famous person crosses our paths in our "ordinary" and "run of the mill" lives, we are usually unprepared for the moment. That is, unless you have something to loosen yourself up and help you to act relaxed and natural...something perhaps like alcohol. This is sort of what happened to Bradley, Walik, Rhundel, and Rossovich at this moment, in a nondescript hotel bar. Bradley's backstory information provides some necessary explanations:

"I had gone out to Las Vegas before, to see a couple of girl*friends* with James Street and a couple of other guys who I played football with at (the University of) Texas," continued Bradley, "and I had watched Evel Knievel try to jump that fountain at Caesar's Palace (Author's Note: Yes, Knievel's first name is spelled Evel, not Evil). Of course, he was all dolled up with a helmet, his jumpsuit, and all that stuff. We were standing there at the end of the crowd, and there was a giant crowd around him where the takeoff was. And he jumped and he gets catawampus on the landing, and starts crashing, and he broke his pelvic bone. He lived, though...he didn't get knocked out or anything. So that jump was before our meeting with the two guys sitting in regular street clothes behind the pool table.

"We go up to them and say, 'Hey, would you all like a drink?' So we bought them both a drink and we shook hands with them. And one of the guys says, 'I'm Knievel.' And I'm looking at him, and he looked familiar. And the other guy says, 'I'm Amarillo Slim.' Now Amarillo Slim was known as the best Hold 'Em poker player in the United States. Then the first guy says, 'My name's Evel.' And I'm thinking to myself, 'Oh God. This guy named himself after Evel Knievel!' Now mind you, I'm feeling the full effects of my drinks by this time."[14]

The full effects of meeting the actual daredevil Evel Knievel eventually occurred for Bradley, however. He ultimately came to the realization that he had just met a couple of famous people...much more famous than himself, in his opinion. Bradley was probably also thinking in this particular moment of introspection, that in the case of meeting Evel Knievel, he had finally met someone in his life who was quite possibly even crazier than himself, if such a man ever existed. But the story certainly does not stop there.

"So the bar is closing down," Bradley recalled, "and we still have my dad's pickup truck. So we get in our pickup truck, and Billy (Walik) is sitting in the back, Cis was in the middle, and Timmy was by the window. I said, 'Timmy, you need to drive. I don't think that I can drive back to our room,' which was a little way away from the bar."[15]

To the average person, this would appear to be a smart move. Calling for a designated driver during this situation was probably one of the most cognizant and logical moves that Bill Bradley made throughout this evening. Unfortunately, Tim Rossovich was likely no more sober than anyone else in the truck. That fact soon became apparent to all concerned.

"So we're in the truck, and we see Evel walking with his cane, and he had about 200 yards to go to get to his hotel room," remembered Bradley. "So I told them (Amarillo Slim and Evel Knievel) to "...get into the back of the truck, and we'll drop you off at your room on the way down to ours."[16]

Getting into Bradley's Father's pickup truck was probably the biggest mistake that these two gentlemen made on that night. It was a mistake that they fortunately were able to live through to tell the tale about. But for a few unnerving moments, that fact would be touch and go for a while.

"So they told me their room numbers and we headed down the bank," recounted Bradley. "Well down the bank they had what we called a 'Sleeping Policeman,' which is commonly called a speed-bump. Timmy was driving, and he wasn't being wild or anything. I told him to go slow. In the back of the truck, we were sitting on one side of the bed to the other, and our feet are hanging out the sides and the tailgate. Billy (Walik) is sitting in one spot, and Evel is sitting next to him. I'm on the other side with my feet hanging out the side, and Amarillo is on the same side. Well, Timmy takes off, and remember, he is not going very fast. And he didn't know that there were speed-bumps in the road."[17]

Sometimes, a lack of common or basic knowledge presents a major problem for many people. And as is usually the case, we humans do not seem to acquire common or basic knowledge until after we make some mistakes...or drive over a few speedbumps in our lives.

"I remember this like it was yesterday," admitted Bradley, as he anxiously explained what happened next. "So Timmy hits a speed-bump going about maybe three miles an hour. And you know how riding in the back of a truck feels? Well, he hits that bump, and we start rattling around, and I hear a cane flying on the ground. And then we hear Evel. We know by now that it's Evel Knievel! By now! And Evel starts screaming, 'Stop this motherfucker now! Stop this son of a bitch right now!' And we're all rattling around in the back of the truck.

"So we stop and let Evel out, and we dust him off, and we're standing around the back of the pickup. And he says, 'Man, this is painful!' He gets his cane and says, 'I'm walking back to my damn room!' As he and Amarillo start walking back to their rooms, Evel looks back, and he sees us all disheveled a little bit, and he says to us, 'I just jumped 30 buses in London, and I tried to jump Caesar's Palace, and that's why I'm crippled! This is the worst fucking ride that I've ever been on!' And keep in mind, he almost got *killed* at Caesar's Palace! And he was almost crying from laughing so damn hard. All of us were. And that's how I met Evel Knievel."[18]

As strange, implausible, or hilarious as this story was, Bill Bradley also met some other people on this trip to Dallas. But they were the type of people that he would have preferred to avoid, because they were officers of the law. You see, Bradley still had to report to practice for the Pro Bowl, and during the week of practice for that game, the players selected to play in that contest are granted plenty of free time in the evenings, to explore the host city, or take in a movie, or whatever. For some of the players, that free time was spent relaxing after a tough and arduous season of pro football, and this Pro Bowl game was their reward. But for Bill Bradley, however, that free time needed to be spent having fun. Remember, he was a free spirit after all. He had to be true to his nature.

"After that adventure with Evel Knievel and Amarillo Slim, we were riding around in that pickup truck, and we got arrested," admitted Bradley. "I was drag racing the truck from one red light to another for $25. This guy in a red and white Cadillac Eldorado rolled his window down, and I rolled mine down. All right, we agreed to race for $25 to the next light. We'd take off right there. Well, my dad's pickup truck had a big V-8 engine in it. As long as I didn't spin out, I could give that big old tank (the Cadillac) that he was driving a run for his money. So when the light goes green, I slam on the gas pedal and beat him to the next light. Well we both pull over after the race, and he (Bradley's competitor) pulls over in front of us."[19]

Have you ever had someone stiff you of the money that they owe you? Whether it be from a loan that was not repaid, or from giving you the incorrect change at the supermarket...or when you beat them in a drag race, and they fail, or rather, refuse, to pay you what rightfully belongs to you (i.e. your winnings)? Well, that is the position that Bill Bradley and Billy Walik found themselves in at this moment. Unbeknownst to them at the time, there was also a witness to all these shenanigans.

"I tell Billy to jump out that side and go over there and collect our money," Bradley explains. "Well Billy walks past my truck, then he gets to the front headlight of that Cadillac, and the guy that we just beat in the race floors it! He floors it! And Billy has to jump out of the way! That Cadillac almost hit him, but he jumped out of the way and rolled a little bit on the road after he landed on the road. Well, we chase this guy down to the next light. Well we didn't know it at the time, but there were cops who were hiding in a nearby parking lot, and they chase us down. I pull over once I see their flashing lights, and to make a long story short, they bust us for speeding and for illegal drag racing. So, they arrest us and take us down to the local police precinct and book us. And so we go to jail." [20]

By this time in this unique adventure, Bill Bradley has probably felt that his luck had run out. You readers probably have too. But even the unluckiest people now and then have a special angel watching over them, to give them a break that they probably—in all reason and likelihood—do not deserve. That is exactly what happen to the two Bills on this winter's night in Dallas, Texas.

"This is an amazing story," declared Bradley in an obvious understatement. "So we're at the jailhouse, and they're taking my fingerprints. They're taking my front picture, my side picture...like they do when they're booking you. Now, flashback for a moment. The man who was coaching the NFC team in that Pro Bowl (following the 1973 season) was Tom Landry and his staff (Author's Note: Hall of Famer Tom Landry was the head coach of the Dallas Cowboys, a division rival of Bradley's Philadelphia Eagles). Now we had a meeting before the Pro Bowl with our team, and with all of our coaches. Tom Landry told us at that meeting...he said, 'Listen, if you all get in a bind, or any kind of deal, here's my card. Call me.'

"So the officers take us into a building, and I was given the right to make a phone call. I had one (business) card, and it was Tom Landry's card. I called him, and he didn't say much. He said, 'Where are you?' I said, 'I'm at the police precinct, behind the airport at Love Field.' And he knew where it was, and he came over there."[21]

Famous people often become the victim of stereotypes in the public eye. It is frequently unavoidable. Tom Landry's stereotype was that of a stern, rigid, and yet extremely intelligent man. He was very analytical, and he was also a man of few words. Many people felt that his often-cold persona was an accurate indication of his personality. But that was not the case. He had other sides to his personality as well, and all too often, no one ever got a chance to observe some of those other sides. You see, stereotypes—at least those of Tom Landry —are true to a degree. But sometimes they are not. Are they fair? Possibly. But on many occasions, as in this narrative, Tom Landry proved to Bill Bradley, and possibly to some others, that he was also a compassionate and understanding man, and that some of the stereotypes that often accompanied the name of Tom Landry were undeniably false.

"Tom Landry got me *out* of jail," said Bradley. "He didn't say a thing. He just got me out of jail. The cops saw that it was Tom Landry coming into their precinct, and they said, 'Hey, that's Tom Landry! We better let this guy (Bradley) and his friends out.' And not one word was said in any print media or on TV. Especially print media. He came and got me, that man did. And we didn't talk to each other, but he got me out of there, and not one word was ever said in the newspapers.

"We were rivals with the Cowboys, and he could have probably gotten me kicked out of football. (Author's Note: Tom Landry was a person who had an irrefutable reputation throughout pro football. He was so honored throughout the league, that when he talked, everybody in all offices of the NFL listened). But the man took care of me, and I have all the respect in the world for him...even though the Cowboys still suck (laughter). When (fellow Eagles teammates) Jerry Sisemore, Steve Zabel, Billy Walik...when we'd get together today and text each other, the first line in our texts isn't 'Hi! How are you doing?' It's, 'The Cowboys still suck.' And then we'd talk about it (laughter)."[22]

After all these incredible adventures, Bradley knew that it would still take a lot of hard work to prove to the rest of the league that his refrain of "The Cowboys still suck" would be more than just a braggadocios group of words. The only way to do that was to beat their divisional foe on the gridiron. He and his Eagles would indeed get another chance in 1974 to prove that they were better than Tom Landry's Dallas Cowboys, and as it turned out, they would do so, and on national television to boot.

8

FIGHTING FOR SOME HOPE

The 1974 National Football League season would be one of the most unique in the history of the game, at least up to that point. But before Bill Bradley and his teammates would ever step foot on the practice fields at Widener University in Chester, Pennsylvania, for summer training camp, they had to address a problematic situation that surfaced across the league. In fact, every pro player would have to deal with this predicament, which was a labor dispute between the team owners and their players. The business side of the game once again made a showing on the scene, and whereas players of past eras would never have given thought to demanding more money or better financial benefits from the team owners—for fear of being cut outright from their teams—the players in 1974 were bolder than their predecessors, with a stronger sense of themselves, and of what their worth was to the owners, and to the game itself.

The 1970s had a moniker in American society, that of being "The Me Decade." It was hard to disagree with that label, as almost everywhere you looked, people across the nation were paying much more attention to their own lives, their own futures, and their own financial well beings. The players across the landscape of the NFL were no different. Despite what many people today might believe, professional athletes did not on average make the millions of dollars in the 1970s that they do today. One look at Bill Bradley's previous holdout (See Chapter Six) confirmed that only a token few players were granted a six-figure salary in that era, and obtaining such did not come about without one heck of a fight. If you were not a superstar, then you were usually subjected to a salary that rarely paid you a living wage for a season. And if you did not like it, too bad. You really had few rights to obtain a trade to another team. You had to sign what contract your team presented to you, especially if you wanted to continue playing pro football. Your only real alternative was to do what Bradley did...hold out and hope that the ownership would change their minds.

Terry Hanratty, a former All-American quarterback from Notre Dame University, and a guy whom Bill Bradley played against in the famous Big-33 Game back in 1965 (See Chapter One), and who during the early 1970s was a starting quarterback for the Pittsburgh Steelers, was a witness to the financial dilemmas that were faced by 99 percent of the players in the NFL prior to 1974. His memories of what he and the rest of his teammates faced during the summer of 1974 are identical to what all the other veteran players across the league observed at that time.

"People don't realize that back then, the minimum salary in the NFL was $12,500," explained Hanratty, who was a union representative for the Steelers in 1975. "That's hard to believe. Today the minimum league salary is $650,000 I believe, or somewhere in that range. After taxes (in 1974), you're probably taking home $9,000 a year. You probably had a couple of kids. You know, we all had to work in the offseason. And if your team was not in the playoffs, and your final game was at home, your car was packed with all of your shit in there. After the (final) game, you drove to wherever you may have lived, because you started work (at your second job) on the following Monday morning."[1]

Guys like Hanratty and Bradley were not in the same economic ballpark as noteworthy celebrity players such as Joe Namath or O.J. Simpson. Those household names were taking home salaries that were well over $400,000 each year, not to mention the enormous amounts of money that they were making by endorsing numerous consumer products on television and radio advertisements every year. No, the average NFL players—even longstanding veterans with over 10 years of service—were certainly not in the upper echelon of income earners, compared to the mere handful of icons in the league. Because of this, and because they were simply sick and tired of working two jobs to make ends meet every year, they expressed a redress of their economic issues with the only entity who would listen: the players union.

The leader of the NFL Players Association, or NFLPA for short, was a lawyer by the name of Ed Garvey. He was really the first labor leader to take up the cause for the players in a strong and dramatic way. Garvey kept the players' plight in the headlines, which was most distressful to the team owners. He insisted that each team designate a union representative, which they did. Some of these delegates also vocalized their grievances in the media, which just added on to Garvey's invective. Matters all came to a head as the 1974 summer training camps began. The attendees to those summer training camps on day one were a bunch of rookies. Across the league, it was nothing but rookies. A strike had been called, and most of the rank-and-file veterans across the league supported it.

This 1974 NFL Players Strike was not the first players strike in league annals, but it turned out to be the biggest one, at least before 1982. Picket signs were painted ahead of time, for the worst was expected. In cities across the league, veteran players were protesting team practices, and in a union-based town like Philadelphia, work stoppages were second nature to most. It became common to see popular guys like a Bill Bradley or a Harold Carmichael pacing around in front of Veterans Stadium, carrying picket signs. Garvey joined with the team representatives and came up with a total of 90 demands for the owners to address. Yes, 90 demands! This, in retrospect, was not a good move on the part of the player's union, because it automatically put the owners in a defensive posture. If the ultimate goal among the players was to gain a reparation of at least some of those demands, and to obtain a solution to the grievances over annual finances and salaries, the veteran players found out that they faced an uphill fight against the rigid and unbending 26 league owners (Author's Note: In 1974, the NFL had 26 teams, whereas today there are 32), who were content with filling out their rosters with rookies and walk-ons. The veteran players on strike had another name for those players.

"We called them scabs, and we were harassing them as they came into the preseason games," recalled Bradley. "We were out there striking, and holding up signs that said 'No Freedom, No Football.' Some of the Redskins players would come up and they would picket with us. It had a lasting effect on us. It ended up that we were throwing whiskey bottles and shit like that at the buses that were coming in with the scabs in them."[2]

Bradley's anger paralleled those of his striking teammates, and in many respects, it was justified. The team owners were getting very wealthy, thanks to the arduous labors, and the blood, sweat, and tears of the players. But where a large amount of bitterness came from, ironically, was not how the players were treated during the regular season. No, that acrimony came about during the preseason.

"Now you can't tell me after six preseason games and with the stands filled," explained Bradley, who is still caustically bitter over this mistreatment, "...you cannot tell me that (Eagles owner) Leonard Tose and all the owners didn't generate *way* more money from those (preseason) games than what money is generated in sports like basketball and baseball. It was a travesty!"[3]

Another travesty was the fact that while the veteran players were on strike, they were not making a dime. These were exceedingly difficult days for many players, but especially for the guys who only had one year under their NFL belts, and who did not have a whole lot of money to begin with. Bill Bradley saw these problems with some of the friends that he had on the team, and he saw them up close. He was determined, at least in one way or another within his own abilities, to help some of those players out when and where he could. That included helping them find something to do with their free time, helping them find some places in which to do those things, and perhaps most importantly, helping them find a place to live.

"I knew (offensive linemen) Jerry Sisemore and Wade Key, because both are from Texas," said Bradley. "I knew them before I even went to the Eagles. Well Sisemore was a number one draft choice from my college (the University of Texas). I picked him up at the airport after he was drafted in '73, and I told him the places to go to, which incidentally was all of the places that the NFL representative—who came in to our first meeting every year—told you not to go to (laughter). I wrote down every one of those places, and then we got to pick and choose which ones were okay. Most of the places that they (the NFL brass) would tell you not to go to were the most fun places (more laughter).[4]

"Well Sisemore, who was only in his second year in the league, had a brand-new baby in '74. He was living with me on 22nd and Spruce Street in the bottom floor of a row home in Philadelphia. He needed a place to live, so I let him stay with me. I let him come in there and sleep on my couch. He had a shower, and a shitter...all that stuff. And it helped him because he was out of money. He couldn't afford to stay in a hotel, so it was a relief to him. Staying with me enabled him to spend his money to fly home when he needed to, and then fly back to Philly."[5]

One person who really could not afford to see his team go on strike was Philadelphia head coach Mike McCormack. He was beginning his second year at the helm, and he could ill-afford to waste the momentum—if one could call it that—that the Eagles had built up with their five wins during 1973. But McCormack really had no say in whether the veteran players would go on a work stoppage or not. He also did not have any choice but to coach the large batch of rookies and walk-ons who permeated the Eagles' training camp in the summer of 1974. McCormack was a successful assistant coach at Washington prior to coming to Philadelphia, and he had the persona of being what we call now a "player's coach." That was just what the press and the public may have seen, however. In reality, McCormack was more closely aligned to Leonard Tose—the man who signed his checks—than to his players.

"Well he (McCormack) stood up at one time in front of the players, right before our strike was declared," remembered Bradley, "and he made a speech to the team. His speech was totally in favor of the owner and the money. And that was his job too. And after he gave us that speech, everybody was just looking at each other and saying to each other, 'This guy ain't even *close* to being on our side.' So, we basically boycotted him."[6]

The player's union certainly boycotted—or at least rejected—the owners' efforts to end the strike. Garvey's numerous demands were not even close to being met as the preseason games began. This drama of seeing nondescript rookies playing on every team was being witnessed across the league, and in what appeared to most as a spiteful measure, the team owners refused to discount the ticket prices. The whole mess was unseemly to the public. From the veteran players' perspective, the strike would also have the unexpected and unwelcomed stigma of seeing certain players crossing the picket lines. Some of those less-wealthy players had a legitimate reason to do so, as the pressures of not making any money, and thereby not being able to pay one's bills, was a hopeful strategy of stress that the team owners across the NFL employed. It was a battle of attrition, and by the second week of the strike, that became obvious for all involved.

"If anybody should have crossed the picket lines, it would be a guy like Jerry Sisemore," declared Bradley. "But he didn't. He was damn near broke, but he stood strong with us on the picket lines."[7]

Some veteran players did not show the strength and resolve of guys like Sisemore and Bradley, however. As it turned out, the 1974 NFL Players Strike became a referendum on personal choice, and on what was more important to each individual player. Their willingness to stay on the picket lines thus became a badge of honor of sorts with their teammates. Conversely, some veteran players across the league finally had enough of carrying their picket signs. The owners knew that this would happen. To entice some of the bigger names in the NFL to cross the protest lines and come back to training camp, the owners—in a clandestine way—sweetened the pot, as it were.

One of those owners was the dynamic Al Davis, whose Oakland Raiders were a perennial contender for a conference championship. Davis was not really a fan of attempting a measure of collusion with the other owners. Rather, he just wanted to see his players get back into camp. To accomplish that meant doing whatever it took, regardless of how improper it might have appeared to most.

"The word was that Al was paying certain guys a bonus just to come in (to camp)," said veteran Oakland outside linebacker Phil Villapiano, "and that *really* ruined things. I remember the thing that broke us (our team's determination to stay on strike) was when (starting quarterback) Kenny Stabler and (starting wide receiver) Fred Biletnikoff went to training camp. They were two of our big leaders. You see, nobody had any money. We also wanted to go to training camp, but we stuck together. And then two of our big shots (Stabler and Biletnikoff) went in and kind of ruined the whole flavor of things.

"On our team, they (Stabler and Biletnikoff) were a couple of guys that really mattered. If anybody else went in, they were probably going to be cut from the team, and they were kissing ass or something. Stabler and Biletnikoff hurt us. They went into camp without telling us, and that wasn't good. And then all of a sudden, another guy goes into camp. And then another guy. And then another guy.

"You know Al (Davis) was like that. He just knew what to do to end that strike. All he cared about was getting us back into camp. He didn't care one bit about how he had to do it. To him, the ends justified the means."[8]

Davis was not the only owner who was offering secret payments to players to get them to cross the picket lines. In Miami, Dolphins owner Joe Robbie presented star halfback Mercury Morris with a whole new contract, complete with incentives, if he refused to strike. Morris agreed to the deal, which did not really place him in the "favorite teammate" classification with the rest of the Dolphin players.

"I remember they (some of Morris' teammates) had a Winnebago out in front of Biscayne College (where the Dolphins held their summer training camp), and the guys were out there marching with their signs," said Morris. "When I came driving out there in my new Ferrari 365 Berlinetta, (offensive guard) Larry Little called me a turn-coat! I said, 'Yes, but I'm a rich turncoat!' I was hurt so I wasn't prac-ticing, but Joe Robbie just wanted the optic of Mercury Morris breaking a strike line."[9]

In Philadelphia, the situation was identical. The Eagles' front office would try to induce certain players into putting down their picket signs and picking up their shoulder pads and helmets with cash bonuses. Most of the players shunned such enticements. Some, however, did not. One of those who took the bait was one of the team's most important players.

"Well, it was a big deal," recalled Bill Bradley. "And the way I understand it, they tried to pay (star wide receiver) Harold Carmichael to cross the picket line, but he wouldn't do it. He was one of my best friends, and they talked to him. He refused the few thou-sand dollars that they offered him, and he chose to stay out there on the picket line with us. So, they tried to pay some of the other players to cross the picket line. I know that they did. A lot of them did go across, and I'm not going to name names, but some were big-time names, who were really scabs. One of them was one of our quarter-backs, and you can figure out who that was on your own (research). It caused a split on our team."[10]

Everyone knows what a traitor is. Commonly referred to as a Benedict Arnold, or in biblical terms, a Judas Iscariot. Well, in foot-ball terms, there is probably no one so hated on any team, as a traitor —a teammate who sides with the team's ownership over his brothers in the huddle. What happened in Philadelphia happened on practi-cally every team during the 1974 NFL Players Strike. One (or more) players decided to stop protesting and start practicing. Most of the times, the players who remained on the picket lines eventually forgave their errant teammate. Sometimes, however, that forgiveness would come with a price.

"The Redskins came up to play us later in the year," Bradley recalled, "and they included guys like (mammoth Washington defen-sive tackle) Diron Talbert. Well, some of our offensive linemen remembered what happened during the strike, and they used what was known as a 'Lookout Block' on certain plays. Do you know what a lookout block is? An offensive tackle falls down and makes it look like he missed his block. As he is on the ground, he looks back at his quarterback and screams '**Lookout!**' A well-known quarterback for us...one who crossed the picket line during the preseason...got his knee hurt on a lookout block."[11]

The efforts of the players who stayed on strike were indeed hurt by those growing numbers of teammates who decided to eventually cross the picket lines across the league. Nevertheless, the Eagles players who kept striking also kept training, in the hopes that, some-day, an agreement between the two sides would come about. Their training site had to be at a different location than the team's training spots at Veterans Stadium and JFK Stadium, however. Those venues were forbidden for those players who were still actively on strike.

"We went to this little university called Drexel Hill College in Drexel Hill," confirmed Bradley (Author's Note: Philadelphia has no less than a total of 37 colleges and universities in the city environs, not to mention dozens more in the surrounding suburbs). "We prac-ticed there every day while we were on strike. Everybody met there, and we went through our drills and all that kind of stuff. We worked our asses off during that time."[12]

But knowing Bill Bradley as we do, he was not about to allow certain opportunities to pass him by, especially if those opportunities involved having fun. The city of Philadelphia is teeming with recreational prospects, not to mention the food. Even back in the early 1970s, the cuisine in and around the "City of Brotherly Love" was second to none in America, and that included the city's world-famous cheesesteaks. A guy like Bradley was more than willing to experience all that Philadelphia had to offer, even during a pitted and acrimonious NFL player's strike.

"At night after our practices at Drexel Hill, we'd go out drinking around the block at some of the pubs," Bradley admitted. "You know I love Philly because all of those bars are just meeting places. Boy, and let me tell you...they've got some really good food in those places. So, everybody would be working out hard during the day, and then having some fun at night."[13]

But the 1974 NFL Players Strike was certainly not a fun thing to experience, especially as it dragged on. More and more veteran players across the league were soon feeling the ill-effects of this battle of attrition with the owners. After 42 days, the strike ended on August 10, when the players union, noticing the growing number of defectors crossing the picket lines, decided to agree to a "cooling off" period. Union president Ed Garvey then employed a mediator and the National Labor Relations Board to continue the players' fight with the owners. This decision thus allowed the players to return to their training camps and doing what they did best—playing football.

It was a bitter lesson for many of the athletes. Most did not possess the business acumen to understand exactly how they were being taken advantage of by the owners. Indeed, throughout the preceding 55 years that the NFL was in existence, it was the players who were getting the short end of the stick. For Bill Bradley, the strike of 1974 turned out to be just another loss to take.

"We were lobbying for our futures, and for the futures of the future players," explained Bradley. "I thought that we needed to have better salaries. That's why we were out there (on the picket lines). We wanted something better for our futures."[14]

The immediate future of the Philadelphia Eagles, however, would now finally leave the board rooms and the picket lines behind, and would be played out on the football field. The 1974 version of the Eagles optimistically turned out to be the best one that Bill Bradley would ever experience as a member of the team. But it was also not without some difficult moments. From the first game of the year, almost every play would be a pensive mini drama of sorts, where one snap of the ball could mean the difference between winning and losing. This was evident in a pitched battle on opening day at St. Louis. Bradley and the rest of the Eagles defense offered up one of their finest efforts against a team that would eventually win the NFC East Division by season's end. Philadelphia limited the Cardinals to just one meager touchdown. You would think that with the explosive passing attack that they displayed in the previous year, the Eagles offense should be able to outscore those red and white birds of a different feather.

But such was not the case. Philly's offense could only account for one paltry field goal in a 7-3 loss. Especially galling was the fact that the Eagles were perched just nine yards away from the winning touchdown in the final minute of the game, and they had four tries to make those nine yards. They fell short each time on four Roman Gabriel pass incompletions. It was just another flashback of futility for the team.

"I'm thinking, here we go again," lamented Bradley. "Even though we didn't win much, we had a lot of games like that. And I don't want to bring blame upon the offense, but golly, four straight tries! I thought that we could have used some of our really good running backs, like my friend Norm Bulaich."[15]

Bulaich was brought into Philadelphia by Coach McCormack at the beginning of the 1973 season. He had previously played three years in Baltimore, and he helped the Colts to win Super Bowl V. But before that, Bulaich also played on the same Texas All-Star high school team that Bradley was a member of when the two played in the legendary Big-33 Game up in Pennsylvania in 1965. Several years later, Bulaich came to the Eagles still sporting plenty of talent and speed. He was also an exceptionally good blocker. He was just an all-around versatile running back, the type that every team needed in the 1970s to become a winner.

"Norm was something else," said Bradley. "He and I are still really good friends. He lives in Fort Worth and we stay in touch all the time. The guy was really built for football. He had a high butt, and he could run. You know I ran track against him in high school in the state tournament. I didn't run in the 100-yard dash (like Bulaich did), but I did run in our sprint relay team when Bulaich was at Lamar High School. And I watched that rascal, as big as he was even in high school, run about a 9.7 time in the 100-yard dash back then. And that was fast."[16]

McCormack would also bring in another key player in 1974, but the price to get him was high…exceedingly high in fact. Philly's defense did not receive much attention in the annual NFL draft, so the Eagles brain trust did the next best thing. They traded to get a proven performer. McCormack acquired former Cincinnati All-Pro middle linebacker Bill Bergey. To obtain his services, McCormack surrendered two number one draft choices to the Bengals. The deal—barring injury—virtually promised that Cincinnati would be a competitive team for several years into the future. The Eagles in exchange would get a fiery team leader in Bergey, who would lead their defense into the early 1980s. Like most middle linebackers, Bergey was boisterous, demanding, and at times, somewhat egotistical. Philadelphia's fans loved him immediately, just as they had loved Bill Bradley. Bergey's teammates, however, were not all on board with his personality.

"Bill could never seem to remember anyone's name on our defense," said Bradley. "He called everyone Bubba. So we all just started calling him Bubba. He was our Bubba. His wife once asked me, 'You don't like Bill, do you?' I told her, 'No, I don't. But I love him.' Being married to him, she immediately understood what I meant. He was a son of a gun, but he was *our* son of a gun. He was our Bubba."[17]

Another Eagles player would get a chance to display not so much his personality, but rather his speed in the next game, and practically everyone would see it happen. The nationwide stage of Monday Night Football during the 1970s was an opportunity for every player in the league to show how well he could perform, because everyone in the NFL knew that nearly everyone else in America was watching those games. It was a big deal back then to be on Monday Night Football. The television ratings soared all throughout the decade when families from coast to coast would sit down in their living rooms and watch professional football on Monday nights. It did not really matter what teams were playing. It was pro football, and it was entertaining and exciting.

The Eagles seldom displayed exciting football during the majority of the decade, and so they rarely got a chance to appear on Monday Night Football during those years. But on September 23, 1974, they were slated to take on their division rivals, the Dallas Cowboys, at Veterans Stadium. It would be a contest that no Philly fan who was either at the game, or who watched it on television, will ever forget. Bill Bradley would never forget it either. He observed how his team kept fighting back and regained the momentum, which in turn kept the game close. Then came that one incredible play. Dallas was within the shadow of Philadelphia's goal line when their rookie running back, Doug Dennison, ran a sweep to his right, and cutback toward the end zone. Dennison fumbled the ball after hitting the ground, and Eagles corner back Joe "Bird" Lavender picked up the bouncing pigskin and started running. He never stopped running until he reached paydirt 96 yards later. The memorable play boosted Philly to an incredible 13-10 triumph over the Cowboys.

"Well we went into every game defensively thinking that we could win," asserted Bradley. "And 'Bird' Lavender was a piece of work man. That guy could *run*. And he was a bit tall for a cornerback (Author's Note: Lavender stood 6-foot-3). Joe Bird was a great, great friend of mine, and he still is. And just a wonderful guy. That fumble return (against Dallas) couldn't happen to a better player. Man, watching him run that whole length of the field was like poetry in motion."[18]

Philadelphia's next three games were quite beautiful as well. The Eagles defeated the Baltimore Colts (30-10), the San Diego Chargers (13-7), and the New York Giants (35-7) in succession, giving them an impressive 4-1 record to begin the 1974 season. It was the best start that Bradley had ever experienced as a member of the team, and optimism abounded. Both the offensive and defensive units of the team were making big plays all throughout these three big victories. Never mind the fact that the Colts, Chargers, and Giants were each unimpressive by most onlookers' standards. These were three straight wins for Philadelphia, and that accomplishment deserved to be lauded.

"We were sniffing the playoffs at that time," admitted a hopeful Bradley. "When we win some more, the odor will become stronger. Right now I'd be willing to sacrifice my personal goals, such as getting so many interceptions and being selected as an All-Pro, for a chance to make the playoffs. I'd welcome such a sacrifice. And really, it wouldn't be a sacrifice at all, but a gain."[19]

During this time, Bradley's strategical decisions on the field were also considered by some as a sacrifice. His movements and decisions on the field were scrutinized like never before, but that was a good thing, especially when one considers how well the defense was performing. He was now required to stay deep in the middle zone, which in turn would deter opposing quarterbacks from throwing the ball deep downfield and gaining a lot of quick yardage against the Eagles.

"I don't have any problems with that, as long as the win-loss record holds up," admitted Bradley back in 1974. "My (main) responsibility is still the deep middle, but there hasn't been any really interceptable balls thrown out there (lately). There are a lot of shrewd quarterbacks in the league and many of them key on the free safety as the most important man in the defense. They like to throw where I'm not, and if they can move me out by showing a run, I better be damned sure it is a run or its going to be six points for the other side." [20]

His efforts at keeping those six points from occurring involved his employment of plenty of intelligence. Bradley was becoming a strategical team leader during this time in his career. His efforts as a policeman of sorts in the defensive secondary also became more pronounced, and indeed, more visible. By 1974 and considering his background from both his college years and his early years in the pros, Bradley owned a good working knowledge of what he had to do as a free safety, and how best to do it. He had also acquired a firm idea as to what opposing offenses were trying to do in any given situation, regardless of the down and distance. One of his goals now in this year was to disseminate that information to his defensive teammates, to help them become better at their jobs, which in turn would help the team to continually improve.

"As a former quarterback in college, I know how a quarterback thinks and what his problems are," explained Bradley. "I try to be where I never liked to see a safety when I was a quarterback in college. Mentally, the thing is an overall understanding of both offense and defense. It was a great help for me to have been trained as a quarterback in college.

"I know where the help is coming from, because when I was a quarterback in college, I always saw the spots where I didn't want the safety to be. I have to call defenses too, at times. So you need that all-inclusive knowledge of football. And you must be firm with the other guys on the defense. I'm in the position of seeing everybody play, of knowing where everybody should be, so when I correct somebody, or suggest how he should handle a situation, I'm not doing it because I made it up. I saw it, and I know if it worked well or not." [21]

The Eagles appeared to be working well as they neared the midseason point of the 1974 season. But their competition would become tougher as the games wore on. Philadelphia would be tested in a series of games which would require a better effort from everyone on the team. Their offense at this time was not producing as well as they did the previous season (1973), and so their challenge would be especially difficult against some of the tougher teams that were coming up. The first of those tough games was a rematch with Dallas at Texas Stadium. The Cowboys were languishing in one of their worst seasons ever. They were a woeful 1-4 going into their second tilt with the Eagles, and they were smarting for revenge after losing to Philadelphia earlier in the year. As it turned out, they would take out a lot of their frustrations against the Eagles, and against Bill Bradley in particular.

One specific play ignited the spirit that these teams displayed whenever they went up against each other. Eagles running back Tom Sullivan was knocked out of bounds by Dallas middle linebacker Lee Roy Jordan. Bill Bradley was standing along the Eagles sideline, right in full view of the play. It was obvious from watching the replay that Jordan hit Sullivan just a fraction late, but his hit did not draw a penalty. It did, however, draw some of Bradley's ire, who wasted no time in explaining to Jordan—in his own way—that he was wrong to have done such a thing. Now keep in mind, Bradley himself had been guilty before of giving extra-curricular hits to his opponents on quite a few occasions, but that fact did not really matter in this instance. Jordan took offense to Bradley's sentiments, and immediately shoved Bradley in his chest. A melee ensued, as players from both teams began hitting each other in the midst of flying penalty flags and the piercing sounds of shrill referee whistles.

"I can't really remember what I said to Jordan," Bradley claimed. "I might have called him a spoiled brat or something like that, I think. But you know he was a great football player. He was light for his position, but man that guy could run and make plays. And he was just like me...he was as competitive as heck."[22]

The competitive aspect of this rematch with Dallas ended when a costly fumble by Philadelphia punt returner Marion Reeves led to the go-ahead Cowboys touchdown in the fourth quarter. The Eagles thus lost their first game in almost a month by the score of 31-24. It would be the first of six straight debilitating losses for Mike McCormack's team, which effectively knocked them out of any chance that they may have had of making the playoffs. Following the loss at Dallas, the Eagles suffered a 14-10 loss to the New Orleans Saints. Philadelphia allowed New Orleans to score the winning touchdown with less than a minute to play, and what made matters worse, Eagles tight end Charle Young would have scored a touchdown earlier in the game on a pass from Roman Gabriel, if he did not have a small portion of his left foot over the end line. That was two straight losses that could have legitimately been wins.

"We really had a tight-knit team at that time," said Bradley, "and we were coming together. We really just got the short end of the stick when it came to those close games. Some of them had to deal with the possibility that we really didn't know how to win those close games, you know what I mean? We were trying...it wasn't like we weren't trying. In a lot of our games, we would either get down early, or we'd be ahead early, going into the fourth quarter. And sometimes, after losing so much, you start doubting yourself toward the end of the game. You start waiting to make a mistake if you're ahead, if you know what I mean. It always seemed that we were just underneath the line."[23]

The Eagles would certainly fall underneath the lines of the Pittsburgh Steelers the next week, as the Super Bowl-bound Steelers pulverized Philadelphia, 27-0. Next up was a 27-20 loss to the Washington Redskins at Veterans Stadium. As with their current trend of making a costly mistake late in the game, Gabriel followed suit by fumbling the ball near his goal line without even being hit. Washington linebacker Chris Hanburger fell on the ball in the end zone for a margin of victory touchdown. The Eagles offense could only obtain a mere field goal the following week in a 13-3 loss to the St. Louis Cardinals. A rematch at Washington produced another defeat, as the Redskins once again prevailed over Philadelphia, 26-14. Six straight losses. Some games winnable, and some games not. In a season where so much optimism was evident in September, the Eagles were eventually left with the sour taste in their mouths of earning another losing record in the final month of the year.

But that did not happen in 1974. There were three games left on their schedule, and those three opponents were not having great seasons by anyone's estimation. The first was at home against the Green Bay Packers at Veterans Stadium. It was a cold and blustery day on this first day of December, but the weather did not matter to Philadelphia's offense. The Eagles scored 36 points, the most points that they would score all throughout the season. Moreover, their defense only permitted 14. Philly's record now stood at 5-7. They followed the victory over the Packers with another one in even worse weather conditions. Philadelphia defeated the New York Giants up in the Yale Bowl in New Haven, Connecticut, 20-7. The field was a muddy bog, and sure footing was nearly impossible. Nevertheless, the Eagles did enough on both sides of the ball to squish their way to their sixth victory of the season. One game remained, and if they managed to beat Detroit on the final day of the season, the Eagles would finish 1974 with a 7-7 record.

Their hopes came to fruition on December 15. The Philadelphia offense excited the Veterans Stadium crowd to four touchdowns, en route to a 28-17 win. The Eagles had finally achieved a .500 mark; the first time in Bill Bradley's pro career that such had ever occurred. The final three games of the 1974 season delivered some hope to the team, to the fans, and to Bradley himself.

"In those last three games of '74, we kind of hunkered down and tightened up our chinstraps and belts and went after them, you know," stated Bradley. "That three-game winning streak to end the season was really cool. It was a great group of guys who did that."[24]

Some of the members of that "great group of guys" included the players on the Eagles defense, a unit which permitted only 217 points in 1974, which was an incredible 176 points less than what they surrendered in 1973. How did they accomplish such an outstanding feat?

"Well, we had some guys who had been with the team for three or four years by that time," Bradley explained. "And we drafted well, and we practiced well. There wasn't any crap going on in our practices or stuff like that. We were starting to develop some level of cohesion."[25]

That cohesion would not last, unfortunately. But that was unseen and still in the future. The moment at hand brought a new label for the Eagles: one of contenders. They were not where they wanted to be, for certain, but they were on the road toward getting there.

Philadelphia's 1974 season thus ended on a positive note, something that rarely happened during Bradley's years with the team. Their 7-7 record was a sign of hope for the players and the coaches. It was also a time for optimism among the city's football fans, most of whom were dreaming of the day when their beloved birds could regularly remain at this level of competition in the league. But even though the Eagles had finally notched a respectable season for the first time in the past three years, Bill Bradley would not be an invitee to the annual Pro Bowl game. To his credit, he did not take this slighting too seriously. He knew that statistics often determine who goes to the Pro Bowl, and for defensive backs, the only statistic that seemed to matter to those who select the Pro Bowl rosters was interceptions. It was that way in 1974, and it is still that way today. Bradley's two interceptions in 1974 spoke volumes. "I would almost have to manufacture what interceptions I got during that time," lamented Bradley (Author's Note: as stated previously, Bradley would sometimes bait opposing quarterbacks into throwing the ball into areas where they thought Bradley was avoiding).[26] It was time for the powers that be to select a different free safety for the Pro Bowl honor.

No matter for Bill Bradley, he was nevertheless determined to make yet another one of his off seasons memorable. But he may have even outdone himself following the 1974 NFL season. In some respects, one individual episode...nay, one individual evening during this offseason...had the potential of being the most unnerving night during his young adulthood. It was an adventure that he swears to this day, that he was just an innocent bystander to the following proceedings.

"No, I was a *very* innocent bystander to what happened that night in Las Vegas," affirmed Bradley. "I didn't have anything to do with it. Now I can't say that I was innocent on some other things (chuckle), but on that particular deal, it was all James Street's fault (Author's Note: yes, James Street showed up again. Bradley and Street always seemed to run around together for many years after both left the University of Texas). That was all on Street, and it was as funny as hell."[27]

This "funny as hell" episode begins and ends in Las Vegas, a place which might be regarded as Bill Bradley's second home, considering how many times he and his buddies went there following so many different football seasons. As a reminder, Bradley was not into the gambling aspects of Vegas. He could see how easy it was for people to lose their money in such a location, with so many casinos all about. Instead, Bradley enjoyed watching the entertainers. Being one himself on professional football fields across America, he had a certain appreciation for those performers.

"So every time that we would go to Vegas, we would go to the Dunes," recalled Bradley. "We had lots of connections, mostly through UT (the University of Texas), and from guys like Bobby Layne and Doak Walker, and some big-time oil men, several of whom owned stock in the casinos. So James (Street) and I forged connections through those folks out in Vegas. Anyway, the man who ran the Dunes Casino was a great friend of Bobby's, and his name was Abe Schiller, and he was from Dallas. And Bobby got to know him because Dallas is where Doak Walker went to high school at Highland Park. So those guys knew Abe from high school!

"And so we'd go out there, and Abe gets us front row seats to see the Rat Pack. They were Frank Sinatra, Sammy Davis Jr., and Dean

Martin, and Abe fixes us up with front row seats to see those performers. They were great singers, and Abe gets us 50-yard line seats, right
in the middle of the stage, and within spitting distance from the
stage!"[28]

Bradley, Street, and their friends were very appreciative of
Schiller's kindness in getting them several choice tickets whenever
the group of Texas natives got to visit the Vegas casinos. In fact, they
enjoyed treating Schiller as if *he* were just as much of a celebrity as
those singers on stage. Well, with a little help from a liquid agent
anyway.

"We'd stand at the hotel's front desk, and they'd have a room or
two or three ready for us," said Bradley. "And Abe always hung back
at the bar, where he could see the front desk, about 50 yards away.
And he knew when we were coming in. Well we came in there, and
we were shellacked, and we were rowdy...oh boy were we rowdy
(laughter). Once Abe sees us coming in, he'd come running toward us
(more laughter). And Abe would look like Porter Waggoner. He wore
a ten-gallon hat, with sequins and all that stuff. And he was a good
guy...a good businessman. He ran that casino. And like I said, we
were shellacked. It was about six or eight of us, and we were all
yelling out loud for Abe. And we would be in tune too! We would
start really low, and then we would get to a high pitch...and we would
stretch his name out, like Aaaaabe Schiller! So finally, all of us are
screaming together, Aaaaabe Schiller (still) tables and be quiet!'"[29]

Little did Schiller know it at the time, but one of Bradley's gang
had no intention of being quiet. In fact, James Street's shenanigans
on this particular evening were just beginning.

"Well we started down between the blackjack tables and the dice
tables, and the bar is down there on the right," mapped Bradley.
"Well we headed for the back bar, and before you know it, we lose
James! We all were just walking around and wondering, 'Where's
James?' Then all of a sudden as we're walking back through the
casino, we'd see several ladies who were sitting at their stools playing
blackjack. Well, we saw those women jump up, one by one. And up

on the chairs...you know the higher chairs...well James was walking back there and pinching those women on their legs and on their butts (still more laughter)! He was doing that all the way back to the bar where Abe was! And all you could see was the ladies jumping up and down near the aisle where we were (continued chuckling)."[30]

Street was just getting warmed up for his even greater prank, however, which unbeknownst to the entire group of young men, would be something that each of them would remember for the rest of their lives. According to Bradley, the genesis of this adventure really began when he and all of his friends tried relentlessly to get Street to see another act in Las Vegas besides Elvis Presley.

"We said to him, 'James, you've got to come see some other entertainers, because they're pretty cool,' affirmed Bradley. "We told him that he 'would fall in love with some of those acts.' Now we got to meet some of those guys (Dean Martin, Sammy Davis Jr., etc.) backstage, but James never did, because he always went out and hung out with Elvis!

"Now James wasn't a bad drunk, and it's important to mention that because it plays a part in this story. He wasn't a sloppy drunk. But we didn't care. We wanted James to experience watching the acts that we had already seen. On this one particular night, however, we finally were successful in getting James to see another act besides Elvis. We get him to go see Frank Sinatra with us. We've got two front row booths, and James is sitting in one of them at the end of the booth, because thanks to all of that alcohol, he had to get up and use the bathroom some. The booths were those half-moon booths, and we were all right in the front row."[31]

It is important to note that we usually remember the first time that we do something, as in the first movie that we ever saw, or the first base hit that we ever got as a little leaguer, or in this case, the first time that James Street ever saw Frank Sinatra sing in a Las Vegas showroom. Coincidentally, it was also the last time that James Street ever saw Frank Sinatra perform. The evening took on a surrealistic quality, where you just had a difficult time believing what you just saw. Bradley's narrative of the events of that evening explain how Street's sophomoric actions served as the springboard for a rather worrisome few minutes.

"The performers at Vegas had a pre-act," remembered Bradley. "Oh God, the pre-act was one hell of a singer, Jim Neighbors. Then they got to the Rat Pack of Dean Martin, Sammy Davis Jr., and Frank Sinatra. It was a great show, and Sinatra was the final singer. And as you watched the show, you also got food. It was a dinner show. You had your roast beef. Some folks got lobster. And you also got some of the side dishes and vegetables. It turned out that James got English peas, and he didn't like English peas."[32]

As strange as this may sound, that evening's incident—and indeed it was one heck of an incident—could rightfully be blamed on those English peas! Had Street been given some other vegetable, what happened next might never have happened. But fate has a way of showing up in and around the people that Bill Bradley meets or knows, and as a result, Bradley becomes involved. You might call it the time-honored "guilt by association" situation. Now mind you, Bradley was not guilty of what happened. In retrospect, he had only one plausible response: to plead his ignorance and lay the blame on someone else. As it turned out, that is exactly what James Street did too.

"And so Sinatra's up there, and he's singing his signature song, *My Way*," recalled Bradley. "James is over there in the corner, and we (Bradley and the rest of his friends) can't see him. Well, James has a spoon, and he's flicking those English peas up on the stage at Frank Sinatra! With a spoon! And nobody is catching him! He was sneaky. Well, one of those peas flies by Sinatra's head. We're sitting there watching it, and we saw Sinatra flinch. His head went sideways, but he kept singing. And we thought that maybe it was a bird that had gotten into the theater or something like that.

"Well the next thing that we know, James flips a few more of those English peas toward Sinatra, and one of them hits him right in the cheek (laughter)! Right in the cheek! We're sitting there, and we still didn't know that it was James who was doing this. Well Sinatra yells out 'Stop this motherfucker right now! Bring the lights up!' So the lights in the whole place go on. We're all looking around. James is acting as innocent as hell. You wouldn't even know that he ever was the one who was flicking those English peas at Sinatra. Then Sinatra yells out again, 'Somebody out there has flipped some of those peas on my face! When I find out who it is, my goons (bodyguards) are going to come out there into the audience and beat the holy shit out of you!'"[33]

There is a certain beauty in simplicity. And there is something to be said for it. Mess with Frank Sinatra, and you get your face smashed in. It was as simple as that. Bill Bradley's only goal—indeed his only focus of mind at this moment—was to escape that venue in Vegas immediately, if not sooner, without getting his face smashed in by Old Blue Eyes' bodyguards. It had to have been a moment of high tension for everyone in the audience as well, as they were seeing and hearing this musical icon of theirs expressing his anger with colorful —nay—outright profane language. It must have also indeed been unsettling to the females in the audience. Prior to this moment, many of those women would probably have left their husbands in an instant for a romantic encounter with Frank Sinatra. After this threatening situation, however, perhaps not so many would have done so. So, in that respect, maybe James Street kept a lot of marriages intact with his pea-flicking prowess.

Street was not so intact with the rest of his compatriots on this evening, however. This was certainly true when they found out that it was he who caused Frank Sinatra to verbally explode on stage. Street also wanted—nay, needed—to get away from the Sinatra show as soon as possible. But Bill Bradley wanted Street to stay with their group. He (Bradley) was sweating bullets by this time, and he wanted to prove that the old adage of "misery loving company" was true.

"Well we left that theater and James then tells us that he is going over to the Hilton," explained Bradley. "Then we told him, '...James, no. You're going to stay around here with us (the group of friends that

Bradley stuck with).' Then James says, 'No, I gotta go.' And then in the middle of the discussion, we find out that it was him! Bob McKay (one of Bradley's friends who was there that evening) or somebody else found out. And then we told James, 'Yeah James, get your ass out of here. You go over to the Hilton right now and don't you **ever** come back here with us!'"[34]

Now, it is important to note that few people alive had more of a fun-loving attitude than Bill Bradley. But one must realize that such an occurrence could have led to a *really* distasteful incident. Frank Sinatra's "goons" might have beaten up the half dozen or so people that Bradley was with—including Bradley! But knowing how tempting that mob rule was (and still is), many members of the audience might have gotten their licks in as well. As a result, the Texas fellas were more than happy to leave that theater as soon as possible.

"It was a bad adventure," admitted Bradley. "With Sinatra yelling to 'Stop this motherfucker,' to the threats to '...beat the shit out of us,' to the lights being turned on—and not just the stage lights or the spot-lights, but the flood lights as well! Then James finally confesses to us the next day. Oh we got pissed off at him. He could have got us all hurt."[35]

But time in the form of days or years gone by has a way of dissolving the anger and bitterness. Moreover, life-long friendships often prove to be stronger than certain occurrences. Maybe not to the degree of hitting Frank Sinatra in the face with an English pea or two, but certain circumstances nonetheless. Combined with the time that develops such friendships, chapters such as this one was what made the Bradley and Street friendship one for the ages.

"As years went by, we actually got really prideful at the retelling of that story," admitted Bradley. "Oh, we were pissed at him to be sure. But in time, we ended up laughing about it. James was like a magician. That's why he ran the Wishbone offense so well. He took over for me as quarterback at (the University of) Texas, and people thought that I hated James. That wasn't true at all. Heck, we ran around together. We worked out together. We were like brothers."[36]

Bradley's friendships from his youth have indeed withstood the test of time. But time during the pro football offseason often flies by rapidly, and it was on to the next adventure. As the summer drew near, time would be the determining factor in telling whether the momentum of the pro football team that Bradley played for would last until the next season—the fateful season of 1975.

9

THE DOWNWARD SLOPE

The Philadelphia Eagles entered the 1975 NFL season in a unique state of mind. They were optimistic for a change! You could have asked any player on the team, or any coach on the team, and they would have told you the same thing during the 1975 summer training camp—the Eagles were primed for more victories and a winning record. To a man, they were certainly not overconfident, mind you. But they did possess a feeling of collective positivity. Their regular season record had improved in each of the past two years, and there was no real reason to believe that it would not get even better in 1975.

But as we shall see, that did not happen. In fact, the team regressed, and 1975 was quite possibly the most depressing season that the Eagles experienced during the 1970s. The reasons for the team's free fall from a 7-7 record in 1974 to a 4-10 record in 1975 were not too easy to discern. Yes, several players suffered injuries, including Bill Bradley. But there was an even more lasting cause for the team's failure. It was as if the rest of the league suddenly got wise as to what the Eagles were trying to do on both offense and defense.

It was as if their opponents were all ready with effective answers to whatever problems that Philadelphia might offer them. As a result, few things worked as well as they did in the previous two seasons.

Now keep in mind, a player like Bill Bradley did not let a losing record affect his level of play. He continued to excel as a pass defender, and even though he missed some time on defense due to a sore and stiff knee ailment, he still managed to intercept five passes in 1975. And if you had witnessed him after each of those thefts, you would have observed that he still possessed the same verve and excitement that he showed to his teammates in his previous raucous celebrations from earlier seasons. "He's a hell of a competitor," said Billy Hobbs, a former teammate of Bradley's. "Bill should have been playing right along (since his rookie year). He was better than some of the people they were using, and he knew it."[1]

As we have already expressed, pro football is a team sport. Moreover, it is quite possibly the best team sport in America, as evidenced by full stadiums and huge television ratings every year. Individuals are important in football, but only when they contribute to the success of the team. Nevertheless, an individual like Bill Bradley could do a lot on his own to help his team. The 1975 season would, in retrospect, become more of a cerebral season than possibly any other one that Bradley ever experienced as a pro. The questions from that season were numerous and thought provoking. How do you keep your mind focused on what your duties are on every play, regardless of the score of the game? How do you forget about the previous play, to do your best on the upcoming play? How do you not allow a bad call from a referee, or a blown coverage in the secondary, to ruin what you were hoping to accomplish when the situation on the field becomes more difficult? In a nutshell, how do you help your team to win? These were the types of questions that the members of the Philadelphia Eagles had to address in 1975. For his part, Bradley was brave enough and responsible enough to address them.

"Hey, in this league, the easiest thing I do is clap my hands when we break the huddle," Bradley wryly claimed. "Everything else is tough. But I guess the part I've had the least trouble with is my concentration. I'm 100 percent aware of the play, and I don't let anything else bother or distract me. I can't afford to, because this is my living, and if you don't give it everything you can, it is not going to be your job for long."[2]

Bill Bradley's job on opening day, 1975, was to put a halt to the New York Giants passing attack. This both he and his teammates were unable to do, however. Although Bradley picked off a pass from veteran Giants quarterback Craig Morton, the Giants offense did just enough damage to register a 23-14 win over their long-time divisional rivals from Philadelphia.

"You know back then, they called the Black and Blue Division the NFC Central Division," remembered Bradley. "But people didn't really understand the NFC East was the *real* Black and Blue Division. I mean gosh almighty. Every game was nip and tuck. Washington, St. Louis, Dallas, the Giants, Philly...it was just nip and tuck."[3]

These awfully close verdicts for the Eagles would continue the following week in Chicago, when they narrowly lost to the Bears, 15-13. Philadelphia beat their foes from The Windy City in virtually every statistical category, except the final score. When the game was over, Coach McCormack declared that some of his players performed like a bunch of dogs. He even went so far as to claim that some of his athletes were not giving their best efforts...that they were dogging it. The Eagles fans took the cue, and when their team returned to play the Washington Redskins in the third week of the 1975 season at Veterans Stadium, those fans were loaded for bear...or beagle, as the case may have been.

"Oh I know it," remarked Bradley. "Hell, after he said that...well, you know how the Eagles fans are. They were throwing dog biscuits at us. They were wearing costumes of boxer dogs and bulldogs, and they were barking at us. All of that stuff. You know those fans. They're starved for winners. Really and truly, they are really good fans.[4]

"If you were losing, every game would be a boo fest. If you made a mistake, you would get booed really bad. But the best part of their deal with me was something that I am really proud of, even to this day. My main claim to fame as a former Eagle was not being an All-Pro, or leading the league in interceptions two years in a row, or going to three Pro Bowls. No, my main claim to fame is that I never got booed in Philadelphia. When I think about it, my chest goes out, and that shows my gratitude to those fans. And it didn't matter what your record was in Philly. Those fans were rabid. They hung some guys in effigy. And they had a pretty bad image for being rowdy, but that came from us not winning so much.

"Those Eagles fans are loyal, and they love blue collar workers, and that's what I was. For me to make that team, I had to be a lunch pail guy, and Philadelphia is a lunch pail city. You know, everybody there goes to work, comes home, raises his family, and all that. Well, they adopted me directly, because I gave them everything that I had." 5

Bradley and his teammates gave the Redskins everything that they had on October 5, 1975. The offense produced some big plays in the form of two touchdown passes from Roman Gabriel. On defense, Bradley intercepted two passes, which helped to limit Washington's offense to just 127 passing yards. Even more impressive was how the Eagles shut down the Redskin rushing attack, restricting them to just 66 ground yards. Philadelphia prevailed, 26-10.

"We couldn't afford to lose today," admitted Bradley after the game. "It was a matter of attitude, and I was scared. I play better when I am scared. There was just no way I could lose this football game."6

Philly's ship was now righted, or so it seemed. But unfortunately, overconfidence seemed to get the best of some of the Eagles players at this time. They had a tough game against a particularly good Miami team the following week, and it would not be long before the Dolphins helped Mike McCormack's players forget all about their victory over Washington from the previous Sunday. Miami made the big plays that Philadelphia failed to make, and in the end, head coach Don Shula's players claimed a 24-16 win over the now 1-3 Eagles.

The loss to the Dolphins would mark the beginning of a five-game losing streak for Philadelphia, an event that seemed to occur at least once every season. In the span of a month, any chances that the team had of making the playoffs were gone. Particularly galling among those losses was a 20-17 defeat versus Dallas at Veterans Stadium on October 26. The Eagles were winning that contest, 17-10, late in the fourth quarter, when an over-exuberant Bill Bradley was flagged for a late hit on Dallas setback Robert Newhouse. That play set up the tying touchdown for the Cowboys. A couple of minutes later, Dallas won the game with a field goal with no time left on the clock. It was indeed as depressing of a loss as the Eagles would suffer all year. Immediately after that defeat, Coach McCormack defended his free safety for his late hit. The following day, however, McCormack reluctantly agreed with the official who penalized Bradley for his overzealous hit on Newhouse.

"After looking at the films, I can see why the penalty was called on Bradley," admitted McCormack begrudgingly.[7]

Late hits were not new in the sport of football in 1975. In fact, players have probably been leveling other players in a questionable fashion ever since the very first college game back in 1869. Professional games, which began in 1892, undoubtedly followed with the generous distribution of similar cheap shots. Two weeks after the loss to Dallas, Bradley and his fellows would get a chance to play against one of the best "dirty" players that the NFL had ever seen, before or since. Conrad Dobler, an offensive guard for the St. Louis Cardinals, was notorious for his willingness to hit, kick, pinch, or gouge an opponent before (and after) the referee's whistle. Watching Dobler play was like watching a separate game within a game. It was also like watching professional wrestling—but with helmets and shoulder pads, and still with no holds barred.

The Eagles game versus the visiting Cardinals on November 9 was akin to a war. To say that the game was dirty was accurate. But it was also entertaining, especially if Eagles fans got tired of watching their team lose (which still happened in this game anyway). At least one Eagles player got a chance to get a few good licks in on his opponent, and not surprisingly, it was Bill Bradley. On one play, Dobler blocked Bradley, then followed up his block by slamming the Eagles safety to the ground and then driving his fist through Bradley's facemask. Bradley did not turn his cheek, so to speak. Rather, he waited for his opportunity, then retaliated to even the score.

"We were always in a war with Dobler and (fellow offensive linemen Dan) Dierdorf and (Tom) Banks and all of those Cardinals," recounted Bradley. "They ran that team. I mean, they really *ran* that team, much more than their head coach Don Coryell did. And they (the St. Louis offensive linemen) cheated. They would step on you, they would pinch you in the nuts, they would do all kinds of stuff illegally. They would take these shin guards that were made out of a kind of a hard material. If you took the foam rubber off of them, they were hard. And they would tape them under their socks and have a large sock underneath that. Then with those shin guards that were taped to the back of their legs, they would leg whip you. And believe me, that hurt. They were notorious for that."[8]

Leg-whipping reached the level of an art form during the 1970s, as practiced by the Cardinals. To perform the maneuver, an offensive lineman like Dobler (who was a master of this unfriendly craft) would allow a charging defensive lineman a free second to rush past him and charge toward the quarterback. Then, almost instantly and from a crouched position, the offensive lineman would wheel his outside leg backwards in a lightning-fast motion, with his heel striking the back of an opponent's leg, sending the unfortunate recipient to the turf, where he laid in anguishing pain. Many a defensive lineman would spend countless hours soaking his legs in the team's whirlpool following a Sunday afternoon dealing with Conrad Dobler. It is interesting (and somewhat humorous) to note that Dobler always insisted that he was innocent of all of this, as he regularly complained to the referees that his opponents were offsides.[9]

But back to Bradley's response:

"So on one play, Dobler, who won an award for being the dirtiest man in football, gets knocked on the ground, and I noticed that he's got a broken forearm," said Bradley. "He had a soft cast on it. Well, I saw his arm laying on the ground, so without thinking twice, I jumped up and with both of my cleats, I stomped as hard as I could with all of my weight on his arm. He screamed so loud, you could hear him 20 or so yards away (laughter). He went to squirming and rolling around on the ground (more laughter)."[10]

Bradley was not finished, however. Most of these on-field wars did not just consist of late hits. Verbal mouthing and damning insults were also an important addition to the ensemble of requisite actions (and reactions) of these bitter rivalries. Bradley was one of the better and more experienced "talkers" in the NFL. At times, his yapping knew no bounds.

"So one time, I got in trouble," admitted Bradley. "They showed a wide angle on the films, and I was back in the St. Louis Cardinals huddle, bitching at all of them. In their huddle! I pointed at several of them and called them a bunch of dirty cheaters to their faces, and I pointed at several more of them and informed them that they had no talent and that they were a bunch of bums!"[11]

Landing abruptly and fiercely on Conrad Dobler's forearm was one thing, but going into your opponents' huddle and profanely calling them names? That type of action took chutzpah, and it simply could not be excused. As it turned out, the Cardinals and one of their coaches planned to offer some quality payback to Mr. Bradley.

"Jim Hanifan was a well-known old coach in the league," said Bradley. "He was an old man...a good old son of a bitch. He coached for St. Louis, and he and I got into an argument during the game. He was always a 'dick disturber' on the sideline. He called me an asshole after I accused him of coaching dirty tactics to his players. So at the end of this game with the Cardinals, I was leaving the field to go up the tunnel, and we weren't going up the same tunnel. The Cardinals were going to the left, and we (the Eagles players and coaches) were going to the right. And I'm going up there and I got off the field later than most of the other players.

"And I look over to my left, and Hanifan is looking at me. And he motioned for me to come over there to where he was standing. He said to me, 'Come here you little fucker! I'm fixing to beat the shit out of you, you little asshole! Get over here!' So I saw three or four of their players trying to hide behind a pillar. I saw Dobler, I saw Dierdorf. I saw (Jackie) Smith, their tight end. I was afraid of Jackie Smith (Author's Note: Smith had a well-deserved reputation for pinching his opponents in the midst of pileups on the field). I saw them duck around one of those pylons. He (Hanifan) said, 'I'm fixing to talk to you!' I knew what they were up to. They were getting ready to beat the hell out of me. So I took about three steps toward them, then I turned right and went to my dressing room (laughter). I could see them all shooting me the middle finger (more laughter)."[12]

As we shall see, Hanifan and his charges would get a chance later in this narrative to give Bradley more than just a showing of their middle fingers. The Eagles, however, would give a showing of a desperate football team the following week at Shea Stadium, where they took on the nomadic New York Giants (Author's Note: the Giants' new stadium in the New Jersey Meadowlands was still being built at this time, so they played all their home games in 1975 in Flushing, New York, at Shea Stadium). Philadelphia owned a miserable 1-7 record by this time, which would improve to 2-7 following their narrow 13-10 win over the Giants. The Eagles would then split their next two games, another loss to the Cowboys, and a win at home over the 49ers. Three contests thus remained on their 1975 schedule.

The first of these three games was against a team that Philadelphia rarely played, the Cincinnati Bengals, who were often a playoff-caliber team coming out of the American Football Conference's Central Division, one of the toughest divisions in the entire NFL. The Bengals came into Veterans Stadium and gave the Eagles a 31-0 spanking. Following that disaster, Bradley and his teammates would then face another team that they rarely played, the Denver

Broncos, out in Mile High Stadium on December 14. Unlike Cincinnati, Denver was not a playoff-caliber team, but that did not matter, as the Broncos had some sentimental reason to play their best. Floyd Little, the Broncos' inspirational tailback, was playing in his final home game before retiring. Little scored Denver's final touchdown in their 25-10 victory over the Eagles.

Philadelphia's last game of the 1975 season would take place at Washington. The Eagles had won only three games up to this point in the year, and unlike the previous two seasons, they were seldom competitive in most of their games during 1975. But earlier in the year, they easily defeated the rival Redskins, and somewhat surprisingly, they would do so again on December 21. Philadelphia would turn in undoubtedly their best performance of the season, as they routed Washington, 26-3. Now it is accurate to note that the Redskins were not playoff-bound either, but nevertheless, any win over a divisional foe is a good win. The Eagles defense intercepted an incredible seven passes in this rout, including two which were returned for touchdowns; one by cornerback Joe "Bird" Lavender, and the other courtesy of linebacker Frank LeMaster. This stunning victory over the Redskins would end a forlorn 1975 season for Philadelphia, one that saw them go from the possibility of improving their 7-7 record from the previous year, to the despair in a couple of months of realizing that those optimistic hopes would go unfulfilled.

For his part, Bill Bradley experienced one of his better seasons in 1975. Even though he once again failed to make the Pro Bowl, he continued to play hard all throughout the year. He missed some playing time due to injuries, but he still managed to make plenty of big plays on defense. It all boiled down to his attitude and to his rather simplistic ideology about the sport of football.

"If you're winning or losing, you just play football," explained Bradley. "That's what I did, no matter if we were behind on the scoreboard, or ahead, or tied with our opponent. Yes, it was disheartening when we started losing again. But I just kept playing the best that I could play."[13]

Mike McCormack's best efforts were unfortunately not good enough as the final gun of the 1975 season sounded. He was fired shortly thereafter, which would mean that Bradley would be playing for another new head coach in just a few more months. You really had to hand it to Bradley. Few were the veteran players across the league who could continually adjust successfully to a new head coach every two or three years, and to a whole new coaching staff, and to a bunch of new players to boot. But Bradley managed to do so, and as the 1976 season began, he would have to do so again. Eagles owner Leonard Tose hired a new head coach to replace McCormack who was much different than anyone who had ever been selected as head coach for the Philadelphia Eagles before. The young man whom Tose selected owned a youthful exuberance and a determined hard work ethic that would become the very backbone, marrow, and guts of the new coach.

Tose decided upon Dick Vermeil, a young California-bred coach, who most recently led UCLA to a stunning Rose Bowl upset over Ohio State, to be the man to lead his team. Prior to his college success, Vermeil served as an assistant coach in the pro ranks to Washington head coach George Allen, much like Mike McCormack had done. Vermeil popularized the term "workaholic" in the ranks of pro football's lexicon. He worked 20-hour days, and often slept on a cot in his office at Veterans Stadium. It would not take long to realize that he expected the same amount of dedication to the sport from his players, as he demanded from himself.

Vermeil was like most new head coaches in that he brought in assistants that he had worked with before. But he was also unlike most new head coaches, in that he worked his players harder than any of them had ever worked before. Particularly grueling were Vermeil's summer training camps, where exhausting two-hour practices were almost always held twice each day, and sometimes three times each day. The main idea behind all this physical and mental punishment was primarily to weed out those players who were not going to give

Vermeil every ounce of their skills, abilities, and efforts. Every single ounce.

To his credit, Bill Bradley gave Coach Vermeil all that he had. You must recall Bradley's youth. He grew up giving his father a similar effort every day after school, whether it was playing baseball, or football, or running track. Bradley by this time had almost taken the words "hard work" as his accepted middle names. But Bradley at this point was also entering his eighth pro season, and Vermeil was primarily looking for younger players to fill his roster. The writing seemed to be on the wall for Bill Bradley. His days as a Philadelphia Eagles free safety appeared to all onlookers as numbered.

"Dick and I are really good friends today," said Bradley in a 2019 interview, "and six years ago, I even helped him out as an assistant coach at the NFLPA Collegiate Bowl. But when he first came to Philadelphia, he would grind you. Dick was very well organized. And his practices were long. He tried to change the culture in and around the team, and he did a pretty good job of it really. I played for him for a year, and I gave him a heck of a year. He just wanted to get rid of me to get some fresh players in there. But he grinded you man. You had three-a-days to contend with. He had to turn that atmosphere around, and oh, it was grinding. You can ask any player that was with us. But it did change the culture."[14]

While the foundation of this change in culture was being developed, Bill Bradley would still be the starting free safety for the Eagles as they began the 1976 season. Vermeil may have wanted him gone, but he also knew that he had to keep some measure of experience on his roster, to encourage the younger players and help them out when needed. Bradley provided that experience, and he played in all 14 games that season. He continued to tutor all the defensive backs as to their assignments on every situation. In truth, 1976 was a year where Bradley sharpened his coaching skills. He was gaining some initial coaching experience, if he would ever take on that role after his active playing career ended.

While everyone knew what to expect from number 28 in the

defensive secondary, no one was quite sure what to expect of Phil-adelphia's rookie head coach and his new players at the dawn of the 1976 season. But even though the team only won four games all year long, they exhibited a wealth of raw and relentless effort, regardless of the situation or the opponent. It was the beginning of a whole new philosophy in Eagles football: physicality first, last, and always. Beat your opponent down, all game long. No excuses. Just beat your opponent down, every single play.

One specific play in a game versus Minnesota on October 24 had Bill Bradley scratching his head, however. In fact, assistant coach John Mazur was also puzzled at what he just witnessed. Bradley dropped back into zone coverage and relied upon his own knowledge and abilities to read what the Vikings offense was trying to do. Then he acted on it.

"We were playing a three-deep zone against Fran Tarkenton (Author's Note: Tarkenton was an outstanding veteran quarterback for Minnesota who would eventually be enshrined in the Pro Football Hall of Fame) and the Vikings," recalled Bradley. "I was supposed to be in the middle of the field deep, but I studied so much over the years, and playing quarterback (in high school and college) didn't hurt either, you know. So when their running back checked and swung out of the backfield, and all of their other guys were running crossing routes, Tarkenton was going to throw to that swing back, and try to put him on a linebacker. Well even though I was supposed to be in the deep middle (of the field), I ran all the way up. Now his swing pass is behind the line of scrimmage, where the halfback checks and just folds back. Tarkenton never saw me leave the middle of the field, and I went and intercepted his swing pass, and took it back (52 yards) into their end of the field.

"So immediately after that play, I jogged back to our sidelines, and I kept the ball. I tried to keep the ball on all of the interceptions that I would get, because I never knew how many I was going to get in my career (Author's Note: Bill Bradley would intercept a total of

34 passes during the course of his nine-year pro career). I took quite a few, and I kept 'em all."[15]

A player who makes an interception in the NFL is usually greeted as he comes off the field with applause, a showing of congratulations, and sincere gratitude by his fellow players and the team's coaches. Bradley certainly was saluted in this manner following his theft against the Vikings, but Coach Mazur was somewhat dismayed by what he observed his free safety do on the play.

"So I come off the field," remembered Bradley, "and Coach Mazur comes over to me and says to me, 'Goddamn it, Bradley! What are you doing out there?! You're supposed to be in the deep middle third, and you're intercepting the ball on a swing route?' And I said to him, 'Well Coach, I knew what they were doing.' Now keep in mind, I kept the ball behind my back. And he (Mazur) kept going on and on and on about where I was supposed to be on the play. He said, 'You better start staying in your area of responsibility, or they're (the opponents) going to find out about it, and they're going to pick on you, and it's going to hurt us as a defense!' I said, 'Yes sir, I understand that. I will do it, yes sir.' But he kept hammering me about the play, so I finally had enough. I just pulled the ball from behind my back and put it up right in front of his face and said, 'Well Coach, do you want me to give this back to them (the Vikings)?!' And he stopped for a moment and he said, 'No Bradley, I don't want you to give it back to them. But do your responsibility and get back in the middle zone when you're supposed to be there! That's how this defense works.' And he was almost laughing at me when he said it."[16]

Not much laughter was being heard, however, among anyone else associated with the team in 1976. Yes, the Eagles were comprised of a group of mostly young players, many of whom were just getting their first try at pro football. But Philadelphia's win-loss record was not improving during the middle of the year. During what turned out to be a five-game losing streak, frustrations abounded. Bradley, for his part, was also frustrated at some questionable—or downright bad—

calls from the officiating crews. In several games, Bradley decided to have a conversation or two with some of the referees.

"I have heard of some players cursing out the refs to their faces," said Bradley. "I've done it a time or two as well, but it was in a funny way. I went up to one referee who called a pass interference penalty on me. I asked him, 'What would you do to me if I called you a motherfucker?' I had a unique way of putting it, right? He said, 'Excuse me?' And I said, 'What would you do to me if I called you a motherfucker for making that call?' And he said, 'I'd kick your ass out of the game.' Then I said, 'Well I'm not going to call you that then (laughter).' And then I would walk away (more laughter)! So he couldn't do anything about it (continued laughter). And then for another official, I'd ask him, 'What would you do if I called you an asshole?' He said, 'Well, I'd kick your ass out of the game and give your team a 15-yard penalty for unsportsmanlike conduct.' I said, 'Well then, I'm not going to call you that then.' Then I walked away from him (laughter).

"And then one time, I took back a punt return, and there's a referee who is coming toward me to get the ball after the play. I turned around backwards, and even though he wanted the ball, I didn't toss it to him. He yelled at me, 'Give me the damn ball!' And I just drop kicked the ball backwards. I let the ball drop to the ground, and on one bounce, I kicked it backwards with my heel. The ball flew right into his hands. He didn't even have to move, if you can picture that. He watched me jog off the field and he started laughing. He said, 'Man, that was amazing!' I had all kinds of conversations with the referees."[17]

Conversations of another sort, and of another much more important topic, however, were being held during the mid-1970s all throughout the league. The specter of performance-enhancing drug usage hit the newsstands like a ton of bricks at that time. Several players went public with their stories of how many players in the NFL were abusing anabolic steroids, a drug that would build muscle mass and help the players run faster and become stronger. It is important to note that steroids were not forbidden in the NFL during that time, whereas today they are. It was also a drug that time has proven to be both dangerous, and sometimes deadly to those using them. Bill Bradley heard those stories, and he witnessed the effects of those steroids (and other drugs) on different players that he played against. His comments about drugs in pro football are both candid and eye-opening, to say the least.

"Free thinking and all of that kind of stuff was what was going on during those years," explained Bradley. "Some players started smoking a little marijuana. But what happened in Texas back in the 1960s and 1970s, you could go to prison for life if you were caught by the cops with what they called a roach...an open joint. So, there was a lot of paranoia during that time. But I never did any drugs...period. But the trainers on the teams would hand out valium, or other kinds of muscle relaxers to help you sleep. They had different pills, like Quaaludes, and pills that were called white crosses, which were basically amphetamines. They were used by college kids to help them stay awake to study for exams.

"I never took one ounce of any type of a drug to play a football game. I never took one of those steroid pills in my life. I knew what they did. When you lifted weights, those steroids doubled your muscles, and they would cause you to die early. You could tell if somebody was on steroids. They were hyper-extensive. I played against guys who were taking those white crosses, and you could see it by looking at their mouths. They didn't have moustaches...they had white frothing where their two lips came together. And they kept adjusting their padding...they just couldn't stay still."[18]

Observing all these clues to determine which players were using these drugs was hard to ignore. It was only a matter of time until some teams were able to take advantage of opposing players—particularly linemen—who were taking drugs.

"We'd find those kinds of guys, once we played them, and we knew that they were hyped-up on Dexedrine," explained Bradley. "We would have fake signals that would make them jump offsides. They would jump at the sound of a word or something that was different than what they would usually hear. In a strategic point in the game, if you really wanted to be a real cheater, you could do it, you know. Let me explain: so there's one team that we would play, and I know that some of them took all of that stuff. If we had a term that we would come up with right when the quarterback is going 'ready, set, hut' with their cadence, we would yell out that term, and it would often cause their linemen—those who were taking those drugs—to jump offsides. And the refs couldn't call the penalty on our defense, because when we were yelling out that term, we were pointing to our own linebackers. And so, that team used to get more penalties by being drawn offsides by their opponents, and for committing illegal motion penalties, than almost any other team in the league. And it was because of the speed (drug) that some of their players were taking."[19]

The NFL brass was aware of the drug problem in their game during the 1970s, but it took several decades for the league's hierarchy to really do anything substantial about it, such as declaring the drugs illegal, and imposing random drug testing among the players to curb its use. Current penalties for uncovered and confirmed drug use include being disqualified from playing for one or several games, to being fined by their teams, to being banned from the league outright. In the end, each player made—and continues to make—his own decisions on whether to take drugs to enhance his play and help his opportunity to stay on the roster. Indeed, it was—and still is—a risk, and each player would (and will) eventually deal with the penalties and the outcomes of such if he were caught taking illegal drugs.

There was nothing illegal back in the 1970s, however, about taking hits in the head. It was just regarded as a part of the game. Few are the players who have had a pro career that have not experienced a hard hit to their helmet, especially while they were wearing it during practice or in a game. The results back then of possible permanent and long-term damage to the player's brain and thought processes were never discussed by anyone involved in the game...at that time. Yes, there were immediate results to "getting your bell rung," as it was called. Bill Bradley remembers one occurrence after he sustained a concussion in the pros.

"When the trainers and the team doctor came out on the field to see if I was okay, I could hear the bell ringing in my head," recalled Bradley. "The first thing that I said to the trainers was, 'Would somebody please pick up that telephone? Would somebody please answer that phone.' All I could hear was a telephone ringing in my head."[20]

The bells that tolled for the 1976 Philadelphia Eagles, however, were both pessimistic and optimistic ones, depending upon how you heard them, or how you looked at things. Yes, they finished that season with another losing record at 4-10. But they were a noticeably young squad, and Bill Bradley would continue to help a lot of the younger players get to know the ins and outs of pro ball throughout this trying season. But unbeknownst to him at that time, he played his final game in an Eagles uniform on December 12 versus the Seattle Seahawks, an expansion team that was completing their very first year in the league. Bradley only picked off two passes that season of '76, one versus Washington on September 27, and the other against Minnesota on October 24. They would, as it turned out, become the final interceptions of Bradley's NFL career. All in all though, he gave another brand-new head coach and his new coaching staff another outstanding effort.

Bill Bradley's efforts in the summer of 1976, however, involved having more fun. It was the nation's Bicentennial after all, and numerous colorful and exciting celebrations were being held across the country. In Philadelphia, the parties and parades and fireworks were a regular occurrence. Bradley was a bachelor at this time of his life, and like most red-blooded American bachelors, he wanted to have fun with attractive young ladies. A single sports celebrity like Bradley was—whether he would admit it or not—someone that many young ladies would probably fight over. For his part, Bradley observed the beauty of young ladies...and then acted upon it. Few were the alluring young women that smiled at him who did not receive at least a wink in return. In the populated city of Philadelphia, Bradley practically had his pick of the litter.

But sports were still not far from his mind, and on some occasions, Bradley was able to combine the two entities. In fact, there were times when he did not even have to leave Veterans Stadium to date a girl, discuss sports with a team owner, and be a member of the baseball groundskeeping crew...all in the same evening!

"Oh yeah, I dated some of the Philadelphia Phillies usherettes," admitted Bradley (Author's Note: the Phillies were a Major League Baseball team that shared Veterans Stadium with the Eagles, and their hot pants-wearing usherettes were pretty darn appealing). "They were the girls who controlled—or who ushered—the luxury sections of the stadium. Veterans Stadium, the Vet as it was called, was one of the first to have luxury boxes all around the stadium. On meeting one of those girls? Well, we were all single, and I went to every Phillies game, so eventually, I was going to strike up conversations with some of them (chuckle). I met Debbie Pageant and Mary Ann Szal, and I am still Facebook friends with them. They're now married, and they've got kids, but (former Eagles teammate) Billy Walik and I would run around with them back then. We'd go out dancing with them.

"I also took batting practice with the Phillies, and I even worked with the grounds crew for several of their games. Oh, and Ruly Carpenter (the Phillies owner in 1976) and I became friends. I went up there and barged my way into the owner's box one time, and we started talking baseball. And he said, 'Bradley, how come you know so damn much about baseball?' I told him all about how we have a baseball field in my hometown of Palestine named after my dad... Bradley Field. And then I told him about how I was drafted by the Detroit Tigers to play AA baseball out of Montgomery, Alabama. And then I told him about how I lettered in baseball, track, and football in high school. I got along well with Mr. Carpenter."[21]

Bill Bradley also got along well with some of the Phillies players. He was good friends with former Phillies relief pitcher Tug McGraw and his son, future country and western singer and songwriter, Tim McGraw. In fact, after Bradley's retirement from pro football, he kept in contact with the McGraw's, and with Tim's country and western singer wife, Faith Hill. There are quite a few famous people whom Bradley has/had become good friends with over the years. Many of them are naturally former football players, and quite a few of them are of the household name variety, like Joe Namath and Mike Ditka. The list of famous folks whom Bradley has personally known over the years includes the late former New York Yankees great Joe DiMaggio, Hall of Fame pitcher Nolan Ryan, the late Hall of Fame quarterback Sammy Baugh, and the country and western star Willie Nelson, to list but a few.

Bradley eventually also became good friends with Dick Vermeil, but in the spring of 1977, the Eagles coach stuck strong with his plan. He wanted to bring in new players to the Eagles whom he was more familiar with, and younger players at that. Such an intention can often be a jolt to the ego of any older, veteran player. In that vein, Vermeil came to his veteran free safety one day with news that would abruptly change Bradley's career path.

"Dick made a point of getting rid of me and bringing in some UCLA guys, where he was previously a head coach," recalled Bradley. "And I admit that I was getting a little older in the tooth, and he was correct in trying to get some value for me. So he came down to me one day and said, 'Hey Bradley, I got you traded to the Rams.' And I said to him, 'No Dick, I don't want to go to the Rams.' He said, 'Oh yeah you are. I just traded you to them.' Then I said, 'Oh no you're not.' Then he said, 'I've got you traded. You've got to go to them.' Then I said to him, 'No Dick. What you need to do is go up into the general manager's office and read my contract a little more closely. I'm not going to the Rams.'"[22]

Most pro players rarely had anything to do with a team's general manager, and Bill Bradley was no different in that regard. But on occasion, Bradley did have to express himself to a general manager, if for nothing else than to claim his rights, based on what was previously agreed to on his contract. That was also true if there was a discrepancy which involved a bonus or two.

"So in '76, I had two interceptions," said Bradley. "I was tied for the team lead with two interceptions! Jim Gallagher, our general manager, said to me, '...I'm not going to pay you your bonus for that! You just *tied*!' So I said to him, 'There's no statement in there saying if it's a tie! I led the team! I know that it was tied, but I led the team!' So I got $5,000 for two interceptions that year (chuckle)!"[23]

When the discussion between Bradley and Gallagher drifted to the subject of remaining on the active roster of the team or being traded, however, the level of scrutiny increased. In moments such as those, it helped to have someone in your corner who not only would fight for you, but who knew the ins and outs of contractual law. Fortunately for Bradley, he had such a lawyer defending him. This was important, because his lawyer included more clauses in Bradley's contract with the Eagles than what could have been found in Kris Kringle's extended family.

"My attorney was Lyndon Baines Johnson's attorney, and his name was Frank Denius," said Bradley. "Mind you he was a very well-decorated World War II veteran, and just like me, he also went to the University of Texas. Being a strong alumnus, he decided that when I got drafted (by the Eagles), he wanted to be my agent or representative. So he became my attorney, and we became good friends until the day he died.

"Well I had a clause in my contract that stipulated that if I was traded to another team, I would have the right of first refusal (to go to that team). That was just one of many clauses in my contract. Frank put clauses in there that said that if I ever punted for a season average of over 40 yards per punt, I would get an extra $5,000 bonus. If I led the league in interceptions, I would get a $10,000 bonus. If I led the team in interceptions, I would get another $5,000 bonus. I had all of these clauses in my contract. And you know we had some unique ones in there too, just to see if the management was even reading them that far down the list. Like if I beat off at halftime during a game, or some crazy shit like that, I would get $1,000, or some cash bonus like that (laughter).

"We put in about 60 clauses. After reading about 50 of them, the Eagles management just stopped reading them, which was stupid. Pete Retzlaff and Jim Gallagher…they just started initialing them. You know how contracts are. I read everything that comes my way. I learned that from Mr. Denius."[24]

The written words on Bradley's contract with Philadelphia meant that Dick Vermeil would have to find another team wherein he could send his erstwhile free safety. Vermeil did just that, and this time, Bradley accepted his effort. Bradley would be going up north to play for the Minnesota Vikings, a team that was a perennial playoff contender.

"After Dick Vermeil read all of my shit (contract), he altered every player's contracts," Bradley explained. "In the future, the team would have to go to the playoffs before that would trigger any of every player's individual clauses. Vermeil got a third-round draft pick for me from Minnesota," recalled Bradley. "I went there and made it all through training camp. Six weeks of training camp. And you know with (Minnesota head coach) Bud Grant, he was late on doing anything. So I made it through the final preseason game, the deadline for getting cut had come and gone. I was excited about being on their team. I remember telling my wife that 'I got this team made.'"[25]

Bill Bradley was premature with his optimism in this case, however. That was in part because virtually every head coach in the NFL has some idiosyncrasies that are displayed every now and then. Coach Grant was no different. Bradley's fate with the Vikings came about because of Grant's peculiarities as much as anything else.

"For somebody that got traded to Minnesota, I had to earn my right to be on that team," said Bradley. "And I thought I did. The most degrading thing that I went through during the 1977 preseason was when Grant had all of the rookies line up on the field at kickoff, and they would play the National Anthem. You were expected to hold your helmet in your left hand and not move an inch. And I had to do it right alongside all of the rookies. I thought that it was kind of degrading, you know. Of course, all of the veterans were on the sidelines standing. So he had me standing out there on the field with the rookies, and it *pissed* me off. So as they start playing the National Anthem, I was standing there at attention, and we all know what that deal is, with your hand over your heart. And I did so, but I started walking. I walked all the way down the field just to prove a point. You know, Grant didn't like that.

"So I was late in getting cut from the team. Well they kept (free safety) Paul Krause, but they should have kept me. I was the last person cut. Krause was getting up in age, and everyone on the team knew that Paul Krause wouldn't tackle (Author's Note: practically everyone all across the league knew that was the case as well). The next thing I knew, I was told to '...bring my playbook to Bud's office.' Bud Grant ran that show, and he took care of his veterans. The veterans on his defensive line were mostly in their mid-30s."[26]

And the veterans in the defensive secondary were commiserate with Bradley's plight. They got word of him being released by the team, and they did something that no other group of players ever did during the reign of Coach Grant. They refused to attend practice the next day, in a showing of solidarity, and in a statement of dissent.

"Two or three of the defensive backs actually struck," remembered Bradley. "They didn't go to practice when I left the team. Because they thought that I had earned the right to belong on the squad. Because they knew that I could cover their backs and receivers, and they knew that I could make a tackle, and all that kind of stuff. So they didn't go to practice. They were mad."[27]

Bill Bradley might have also been quite perturbed at this time as well, having been cut for the first time ever in his pro career. But those feelings did not last long. He still had some life left in his 30-year-old legs, and he still possessed the one important talent that every good defensive back needs to have if he wants to stay in the NFL: the ability to read what a quarterback and what an opposing offense was trying to do. It would not take long before other teams brought him in to see if he could obtain a position for their team. Unfortunately for Bradley, his experiences with several other teams were all brief and unproductive. The Houston Oilers suited Bradley up for a week, then released him. His stay with the Oakland Raiders lasted an even shorter amount of time. As a member of the Pittsburgh Steelers, Bradley got a chance to experience a depressing lack of communication, courtesy of their head coach, Chuck Noll.

"I went to the Steelers and I was in my uniform, and at the end of practice, he (Noll) called for one of those board drills," related Bradley. "That was a drill where a defensive back had to shed a blocker, and within five yards of each side of the board, you had to try to make a tackle before a running back got passed you. And so I was doing some punting at the end of practice, when we go to this board drill, and it's live contact. And the first time, (offensive lineman Jon) Kolb came out and blocked me, and I got under him and made the play. Then the coaches overseeing this action yelled out 'Do it again! Do it again!' Well the next time, Kolb just pancaked me. That's how that practice ended.

"Noll didn't even have a word to say to me...not about my punting, not about anything. So I'm leaving to go call a cab to go to the airport. And I reasoned to myself, 'Man, this ain't right. Man, I'm 30 years old. Golly, I think that I've already proven myself.' And so I'm going out to get in a yellow cab, and he (Noll) comes out and says, 'Bill, we never got to see you punt.' I just looked at him and got in the cab and said, 'Well, you ain't never going to see me punt.' And I took the cab to the airport. I was full up with that stuff. I got tired of that shit."[28]

There comes a point in every pro athlete's life where they know that they have had enough. Sometimes it comes in the form of what an athlete can or cannot do anymore with the minimum acceptable performance level of his body. Sometimes it is more a mental awareness or feeling in his mind that he just does not want to think about the pressure of dealing with coaches, of making mistakes, or of letting his teammates down. For Bill Bradley, pro football had become more a mental game than a physical one. He could still run fast, cover receivers, and make tackles. But when he had to deal with numerous coaches over the years, where no stability could be had, and when he had to deal with head coaches like Chuck Noll, who did not—at least in Bradley's case—possess the mental faculties to communicate with his assistant coaches or his players...well, Bradley reasoned that his time in the NFL was done.

Despite what you might think, few of us get to retire the way that we want to retire. Often, we never get the chance to offer a proper goodbye to our coworkers (or teammates). And on occasions where our bosses are not the best of bosses (by a longshot), we often just dream about telling them off as our official sendoff to a new chapter in our lives. Sometimes, our retirements are forced on us, and in some cases, they are or can be premature. Usually, however, we employees just end up taking the high road and keeping our mouths shut. After eight seasons in pro football, Bill Bradley felt comfortable to call it a career. His sojourn through the pathways of pro football had officially ended...for good. Well, that was until he happened to get a phone call from a guy who admittedly was his hero in his younger years.

"Gosh I was done," said Bradley, "and I was still getting paid by the Eagles from my previous contract. I had gone back down to Palestine, and I was trying to be married to my first wife. But one day during the 1977 football season, I got a phone call. It was from Jim Hanifan, the assistant coach from the Cardinals who kept flipping me the bird and calling me an asshole from the sidelines. Hanifan told me that 'Larry Wilson is going to call you.' Now Larry Wilson was my idol at free safety. I remember him playing for the Cardinals, and he intercepted a pass with two broken hands! With casts on both of his hands! Well, he was the general manager for the Cardinals at that time.

"So Larry calls me and says, 'Bill, we would like you to play for us. Coach Hanifan said that you are a great football player. I started looking at film, and you have played very well. And Coach Hanifan swears by you.' And I thought that Hanifan was my enemy. Well on the phone, Larry says, 'Bill, I really need you.' I said to him, 'Larry, I really respect you. But you don't know what I've been through for the past six weeks. It's a long story. It's a personal story. And I'm not going to bore you with it.' He said again, 'Bill, I need you here. Mike Sensibaugh (the Cardinals free safety) is hurt, and we need a punter and a safety. Can you make it up here?'"[29]

The chance to play once more in the NFL is indeed enticing. Bradley weighed his options in a very quick fashion. He knew what he had waiting for him at home. He did not know what waited for him if he accepted Wilson's request. He decided to tell Wilson no, in the hopes that Wilson would give up on his plea. As it turned out, he did not give up.

"So on the phone," continued Bradley, "and I told him, 'Larry, I'm on an 86-acre hay farm, I'm trying to stay married, I'm trying to make another life, I've got a country grocery store, and I'm still getting paid by the Eagles.' He said, 'I know that, but I need you here.' So I said, 'Larry, I'm not coming.' He said, 'Bill, I really need you. I swear to God.' Finally, I said to him, 'Larry, do you swear on a stack of Bibles, and on your mother's grave, that if I come up there, that I will be playing this Thursday (they had a Thursday night game that week)?' He said, 'Bill, I swear on a stack of Bibles and on my mother's grave. Hanifan has sworn by you (Author's Note: besides swearing *at* Bill Bradley, Coach Hanifan as it turned out also swore *by* Bill Bradley).' He then said, 'Bill, I need you. You need to come. You don't know me. I'm a man of my word. You'll be returning punts for sure, and you'll probably get into the game as our free safety.'"[30]

Bradley at last decided to trust Wilson, a man who he held in the highest regard from all of his numerous exploits as a player in the league. So he packed up his stuff and took an airplane flight up to St. Louis.

"I trusted him," said Bradley of Larry Wilson. "And I finished that season (1977) with the Cardinals. And Hanifan was the one that got me there. And I'm sure that he (Hanifan) said something like, 'I know that little asshole Bradley is a damn good player. He's played very well against us every time that we played them (the Eagles). So bring him in.' But I came to realize over time that I had misjudged old Jim Hanifan. I found out that he was really deep down a really nice guy...he was a good guy. Sometimes that happens. We don't really know a person until we really get to know a person, if that makes any sense."[31]

Making some semblance of sense was difficult to determine at this point in Bradley's life. It had to have been at least a little bit strange, or maybe even unsettling, to sign a contract to play for a team that for his entire career, had been one of Bradley's hated rivals. In truth, Bradley really was not sure what to expect when he walked into Busch Memorial Stadium. Keep in mind, he had endured tryouts from the Oilers, Steelers, Raiders, and Vikings just prior to the start of the 1977 season. He probably felt that his trip up to St. Louis with just one month left in the season would produce no different result. But it certainly did, in more ways than one.

"Well I go into their dressing room, and they have my uniform ready and all that," recalled Bradley. "And nobody is in there. And they're about to practice in about three hours. Not one fellow was in there. So I walk up to the equipment guy, and I see him pick up a bell and start ringing it. And they—the Cardinals players like Conrad Dobler, Dan Dierdorf, Tom Banks, Jackie Smith, and several others—they all come running out of the showers and the bathroom and they dogpile me in the middle of the damn dressing room. I immediately thought, 'Oh my God. I'm going to have to fight my way out of this one.' From what I understand, Jim Hanifan told those guys that I was joining their team. They were ready for me, and they dogpiled me. They beat me up. They said something like, 'Welcome Bradley. We hate your ass. We're glad that you're here man.' That was unbelievable. You know how people celebrate when they jump on the pile? They all dogpiled me. But they accepted me because as it turned out, I was a lot like them."[32]

At least Bradley *thought* that he was a lot like his new teammates. The Cardinals only had four games remaining in their season. If they won those games, they would go to the playoffs. If they lost, they would not go to the playoffs. Bill Bradley was now an active player in his ninth NFL season. He had yet to go to the playoffs. Unfortunately, that streak would continue thanks to what happened during the final month of his pro playing career.

"They (the Cardinals) were on their way to the playoffs," said Bradley, "but they didn't win their last four games. The players were tired of playing, and that made me so mad, but I couldn't say anything. It all came down to four games. And they lost them all."[33]

The perpetual losing seemed to be getting the best of Bradley at this time. He knew that there was really no hope of him sticking around to play for St. Louis in 1978. To get his mind off of one defeat after another, Bradley decided to have some fun with his new teammates. That fun involved another opportunity for their new free safety's penchant of displaying his unique personality.

"By that time, I was already running around with Waylon Jennings, a buddy of mine who was a country and western singer," said Bradley. "And we hit it off pretty good. I ran around with him and I got to know him. So when I went to the Cardinals, he (Jennings) had a concert coming in at the nearby hockey arena, with like 15,000 people attending. Well I called him and said, 'Waylon! I want to take care of these guys (Bradley's new teammates)...guys like (St. Louis quarterback) Jim Hart, Dobler, Dierdorf, Banks...you know, all those guys, about six or eight of them.' I said that I wanted to bring them to his concert. Well he got us front row seats, right by the stage. I told the guys (Bradley's teammates) that I would meet them there. Well because Waylon's my friend, I decided to kill time before the show started by drinking some whiskey and beers, and by going backstage. While Waylon is practicing and getting his sound system squared away, and time got away from him...and from me. Waylon was married to Jessi Coulter, who was the daughter of a preacher man. The Hell's Angels were his bodyguards (Author's Note: the Hell's Angels motorcycle club served as bodyguards for several musicians and musical groups during that period, including The Rolling

Stones, among others), and they were fixing to move down (into the audience).

"And Jessi is tuning up the baby grand piano. She plays the piano and sings background vocals. She's an absolutely gorgeous woman. I sat down on a stool at the end of the baby grand piano, right next to her. Keep in mind that the curtains were still closed. And the time got away from me. I forgot about the time! Now I told all of those Cardinals players to pick up their tickets to the concert at the will call window. I told them that I didn't know for sure what I would be doing, but that I would catch up with them at their seats. So they came in, and I didn't show up at the seats like I told them I would. I'm just sitting next to Jessi Coulter at the baby grand piano and listening to her sing. So anyway, I'm shellacked on bourbon and beer, and all of a sudden, the curtain goes up! And there's 15,000 people looking at me sitting at a stool at the baby grand piano, right next to Jessi Coulter!"[34]

Did you ever have to go onstage in elementary school or high school for a school play, or a recital, or to sing a song? You know the feeling of nervousness that you probably felt at that moment? Bradley may have felt those same feelings at this moment, and it is possible that they were made even worse with the alcohol that was in his system. No, he did not toss his cookies because of the drinks that he had previously consumed. But he did have plenty of enjoyment on that evening. There is one fact that you must understand when it comes to Bill Bradley: he was born to have fun, regardless of the circumstances. On that evening, he certainly did.

"So I helped Waylon and Jessi sing a song to open the concert," said Bradley. "And all those Cardinals guys down there in the front row of the audience? I knew what they were doing. I'm sure that they were saying stuff like 'Bradley...he's a no-show son of a bitch. He ain't never coming. He didn't even know this guy (Waylon Jennings).' Well after the curtains came up, I looked down at the front row, and there they are. All of them to a man just stuck out their index fingers and pointed at me! They went into shock! They put their hands over their mouths and then just started laughing their asses off. From that point on, I was a hero around the Cardinals dressing room."[35]

The full-time hero and part-time free safety had certainly made an impact on his new teammates in just a few short weeks. But the 1977 season was soon over, and that was simply fine for Bill Bradley. It was time for him to get back home; back to Palestine, Texas, where he was born and raised. His life was meant to continue down there in the Lone Star State, for another new (and likely a less exciting) chapter. His sojourn through the world of football was now officially at a permanent end. Or was it?

10

VISITING THE CROSSROADS

The most recognizable signs that point to a successful person can often stand out with just one glance. Sometimes, how much money one has or what quality of clothes one wears serves as obvious marks of success. At other times, a person's possessions, such as the car he or she drives, or the house that he or she resides in, will aptly provide an indication of their accomplishments. All those tangible items, however, can be misleading to the casual observer, especially if we do not really know the person in question. There is one sign or fact that is undeniably a constant sign of success, however, even if a person does not show any outward signs of triumphs. A successful person will always be able to make the best of any situation. Such a person is usually also able to favorably adapt to a variety of changes in his or her life. Despite the familiarity that one has performing one task, he or she can still acclimate themselves to a new challenge, or even a whole new occupation.

Bill Bradley led a contented life after he retired from playing pro football at the end of the 1977 season. That is because he was a happy-go-lucky person, and he enjoyed the basic and relaxed life that he had carved out for himself. Bradley had migrated back down to his home in Palestine, Texas, where he stayed busy with several projects. He applied himself to working on his 86-acre hay farm, and to owning and operating a small grocery store and a filling station. He lived in the back room of the store, which was a rather sparse existence for someone who only recently became the first man to ever lead the NFL in interceptions two years in a row.

But Bradley never outwardly allowed a prideful persona to inhabit his frame of mind. Rather, he was always willing to adapt to any background, to any occupation, or to any specific situation. That is probably why he always got along so well with virtually everyone. He was simply willing to put the lives of other people at center stage, which in turn allowed those people a certain level of comfort whenever they spoke to Bradley or befriended him. It was as if Bradley already knew a stranger, and that stranger was already his good friend. Indeed, few were the people who could honestly say that they did not care for Bradley, especially after he met them. In short, Bradley was—and is—a people person, and he went about his "new" daily life with the same happiness with which he addressed his former life...as a free safety in the NFL.

"I bought a country store, a grocery store, after I retired from pro ball," said Bradley. "It ain't bad. It was out in the middle of nowhere along my farm. It was what you would call a convenience store. We had all the little staples that people eat out in the country. I also bought a filling station in front of the store, and every time one of the ranchers or their wives would come in, I'd get to know them. I would check their oil, fill up their gas tanks, wipe their windows...you know, the basics. It was called the Brushy Creek store, because it was right alongside Brushy Creek, in a small little church community.

"So the ranchers and the farmers would come in around 5:30 in the morning, and I would have the place opened for them. I might be sitting on the front porch, on a swing, and then buy one of those little Cokes, and then pour all of them damn Planters peanuts in them, like all of the old timers do. And one of them might come in and say, 'Bradley, my nephews ain't around this summer. Can you help me haul some hay?' And I'd say, 'Well let me call my dad or my girl-friend, get them out here to run the station, and we'll put up however many bales of hay to put up.'"[1]

It was Americana in all its grandeur. Small town life and daily living, as pure as it can be. Neighbors helping neighbors. Friends helping friends. Nothing to write home about, but the sentimental stuff of making a go of it in a rural country existence. It was in a world of homespun happiness, where few things were difficult or scientific. No, this was a basic working world that Bill Bradley felt reasonably comfortable in, especially when one considers that he had been born and raised in just such a world not too many years previously. His post-playing life indeed gave him a sense of satisfaction, and a sense of pride as well.

"I built the business back up and lived in the back of the store," said Bradley. "It was a big, rectangular feed store back in its historical days. The store wasn't doing any business because they weren't running it right. So I moved back home to my 86 acres, and I began running the business. I didn't have much else to do. I kept the place clean...I swept up daily, and I sold gasoline, diesel, ethanol, and kerosene. I also had one of those big old porcelain coolers with all of the meat in it like you see in grocery stores now. And I had an ice cream still over on the side in one of those ice cream fold out tops.

"Now ice cream didn't sell that much, so what I'd do is I'd find one of the ranchers out there who was going to butcher one of their cows, and I'd say to him, 'Let's go halves on it.' So I started going halves, and they were stamping their meat, but it wasn't stamped legally (chuckle). I kept the meat in that ice cream cooler, and I sold more meat out of there than anything else."[2]

This was certainly not an exciting living, to be sure. But there was seven days in a week, and Bradley was the type of guy who needed to do other things on his weekends besides just selling food and pumping gas at his store. Now you might think at this time of his life, he did not have enough free time to take another extravagant trip to a place like Las Vegas again. Well, you would be correct. But his lack of free time did not stop him from taking a different kind of trip, and to a different location as well.

"I would also leave Texas on the weekends sometimes," remembered Bradley. "Sometimes for even longer than a weekend. You see, the NFLPA (National Football League Players Association) started this thing with NCO Cruise Lines back in the late 1970s and early 1980s. During the football season, the retired players would go on the cruises. Well I was retired, so I got to go on one. Shoot, I loved it! I helped the staff out with different activities. I went on them mostly because I was bored just working at my country store.

"So I knew a girl from Notre Dame who ran the cruises. Dee Rausche was her name. I told her that I was always available if she needed me to help out on the cruises. You know, when some retired player would cancel on her, she would ask me to go in his place. I always told her that I was just a phone call away. I was actually on almost 30 ship cruises over a period of about five years. Dee would call me and say, 'Can you get to the Port of Miami? Can you fly to Miami? We'll pay for it.' And then they would pay me to go on a cruise, because I spoke at the theater in the bottom of the ship on the very first night that they set sail, with the captain and everybody else that was running the deal. Well I also ran the activities at the ship's pool. I ended up becoming an unofficial assistant cruise director (laughter). I went on so many cruises. I eventually took everybody in my family, and I took my buddies three or four times (laughter). We would go to Jamaica, and all those ports down there in the ocean. For a whole month, I went straight to the Caribbean. I never touched American soil. That was the life down there. So I did become the unofficial, official cruise director (more laughter)."[3]

To get along with so many different people, Bradley relied on his own personality and his own creativity. The rule of thumb on every one of these cruises? To have fun. Bradley made sure that everyone on those ships had an enjoyable time.

"Some of the parents would bring their kids," recalled Bradley. "And there was a lot of singles also on the ship. Well I started these relay races at the pool. And then for the singles, we'd have a day or two for them, and then we'd have a day or two for the kids. And then on a Wednesday night on a ship on a seven-day cruise, I would go to all of the parents and say, 'Look, I got your kids this Wednesday night. You all go do whatever you want to. You go eat, go to the discotheque, etc.' Then I would have about a dozen kids, and they'd have a little romper room type of setup. I would get them in a line, and I'd march them through the discotheque, where they could see their parents dancing! They liked me on a ship. So every time a cruise became available, Dee Rausche would call me, and I got to know her pretty well. She went to Notre Dame, and one year, she wanted tickets to the Cotton Bowl game when Notre Dame played there. Well I got her front row seats. So anytime she needed me for a cruise, I would tell her that 'I'm on my way.'"[4]

But despite his happiness, there was always something gnawing at Bill Bradley. It was almost as if something was missing in his life, and he knew that he would not be able to settle these feelings in his mind until he could answer his own missing ingredient. He had left the sport of football with only a few regrets, namely he never went to the playoffs, and he never won a championship. But there were other people in his life who knew all along that he would not fulfill his life's goals until he got back into the game in some way.

"I knew that he would be a great coach," said former Eagles head coach Ed Khayat, "and I had spotted him to be a coach early on. You know, you can spot them, and he was one that I could spot who would be an outstanding coach. He was a leader in the ball club. Bill was one of the smartest players that I was ever around in my coaching days. I'll give you an example: we were playing Dallas, and they (the Cowboys) punted the ball. Bill was our punt returner at the time. You picture him standing to receive the punt, and he's waving for a fair catch. And he's *far* away from the path of the ball. And the Dallas players who were covering the punt, they're looking at Bradley. They're not looking up in the air for the ball. And they all went over there where he (Bradley) was standing (chuckle). And the ball went into our end zone, and we got it on the 20. His play saved us quite a few yards of field position. He's the first guy that I ever saw do that intentionally."[5]

Whether it was intentional or not, Bill Bradley left pro football back in 1977, and never looked back. At least his backwards glance did not include a return to the game. But most of the players who retire from the game occasionally remark how much they miss it, at least a little bit. Bradley was among that number. He knew that he could not and would not return to the game as a player. But what about being a coach? He eventually admitted that coaching football players was something that would be of interest to him...at least a little more than selling groceries and pumping gasoline in Palestine.

But how would Bradley become a coach in pro football? While it was true that he had some contacts, some of whom might be able to help him out with references, it was also true that he was away from the sport for several years. Indeed, any amount of time spent away from the game would be detrimental to his possible return to the game. Nevertheless, he decided to try and make a go of becoming a pro coach. This is where his ingenuity plus his nerve would equal an opportunity. His first step was to take advantage of a random connection or two.

"I knew this guy named Billy Schott, who was a kicker at (the University of) Texas after I went to school there," said Bradley. "His dad was a referee. Well Billy got hired by this guy named Clinton Manges, and he was helping to start a whole new league, the United States Football League (USFL). They were putting a team together back in 1983 called the San Antonio Gunslingers."[6]

Bradley's ingenuity and his daring were often a pair of working gears in his brain. Those two items operated hand in hand with each other. It is doubtful that what he did back in 1983 would work in this current day and age, but back then, his boldness was to be rewarded.

"Well I bought a clipboard and a silver stopwatch," said Bradley. "My dad was a baseball coach forever, and I always wanted to coach. I didn't go to college to become a businessman, or the head of a country. I went to coach, and I knew I was going to coach. I met a lot of people in the football offseason (between February and July). Billy (Schott) called me and told me that I should go to San Antonio to check things out. So I went down there as a fake scout for the Eagles (chuckle). I had an Eagles polo shirt on, slacks, and carrying my clipboard and stopwatch (more chuckling).

"So I go up in the stands in San Antonio, and as fate would have it, I'm sitting next to the team owner, Clint Manges. He must have recognized me when he started talking to me. He asked me, 'Bill, what are you doing?' I told him that I was scouting for the Philadelphia Eagles (laughter). He then asked me, 'Hey, do you want a job?' I said, 'What kind of job are you talking about?' He said that he would talk to his head coach, Gil Steinke, about hiring me. Well, Gil Steinke was a friend of mine (Author's Note: Bradley's connections once again gave him another opportunity). Gil asked me if I wanted to coach the San Antonio defensive backs, which I did."[7]

This would be just the start of Bradley's coaching resume. By the end of 2020, he would account for no less than an incredible 17 different coaching positions. Bradley coached the Gunslingers very well, and in 1985, he coached another USFL team, the Memphis Showboats. The fledgling league then shut down, and for players and coaches alike, it was every man for himself. The NFL only had 26 teams at this point, but in 1976, that number would increase to 28 teams when Seattle and Tampa Bay became expansion teams in the NFL. Of course, there was a bunch of opportunities to coach college football at schools across the nation. Moreover, for those who were willing, the Canadian Football League (CFL) was often hiring former NFL talent as coaches and players.

"After the USFL folded, I went to the Senior Bowl, and I volunteered at the University of Texas for their head coach at the time, David 'Mack' Williams," said Bradley. "I was a volunteer coach for him, and I also ran their scout team in 1987. I didn't make any money, but I went to classes with Britt Hager and some of those players on the '87 team. We beat (the University of) Pittsburgh in the Astro Bluebonnet Bowl, and Pittsburgh had a good team back then. They called me 'The Best Volunteer Coach in America,' and that's a great honor to have. It was fun, and we turned that team around. We went from below .500 to 7-5 and a bowl win. After that, I got a phone call from Larry Kuharich, who was the son of former Eagles head coach Joe Kuharich. Larry's dad drafted me for the Eagles back in 1969, but I never got to play for him, because he was fired shortly after he drafted me. Heck, the fans in Philadelphia hung him in effigy.

"But Larry never forgot that his dad drafted me. He was my age, and he was the head coach up in Canada for the Calgary Stampeders. He asked me if I would come up there, coach his defensive backs, and run the defense for him. I was glad to do it for him, and from that point on, I was off and running as far as being a coach is concerned. If you can coach in the CFL, you can coach anywhere in the world. They've got a larger field and larger end zones. They also allow 12 men on offense and defense. But they require you to get a first down in three downs instead of four like we do here in America. So they're going to throw the ball on virtually every play. So that's where I weaned my coaching career."[8]

The ability to learn new defensive strategies and concepts, and to adjust to a game with somewhat different rules, is something that the CFL requires of any man who plays or coaches defensive units north of the border. To Bradley's credit, he was a fast learner. Just as he picked up key points as a rookie player from former Eagle Joe Scarpati, so too would Bradley learn rapidly about the way the Canadian teams played the game. It was a situation that fitted this free spirit to near perfection. Calgary was a whole new environment, and just like his offseason trip to Europe following the 1970 NFL season,

Bradley adapted well to the many differences in language, customs, and the sights and sounds of Canada.

Pro football in Canada would offer Bradley a challenge that was similar to what he experienced when he was back at the University of Texas, when Coach Royal switched him from quarterback to receiver to defensive back. If he could help Calgary win, regardless of his role, then he would be deemed a successful assistant coach. The ends would justify the means. Bradley thus wasted no time in "hitting the books." He also hit his new players with tidbits of information that he learned several years ago as a player himself. How can you be successful covering all of these fast receivers on a wider and longer playing field in Canada? Bradley would address that very topic with the young Stampeders defensive backs that he coached. As it turned out, he would use the same methods and reveal the same information to every one of his players over the years.

"I would bring my players (the defensive backs) into our meeting room after their regular meetings," explained Bradley. "And I would say to them, 'Guys, we're going to sit and watch from the end zone film the quarterback's habits. Here's just one example: we would watch a quarterback take his snap from the center, then he'd take his steps and look in the other direction, but his throw went to the right half of the field. What clues could my players find in the film that would tip them off as to where the quarterback's pass was going to, even though he looked in the opposite direction?

"Similarly, when a quarterback took the snap in the Shotgun formation and looked left, then back peddled some more, looked around and setup, then the ball would go to the left half of the field, or the left quadrant of the field. I started studying things this way when I was a player. This is how I learned. In the NFL, you're playing against some of the best athletes in the world. I wanted all of my players to be active thinkers out there."[9]

Those active thinkers who learned Bradley's methods could not help but improve as defensive backs. Trying to discover the tips that a quarterback or an offense was showing to a defense was the key. If a player can get into the habit of studying what is going on out there, he can also get in the habit of making big plays to help win a game. And just as Bradley was a detective when he watched his opponents on film as a player, so too would his young charges also be sleuths in searching for the clues of an offense.

"I coached this guy by the name of Antonio Cromartie when I was an assistant coach in San Diego," said Bradley. "He was the best all-around athlete that I ever coached. I have a photo of him leaping high in the air to intercept a ball...with one hand! So, I wanted to challenge him to get his natural greatness to shine. I inserted him in the lineup, and I bet him that he couldn't intercept 11 balls in a season (Author's Note: Bradley intercepted 11 passes in 1971, hence he used that number as a barometer). We had a $500 bet, and he ended up with 10 interceptions. But I taught him how to study football. I said to him, 'You just watch all of the receivers, and you watch the quarterback, and you come to me before we play that team and tell me what you were able to find from watching the films. I will then inform the rest of the defensive backs of your tip in our meeting before we would play that team.

"So one time he came to me, and we were playing the Dolphins the next week, and a guy named O.J. McDuffie was their slot receiver. And one day after studying the film, Cromartie comes up to me and says, 'Hey Bill, I've got a really good tip for you.' And I'd make my players bring their tip to me, just so I knew that they were studying. And some of their tips were right on. So Cromartie says, 'Every time that Miami breaks the huddle, McDuffie was messing with either one of his gloves, like unsnapping it or pulling it tighter, whenever the play would be a passing play. But if he didn't touch his gloves, it was going to be a running play, because he wasn't going to block...he was going to shadow somebody.' Well, that was one hell of a tip, so when we're playing the Dolphins, we started double-teaming O.J. McDuffie on every third down, whether he was in the slot, or being used as a wideout. So we just killed (Miami quarterback, Dan) Marino. He wasn't mobile enough to move away from the pass rush, so we would sack him or hit him, because he didn't have his go-to guy (McDuffie) anymore. So that's the way that I taught some of my players."[10]

Bradley took his teaching agenda on the road over the next few decades. Different levels of play, and different players to be sure. Most of those coaching venues came with some incredibly unique stories. Take Bradley's time spent in Buffalo, New York, while he served as an assistant coach for the Bills, from 1998-2000. It undoubtedly had him scratching his head wondering what his real purpose was for that team.

"I had coached all over, coaching defensive backs and helping to coordinate defenses," described Bradley. "I talked to Wade Phillips at a coach's convention in Dallas, and he asked me if I was interested in working for him up in Buffalo, which I was. He then asked me if I could get Doug Flutie to come to Buffalo (Author's Note: Doug Flutie was a former Heisman Trophy-winning quarterback from Boston College who played eight years in the CFL, where he first met Bill Bradley). We had just won two Grey Cups (Author's Note: the Grey Cup is the CFL's equivalent of America's Super Bowl) with Toronto in 1996 and 1997. I coordinated the defense for Toronto, and Doug Flutie was our team's quarterback. And so Wade kept asking me to go to an interview for the Bills, but every time that I would go to the interview, he stood me up! But he always made a point to continually ask me if I could get Doug Flutie to come to Buffalo and play for the Bills. And every time, I would always tell him, 'Sure, I've already talked to Doug, and he is interested.'

"So after he stood me up again, I finally caught Wade at a Senior Bowl practice. I said to him, 'Hey Wade...you stood me up again. Do you want me to come and coach for you? Or do you just want Doug Flutie to be your backup quarterback to Rob Johnson?' And he said, 'Oh no Bill...I'm sorry. I didn't mean to do all of that. Go see John Butler (Buffalo's general manager) and work out your contract.' That was my interview with him!"[11]

While an assistant coach in Buffalo, Bill Bradley got a chance to see in person one of the NFL's most controversial plays in playoff history. The Bills took a 16-15 lead with just 16 seconds left in this struggle. On an implausible kickoff return, Tennessee tight end Frank Wycheck carried the pigskin gingerly as he ran a few yards to his right. He then spun around on a dime and threw the ball clear across to the other end of the field, where Titans wide receiver Kevin Dyson was waiting to catch it, which he did. Tyson immediately ran 75 yards untouched along the near sideline to score. The play went down in history as the "Music City Miracle," and it would take a miracle—or some really poor referee judgments—to award Tennessee a touchdown. Despite viewing several angles of instant replays, the officials rewarded the Titans for their pluck with a confirmed score, which knocked Buffalo out of the playoffs.

"We got beat by the Music City Miracle," lamented Bradley. "I'll go to my grave knowing that that play was an illegal forward pass. The referee who claimed that it was legal called it while he was standing behind the play. So it looked like a lateral to him, but it was definitely an illegal forward pass (Author's Note: the receiving team on a kickoff cannot throw the ball forward...they have to throw it backward in order for it to be legal)."[12]

The Titans rode their good luck all the way to Super Bowl XXXIV, where they lost to the St. Louis Rams, 23-16. The ramifications for Bradley and the Bills, however, were quite a bit different.

"We (the coaches) got fired after we lost to Tennessee," said Bradley. "We all got fired."[13]

Such a fate was not unusual. Few are the list of coaches who never get fired, and it does not take a whole lot of reasons for a team owner to fire his head coach, his coaching staff, his general manager, or even his ball boys and cheerleaders, if he (or she) sees fit to do so. Bradley accepted this fate as just another fact of the business side of the game. Unlike a lot of people, he was willing and able to roll with the punches, as it were. His free-spirited nature saw to it. As it turned out, his coaching days were far from concluding. In fact, he was still in his coaching prime following his stint in Buffalo.

Part of the reason for Bradley's success in the coaching ranks flowed from his willingness—indeed, his desire—to coach the fundamentals of the game. Many coaches today fail to spend time on the basics, primarily because they have so much else on their plates to accomplish. Bradley, in contrast, insists on teaching the main tenets that every defensive back should know.

"I still conduct drills," admitted Bradley, "and I have a lot of young players who come to me after each practice to do them. I make all of the defensive players catch a football in the drills, especially while I was a defensive coordinator. They would have to catch it while backpedaling, planting their feet, and then sprinting at a 45-degree angle. I'm the one who throws them the ball. Heck, I throw the ball better now than when I did while I was a quarterback at the University of Texas (chuckle). What it all amounted to was getting turnovers, as in interceptions."[14]

To continue teaching the art of interception gathering, Bradley had to be willing to work for a variety of different teams, which he indeed was. You have undoubtedly heard of the children's show, *Where's Waldo*, haven't you? Well, the sport of football could have had their own version of the show, based on Bill Bradley's coaching stops. It could rightly be called, *Where's Coach Bradley?* He coached in practically every section of the North American continent at several different levels from 1983 to the present day. The litany of the teams that benefitted from Bradley's coaching efforts included the San Antonio Riders of the World League of American Football, or WLAF, from 1991 to 1992. He stayed in San Antonio in 1993 and 1994 as the defensive coordinator of the San Antonio Texans. Surprisingly, the Texans were one of a few experimental CFL teams that were situated for a time in the United States.

Bradley got the chance to coach out west in 1995 and 1996, when he served as the defensive coordinator for the Sacramento Gold Miners, another team that played under the banner of the CFL. He stayed in that league for the next couple of seasons when he coordinated the Toronto Argonauts defense in 1996 and 1997. Then came his three-year stint in Buffalo (1998-2000) as their defensive backs coach. Bradley then moved southeast to coach the defensive backs for the New York Jets from 2001 to 2003. He changed things up in 2004, when he went to the collegiate level, as he became the defensive coordinator for the Baylor Bears from 2004 to 2006. From there, he went back to the NFL, as he was hired to coach the defensive secondary for the San Diego Chargers in 2007 and 2008. While in San Diego, Bradley was coaching for the Chargers' head coach, Norv Turner. Unfortunately for Bradley, he and Ted Cottrell, one of the most noteworthy and knowledgeable defensive coaches of this era, both experienced a bitter and premature departure from San Diego.

"Our defense took Norv Turner to his first playoff game in 2007," recalled Bradley. "He then hired Ron Rivera to be the team's linebacker coach. In the middle of the 2008 season, Ted got fired, and Rivera took over for him as the team's defensive coordinator. We then finished at 8-8 that year, and I was sent packing too."[15]

Ted Cottrell understands how capricious the winds are when it comes to obtaining a coaching job in football, and then keeping one. He also knows how favoritism and politics play a part in who gets a job, and in particular, *how* they get a job. That picture is not always a pleasant one.

"Often it boils down to who you know," acknowledged Cottrell. "There are some guys who will smile in your face, then stab you in the back. And then not just stab you in the back, but then turn the knife from side to side while it's in your back. It's so they can get ahead of you, or it's because they're trying to make themselves look better to somebody else. Make no mistake, it's been going on like that for years, in the pros and in the college ranks as well."[16]

The firing of Bradley and Cottrell was not shocking, considering —as Cottrell alluded—that there have been a multitude of similar coaching and front office removals in both pro and college football history, especially after one or more persons develops a friendship with the decision makers. And as with any other work situation between bosses and employees, jealousies can sometimes develop into gossiping and the telling of falsehoods, where one party is covetous of another party. In that respect, having a connection can sometimes work out poorly for some innocent people, as it did for both Bradley and Cottrell in San Diego in 2008.

The jobs for both Bradley and Cottrell certainly met an untimely end in San Diego. But Cottrell knew a good defensive backs coach when he saw one, and when he saw one, he darn sure tried to keep him. The friendship of these two men still stems from the basic fact that both love the game of football, and both know how to be successful at coaching. As far as Cottrell is concerned, his buddy from the Lone Star State was somebody who he would never hesitate to hire again...every chance he got.

"Bill and I got along so well together in coaching football," admitted Cottrell. "It is almost like we are thinking alike, thinking ahead, and making immediate adjustments based on how well we know each other. Bill's strong points, first of all, is his knowledge of the game. And then his ability to relay it and teach it to his players, and to make them understand it. He can break it down to where it's understandable to his players, to where they could apply those strategies.

"You know, young players today have no knowledge of the history of the game. All they know is what's going on this year or the last year. I have told my younger players to do a Google search on Bill. I told them to go home and do it. So they would come back to me the next day and admit to me, 'Yeah Coach, he (Bradley) was a pretty good player.' And I said to them, 'Yeah, he was. Now when he (Bradley) talks to you, understand that he's saying these things to you after playing the game at the highest level, and going to the Pro Bowl several times. He played for the Philadelphia Eagles, and he was one of the best athletes to ever come out of the state of Texas.' So that's what I always stress to the younger players, and they appreciate that lesson. And when they find out about Bill and his playing career, they always say to me, 'Wow! Damn! He was pretty good!'"[17]

This pretty good Bill and Ted adventure would eventually get another future coaching sequel. But after he left San Diego, Bill Bradley kept his eyes open for other coaching possibilities elsewhere. His search would lead him to the Sunshine State. Bradley signed on as the defensive secondary coach for the Florida Tuskers, a team in the small United Football League (UFL). Bradley coached there in 2009 and 2010. From this point on in his coaching career, however, Bradley discovered that the opportunities were not as numerous as they were when he first started to coach. He was absent from coaching in 2011, but he managed to secure a job in Beaumont, Texas, with the Lamar Cardinals; a college team at the NCAA Division I Subdivision level. Bradley stayed there from 2012 to 2014.

After Bradley left Lamar University, he stopped coaching for five years. The well of opportunities had officially dried up. Moreover, many teams and colleges were more apt to hire younger men to fill the coaching ranks. That has been the trend for the past decade at least. Bradley had already passed his 70th birthday during that time, and he may have been told—in not so many words—that he was getting too old to be a football coach. Coaching, however, was never far from his mind, and it was in his blood. He still knew that he had more expertise to share with other teams. He eventually got another chance to be a coach in 2019, when he strolled the sidelines for the San Antonio Commanders of the Alliance of American Football. It was a league that played its games in the spring, and it was a league which would eventually send some of its players to NFL rosters. But it was also a league that did not have a lot of money to begin its operations. As a result, the league folded prematurely, and filed for Chapter 7 bankruptcy. But it was still football, and it was a welcomed opportunity for Bill Bradley to get back into the game.

"Mike Riley was the head coach of that team," said Bradley, "and he asked me to come on out and work in that new league, and I did that. The general manager was Daryl Johnston, the former Dallas Cowboys fullback who was nicknamed 'Moose.' Well, we ended up being first in our division, and we led the league in interceptions. Moose figured out that we had a pretty good secondary. We were second in the league in quarterback sacks, and a lot of those were coverage sacks (Author's Note: coverage sacks were sacks which occurred when the coverage by the defensive backs of the wide receivers was so good, that time would run out in the passing pocket for the quarterback to find an open target).

"Every day I would go into work and I would go by his (Johnston's) office and say as I walked past his door, 'The Cowboys still suck.' And finally after about the third time that I did that, and he knew that I was just joking with him, he would yell back at me from his office with comments like 'Yeah, you all wanted to be like us, didn't you?'

"Moose Johnston is the salt of the earth. He should be a general manager in the National Football League. We had a lot of talks, and he is just a classy, classy individual. He's just like (49ers general manager) John Lynch. I know John. I've kept up with him when he played defensive back for the Buccaneers, and he was a heck of a player (Author's Note: John Lynch was recently enshrined in the Pro Football Hall of Fame). And Moose is like John Lynch made over, except maybe better, if you could say that. Because I don't know if anyone could do a better job than he (Lynch) did. Those two guys change the atmosphere on their teams...they change the culture, as it is said and often overused in this day and age. To put it simply, they brought wins to the table."[18]

The coaching opportunity and the chance to enjoy more wins with the Alliance of American Football breathed more positive vibes into Bradley's mindset. A new chance to do something that you love often does that. But it appeared that, as 2019 ended, there would be no more coaching jobs for Bradley to send in his application. That appearance was incorrect, however. In the first week of February 2020, a new league, the second coming of the XFL, came on to the scene. With that new league came another new opportunity for Bill Bradley to do more coaching. The city was Houston, and the team was called the Roughnecks. But for Bradley to coach there, he had to display some of his trademark flexibility, as it were.

"Here's what happened in Houston," clarified Bradley. "My friend Ted Cottrell was the defensive coordinator. I called him and he said that he already had a defensive backs coach. I said that was fine. His defensive backs coach is a young man by the name of Darius Bell. He's a very good coach, and he should be coaching in the NFL. June Jones was the Roughnecks head coach, and he called me and asked me, 'Bill, what would you like to do?' I told him that 'I would like to help him (Bell) out. I won't overstep any of my boundaries.' June then asked me, 'Why don't you come on up here and just kind of be a quality control coach?' I was in favor of that idea, and June suggested that I fill that role until the season was over. It was a nice offer by him, and I agreed with it. I ended up coaching for the Roughnecks.

"And I think that I brought a good and positive attitude, mixed in with a lot of fun, for the guys on the team. It was real football, and I felt really good about it. The players on that team still text me, and that's a good payback for me. I knew what Darius Bell wanted, which was right on, because we think the same way. He had worked with June Jones in a couple of different places, and we blended well together."[19]

The new XFL blended the best learned lessons from previous leagues that eventually failed, and it was poised to succeed like none of those other leagues ever did. Unfortunately for the XFL, it too failed, but that was not due to any mistakes of its own. Rather, the looming specter of COVID-19 effectively defeated the new league. The games were all cancelled after the fifth week of play, and that was all she wrote. Even so, Bradley could point with pride to the fact that four of the defensive backs that he coached in Houston eventually made it to the promised land—they made it to NFL rosters.

"I think that the idea behind the XFL was a good idea," admitted Bradley, "because the players wanted to prolong their careers. And we were 5-0. We just kept winning, and we would have made the playoffs if the league didn't fold up because of COVID-19."[20]

If you think that in his mid-70s, Bill Bradley's coaching days are done...think again. He still receives telephone calls and fields a variety of coaching offers. In the spring of 2021, he even got an invitation (which he accepted) to coach a new spring football league in Houston at Rice University. One fact that he can point to when discussing his credentials is a matter of pride with him, and he is sure to mention it to whomever asks about his accomplishments.

"Almost everywhere that I've gone to coach," said a beaming Bradley, "we've had the leading interceptor, or we led that league in interceptions as a team, or we were in the top five listing in overall pass defense in the league statistics. That includes at Buffalo, and with the Jets, and with the Chargers."[21]

Having the lead in any statistical category in pro football will eventually catch somebody's attention. Awards and honors of some sort will undoubtedly be soon to follow. There is one exception to that belief, however, and it is probably the most unfair exclusion that can be found in the sport today. That statistic deals entirely with the time frame that one played pro football. Bill Bradley played in the NFL from 1969 to 1977. So too did hundreds of other men during that era, each of whom gave their blood, sweat, and tears to the game, many for a mere pittance of the money that today's players are making. Many years after their collective retirements, the league has sadly looked the other way when it comes to taking better care of these former athletes. Their retirement benefits only recently improved just a smidgen, but for many years, any monetary aid that these former players would obtain were seemingly distributed with the limits of an eyedropper.

Few are the number of men who played pro football before the early 1990s who will look favorably upon their individual pensions. Keep in mind that it does not have to be that way. The NFL is a money-making machine, and the amount of money that the league pockets is staggering to say the least. Many players today become instant millionaires upon signing their first contracts, and if they can play a few years, and with some common-sense financial decisions, they and probably most of their families will be set for the rest of their lives. The case is vastly different for the men who played the game in the 1960s, 1970s, and 1980s. They never earned a salary anywhere near the amounts of today's players. But those older players do have their supporters. Most of today's American workers and taxpayers (who are not professional athletes) believe that they as well do not make the kind of wages and salaries that they deserve in their individual jobs and occupations. And if questioned, a vast majority of those citizens usually side with the players' belief that at least a little more of the league's surplus money should be distributed to those pre-1990 players in their annual pension plans.

"As far as retirement...we have poor retirement funds," expounded Bradley. "The bottom line is that retired basketball and baseball players make over $200,000 a year, and we (retired pro football players) are still in the $50,000-range. Now I'm not griping about the money, but come on man, you can't tell me that football doesn't generate more money than basketball or baseball. And it still does today!"[22]

Besides money, pro football's popularity today also generates a heck of a lot of fan interest. With the 24-hour coverage from the NFL Network, to the numerous ESPN shows exploring the game, to the multitudes of sports talk radio shows nationwide which focus on the league, there simply is no lack of information and entertainment for pro football lovers across the world. But herein lies the questions which befuddle the men who have played the game in Bradley's era. What about what they accomplished? Where is their notoriety and attention? If you asked a current player about a former player like a Bill Bradley, a Norm Bulaich, or a Tim Rossovich, they would probably look at you with a blank stare, or possibly a quizzical expression. Fame indeed is fleeting in this sport, and in some ways, that is both unfair and unfortunate.

The unfairness is manifested in one annual occurrence: the voting for enshrines into the Pro Football Hall of Fame. It is a sour subject for Bill Bradley, and not so much because he is not in the Hall of Fame, but rather, because what he did out on the football fields from 1969 to 1977 are often only mentioned today as an afterthought.

"Every time that I see a story on (former Eagles defensive back) Brian Dawkins, the article will always say that he is the Eagles all-time leading interceptor with 34 interceptions in his career," said Bradley (Author's Note: Dawkins is a member of the Pro Football Hall of Fame, and he played for the Eagles from 1996-2008. He never led the NFL in interceptions in any of the years that he played. Bradley led the NFL in interceptions twice, in 1971 and 1972). Then the article will state that my 34 interceptions tied Brian Dawkins' number. Heck, I came before Brian Dawkins! He tied my record! It gets me stirred up.

"But I'm in several other Halls of Fame. For instance, I'm in the Texas High School Sports Hall of Fame, I'm in the University of Texas Sports Hall of Fame, and I'm in the Philadelphia Eagles Hall of Fame. But when it comes to the Pro Football Hall of Fame, you know that the only people that we have left to champion our cause for that honor are older writers like Ray Didinger, or Merrill Reese (the Eagles' longtime radio play-by-play reporter). They're the only people that we've got left to talk about us old-timers. I'm not bitching, mind you. I just think that we left a pretty good mark in our day."[23]

That good mark leads us directly to the unfortunate part, and it deals with posterity. Many young people today never got to see Bill Bradley play or heard the stories of his exploits. Those folks have lost out on getting a chance to learn about the game's past, and of the legendary players throughout the sport's history. It is a blight on the current situation in the NFL, but it is not the fault of players like Bill Bradley and his contemporaries. Those guys know that there is not much that they can do by themselves about being honored, or at the very least, being remembered. They just continue their lives, and their individual football journeys, as best as they can.

In June of 2021, Bill Bradley received the word that he would be inducted later in the year into the Philadelphia Sports Hall of Fame. It stands as an honor that will hopefully give more people and fans the opportunity to reacquaint themselves with the numerous achievements of this incredible athlete. And he's one heck of an incredible coach, too! It is hard to believe that a stopwatch, a clipboard, and admittedly a whole bunch of nerve, could land anyone a coaching job in pro and college football for over four decades. But then again, Bill Bradley isn't just anyone.

11

WHAT'S IN A NAME?

Bill Bradley's nickname of "Super Bill" has followed him around since he played in his final high school football game in 1965. All throughout that span of time to today, he has carried that moniker with moments of humility, moments of disdain, and even on the other side of the spectrum, a few moments of pride. It was sportswriters across the country who kept that label in the public eye, and even today, he is still referred to by many folks as "Super Bill" Bradley. It is something that irks him at times, and that is quite understandable. It is a "brand" of sorts, and it carries with it a wealth of stress, practically all of it undeserved.

"We were best friends, good God, for 67 years or something like that," said Bradley's childhood buddy Curtis Fitzgerald, in a 2020 interview. "He went through a phase after he graduated high school. They put all that damn hype on him with that 'Super Bill' stuff. And I felt sorry for him, because of all the damn pressure that nickname put on him. That just put a bullseye on him. And that bullseye stayed on him when he went down to (the University of) Texas, trying to live up to it."[1]

How does anyone live up to the expectations of others, whether they are fair anticipations or not? People will often exaggerate the worth of a person, whether they know them or even if they do not. How does anybody manage to satisfy the masses, who are filled with preconceived opinions of them? Bill Bradley has had to deal with that type of pressure for most of his adult life. In retrospect, and by all accounts, he did a pretty darn good job of addressing those burdens which were deposited—either fairly or unfairly—upon his shoulders.

"What's worth saying is that he was everything that they said he was," confirmed Fitzgerald. "He was one hell of an athlete, and a hell of a competitor. I don't care if you're pitching pennies or playing football. He always played to win. And what's just as important, he handled the fame that he got really well. He never let it go to his head. And he stayed the same later in life. Shit, we're just two old farts, reliving our glory days."[2]

This concluding chapter of Bill Bradley's story will not necessarily focus on his "glory days." But those days will come up from time to time in the following pages. Bradley's friends and family have participated in many of those "glorious" moments with him. They have seen him at his best and at his worst. They have watched him grieve with the death of several of his family members, including his sister Rosemay and his son Matthew. They have also watched him work hard to help his brother Ralph, who requires special needs attention on a daily basis. But they have also watched Bill Bradley give everyone many moments of joy and laughter. They have partaken in his friendship and have enjoyed being the recipients of a big lesson that Bill has known ever since his youth: the lesson that success of any kind is worthless if you cannot share it with your friends. So, the memories of being a friend or family member of Bill Bradley automatically comes with the numerous extraordinary stories that make up the measure of the man...and the extent of his relationships to many people in all walks of life. This chapter will explore several more of those interesting stories and (hopefully) give the reader a more rounded look into Bradley's personality...a personality chock-filled with charisma and character.

The foundation of Bill Bradley's image, besides being a free spirit, was a disposition that practically always displayed a happy-go-lucky nature. He knows that the world and society have serious moments and critical situations. But he also always was determined to keep smiling, to keep laughing, and as much as possible...to keep happy. It was a conscious frame of mind of his that has impressed so many of his friends and family over the years.

"Bill has always been happy-go-lucky," explained another of his long-time friends, Bob Stephenson. "You're not going to take that out of him. That's just Bill. I haven't called him recently, but in the past month, if you listen to his telephone answering machine, you can hear him singing to you before he tells you to leave a message at the beep (chuckling). That tells you a little bit about him (Author's Note: Stephenson is correct, and if you happen to call Bradley once every month, you might hear him offer his renditions of *Shake Your Booty* by K.C. and the Sunshine Band, to *The Dock of the Bay* by Otis Redding, to many more classic songs)."[3]

Bradley is proud of his singing ability. The locals all know him, and he still gets a chance every now and then to get up on a makeshift stage in front of his garage/man cave, and around Palestine and other locales along the Texas Hill Country, to belt out a song or two. It stands to reason that his talents seem to know no bounds. But besides singing, most of his capacities for performing centered on athletics, and as we have previously seen, they began developing at an exceedingly early age. And also, as we have already discovered, he excelled at practically every sport in which he participated. Some of the college sports at the University of Texas did not even have him on their rosters, yet he still made his mark on them.

"I had the chance to meet and talk to Leon Black, who was the head basketball coach at Texas," said Stephenson. "And I said to him, 'Coach Black, I want to ask you a question. I have heard this story all of my life, and I want to know if it is true.' And he said, 'What's that?' And I said, 'I had heard that you once told a reporter, when you were asked who the best basketball player in the state of Texas was, your comment was that the best basketball player in the state of Texas doesn't play basketball...he plays football. Is that true?' And he laughed and he said, 'It certainly is!' When Coach Black had coached the Jacksonville (Texas) Baptist College before he started coaching at (the University of) Texas, in fact when I had first met him, he said, 'I saw Bill Bradley play basketball in high school.' He had followed Bill even while Bill was still in high school!"[4]

The desire to play any sport, indeed several sports, was not an exclusive aspiration for just Bradley, however. Most of his childhood friends played more than one sport as well. But it was in football where people started to really take notice of what Bradley could do with his speed and his smarts. And those observations were happening even before he became a freshman in high school.

"Bill and I were in grade school together," recalled longtime friend Mickey 'Mule' Hubert. "He was in the sixth grade, and I was in the fifth grade. Every day at recess, we'd play football. Most of us at that time, in the fifth and sixth grade...well, we couldn't walk and chew gum at the same time. But Bill was already by that time being recognized for the talent that he had. He just had a finesse that none of the rest of us really had. Anyway, as we progressed on through high school, we were kinda playing at the high school level, and Bill was at the college level."[5]

Bradley's teammates in high school never fail to recall not just his exploits, but also how he was motivated to be a great athlete. Winning had a lot to do with that, obviously. Hanging around with someone the likes of a Bobby Layne during that epic Big-33 Game in 1965 would also get the young Bradley to start planning for victories, and eventually, demanding victories, just as Layne always did. Not surprisingly, if you really want to find out something that motivates an athlete to win, observe them after they lose a game. Such an occurrence is often an eye-opener for those players who are not used to losing.

"You know as far as playing the sports, we had a lot of motivation," expressed Hubert. "In Bill's senior year in 1964, I was a junior on the football team. We were picked by the Associated Press to be number one and win the state championship in football. And boy, we were all flying high and working hard. Then we played our first game, which was in Athens, Texas, and they beat the devil out of us. We were all down, but we worked hard, and we rebounded, and we won the rest of our games. And then we came back to play Athens again in the local championship, and we beat them. And then we went on to win the state championship."[6]

Palestine's motivation to win a state title mirrored Bradley's, as everybody in town yearned for success. The desire to win a championship came from their fans, the local businesses, the local newspaper, the chamber of commerce...practically everyone. It was a prideful thing, this business of winning. Moreover, supporting high school football teams has been a birthright in Texas for as long as anybody can remember. The team and the town were just wrapped up in the excitement.

"You know one of the most memorable events that I can think of probably speaks for everybody that was on that team," remembered Hubert. "Every game that we played at home or away, all the folks in Palestine filled the stands up. And they prepared a line all the way from the dressing room to the sideline. When we came out, we had to walk through all of those fans. Boy I tell you, when you're 16 or 17 years old, that'll really motivate you. And so we were motivated like nobody else. We never really did see that with all of the other teams that we ever played. It was just so far out."[7]

A state championship is indeed an honor for everyone involved. It is a moment in time that somehow never really fades away. It is almost as if it was a snapshot of the final score on a scoreboard, with Palestine High School the victors. And you better believe that every player on that team has fond memories of the event.

"You know as we've grown older, we still get together from time to time, and rehash all of the games and all of the old days," admitted Hubert. "Coach (Luke) Thornton was our coach, and he told us, 'You know, if we win this state championship, it'll be something that you'll never forget for the rest of your life.' And none of us have. You know with Bill and all the others, sometime every two or three years, we'll get together and rehash the old times. And we'll drink some whiskey and have a great time (chuckles). It's the old team, you know."[8]

That old team had to deal with challenges of scheduling back when they were in school. Almost annually, there would be a timing dilemma with the programming of one sport versus another. The football players who wanted to play basketball as well were forced to wait until their games and practices on the gridiron were complete.

"After we won the state football championship," explained Hubert, "we came back on the bus, and I think it was the next day, we had a basketball game that we had to play, because the basketball season had already started. Well, we went to play basketball, and Bill and I were on the team. We ended up beating the other guys on the basketball team, even though we had been playing football all year."[9]

Bradley's prowess at basketball was not unique. What was extraordinary was his ability to excel at several other sports, even though he rarely played them. Sometimes, Bradley accepted encounters that were hard to believe. And on occasion, he even had the nerve to test others.

"I remember him challenging the school tennis coach at Palestine to a game of tennis," recalled Hubert. "And Bill beat him! And get this...Bill was wearing cowboy boots during that match!"[10]

As implausible as his tennis victory over the school tennis coach seemed to be, the origins of Bradley's confidence nevertheless stemmed from his early years, then just seemed to grow over time. He was a student in elementary school when his love for baseball took root. It was an inexpensive sport in which to participate. All you needed at its barest minimum was one bat, a ball, and a glove. That was it. Also remember that this was an era where most kids did not have access to vehicles to get to places, and those adults who did own a car or a truck needed it to get to work, not to drop off their kids at the local ballfield.

"I can remember, even as little bitty kids, how it was in those years," said Bob Stephenson. "Bill didn't really live close to me, but back then, it wasn't anything to walk a couple of miles to play baseball all day. There was a lot right beside his house, and you know, as seven or eight-year-olds, we'd play baseball all day."[11]

As Bradley got a little older, he started to wonder about things like transportation to and from the games. As a teenager, he was also of the age where he started to see the worth in driving a vehicle to get to places. *Any* vehicle.

"We had a lot of great times through the years," admitted long-time Bradley friend Jackie Cherry in a 2020 interview. "I'm sure that the statute of limitations has run out on this, but a bunch of us were uptown one night, and it was during baseball season. The baseball field was a few miles from the high school, and the coach would carry us out to the field in a little old short bus. And when we would come back into the school parking lot after practice, he would put the key (to the bus) in the ashtray. And so Bradley, being the observant type, noticed that. Well one night, we were all in town messing around, and Bill comes into the parking lot where the bus is parked every night, across from the high school. Well we got into the bus, and Bill cranks it up, and he drives around and picks up another two or three guys, and we went to the local drive-in, which was called Buddy's. And he pulls in, and of course we all order a root beer, and we're sitting on that bus. All of a sudden, somebody sees our head coach, Luke Thornton, and his wife, coming from downtown. Those two turn in front of Buddy's, and we see him (Coach Thornton) looking to see what that bus was doing at Buddy's. And of course, he can't turn around for about a half a mile, so Bradley cranks that bus up and we back up with food trays falling off of it, and we fly about a quarter of a mile up the street to the high school, park it, jump out, and everybody scatters (laughter). Nothing was ever said or done about it, because we figured that Coach Thornton knew that Bill was involved (more laughter). We had to play fast on that one."[12]

The young Bill Bradley was undoubtedly not thinking about the possible adverse ramifications of making off with a school bus, such as being in an accident, or being pulled over by the cops. He and his buddies were probably most surprised that they had gotten away with such an escapade. Now to be fair, he surely was not the first youth who attempted a stunt like this, and he indeed would not be the last. He just saw it as another avenue with which to have some fun. The difference between Bill and many other young boys of that era, was that if he was going to do something like driving off in a school bus before he ever owned a driver's license, he was going to make such an action memorable.

Many of the memories from his elementary and high school years were rather plain and mundane, however. He would experience common things, as would every other kid who grew up in Palestine. But the town was not completely backwoods or limited by its lack of businesses. Quite the opposite in fact. There were at least a few high-end business establishments and restaurants in the town, and even though it was a small town that grew slowly in population and businesses, it was still growing, nonetheless. The locals had a fair choice of places where they could sit down and eat a good meal. Bradley's parents, however, felt that saving money was their best option for themselves and for their kids, so they went the commonsense route. They rarely splurged on frivolous things and extravagant meals.

"I ate every day at the school cafeteria," admitted Bradley. "But a lot of kids did. Yeah, Palestine had good country club places, and they were better than going to a restaurant or a hamburger joint. You know we had curb service hamburger places. And so my folks...they never had to give me money all the way up to college. When I got my scholarship to attend the University of Texas, that really relieved my mother."[13]

By the time that Bradley began attending college, his personality was pretty much set in stone. Yes, he was a flexible lad, free-spirited for all it's worth. But he also realized that he was not going to change how he felt about people or things. He knew right from wrong, and he knew that he was his own man. As he stated time and again to anyone who would listen, Bill Bradley believed that he had to be his own man. He also realized that some people—after encountering him—were not thinking of him in the most favorable of terms. Sometimes, a rebellion on the football field would serve as his reply.

"Well, a lot of people at the time kinda frowned on the way you were," recalled Bradley. "I guess that was their way of showing you that you were a little bit out of line as far as the norm was concerned. But I never paid much attention to it. I was just me. I believed in what I believed in, and I stuck by it...and that kind of stuff. I never did it (being rambunctious or rowdy on a football field) for an act, or to be like everybody else. I guess it's just a sensitive side, or a creative side. Sometimes it was different than the norm. Of course a lot of people you know...it wasn't hateful. It never was anything hateful or really out of hand. It was just a different way of thinking about life I guess."[14]

In 1977, a noted graphologist by the name of Michael Zimmer decided to analyze 11 different NFL players' handwriting samples to try to determine if there were any contextual clues to describe that player's personality. One of his subjects just happened to be none other than Bill Bradley. After viewing Bradley's handwriting sample, Zimmer noted that it revealed several important indications about the All-Pro defensive back.

"His writing shows a drive and ambition that is very strong," Zimmer determined. "Bradley is a conscientious man who is always willing to learn and take advice. He plays football with great intensity and is very self-demanding. Bradley does not kid himself or make excuses. The tension seen in his small writing is reflected in a streak of restless behavior and some animosity. If he feels some opposing player is taking 'cheap shots,' Bradley will react strongly."[15]

So far, pretty accurate. But it gets better. Zimmer looked intensely at Bradley's autograph, and focused on his last name of

"Bradley." He noticed several more insightful aspects to the free safe-ty's personality that described him even more accurately.

"There is a break in the letters in 'Bradley,'" noted Zimmer. "The 'a' is not connected on either side. Broken writing is often a sign of musical or artistic talent. It is always a sign of ESP. Bradley is a very intuitive man. He often senses the moves of opposing players and reacts in kind. This talent is an invaluable aid for him and gives Bradley's play an added dimension. Graphically, this formation also reveals a capacity for concrete or visual thinking.

"Notice that the end of 'Bradley' tends to squiggle out like a piece of string. This graphic is called a thread and is frequently found in the scripts of actors and politicians. It enhances our earlier findings of Bill's intuition and shows he is a versatile man with many talents. He can master almost any position. Like all thread writers, he is a born survivor and handles crises very well."[16]

Pretty uncanny, huh? How, just by looking at Bradley's signature, you can possibly tell a lot about the man. Most of Bradley's longtime pals do not really care much about that, though. They just chuckle at esoteric things like that. To them, Bill Bradley is their buddy, and they accept him just as he is. They knew many years before he became a pro football player that he possessed a ton of creative abili-ties and talents, and they were more than happy to grow up with him and experience the "real" Bill Bradley. Today, just knowing him is a token of their pride in him, and in all that he accomplished throughout his life.

"He was a lot of fun," regarded Jackie Cherry in describing his grade school friend from Palestine. "He was such a talented athlete. You could just see it when he touched a football, or a basketball, or a baseball. He just had a knack. I went to elementary school with Bill, all the way through to high school. I was a year younger than he. And I had to wait until he graduated to be able to start at quarterback, so I had to play at other positions until he graduated. I was sad to see him graduate, because he was such a gifted athlete, and such a down to earth good guy."[17]

The "good guy" nature that Bradley displayed stemmed mostly from his foundation of modesty. He knew where he came from, and he knew that he was not born with a silver spoon. As a result, there was no need or desire to put on airs or act any better than what he already believed himself to be. He just would not allow himself to exhibit any showing of braggadocio. Furthermore, he had a group of close friends and teammates who kept him humble, even when it came to observing a simple consumer product in a store. Indeed, one with a familiar likeness on it.

"I got to know all of those old college football announcers," said Bradley. "As a matter of fact, they came out with an album about 100 years of college football. It was one of those albums that had replays of radio and television calls from some of those announcers. It also had several college marching bands playing their tunes on it. Well, I was looking one day, and I saw that album in a record shop. It was a big old LP album, and lo and behold, it had my picture on the cover! It didn't announce anything, but it was my picture, and I thought that was pretty cool. I couldn't get full of myself, however, because all of my buddies wouldn't allow it. Nobody is off limits in a football dressing room."[18]

The humility that Bradley experienced was, as he alluded to, common during his time as an active athlete. Bradley's growing up years were typical of most kids who grew up in the 1950s and the 1960s, especially if they enjoyed playing various sports. Wake up in the morning, eat some breakfast, do some chores, then go out and play ball. It followed a daily cycle, predictable in all its elements. Whatever excitement came about was what you made of your play on the ballfields. It was a time when the basics and fundamentals of life and of sports took their hold on youngsters. And it was a time which many American kids today have somehow replaced with cellphones, their Facebook and Twitter brands, and a sedentary lifestyle. Longtime Bradley friend Curtis Fitzgerald recently discussed the facts about years gone by, about growing up and attending school in Palestine, and about how time has changed things.

"We were all great students," remembered Fitzgerald. "I never made a 'C' in my life until about the 8th grade. That's when I discovered girls, and Bill did too...about the 8th or 9th grade. That's when my grades kinda went sideways. We actually had a remarkable bunch of teachers. The time they spent with us proved that they really cared about us. And the other people living in this small town (Palestine) especially cared for us. If you did something wrong, whoever was around...they generally snatched your butt up by your ears, and they're liable to give you a whipping. And by the time that you got home that day, you probably got three or four more whippings.

"Getting back to the teachers. They didn't let us kids graduate until we learned the basic reading, writing, and arithmetic. I've got some friends today who are retired teachers, but they're still teaching. I guess that they are filling in as substitute teachers. It's unbelievable what they tell me about today's students. I mean it's unbelievable how many kids are graduating, up to 75 percent, who can't do basic math, or who can't read or write. And it's like...why are we spending money educating them if they aren't learning anything? And of course, they've taken all of the discipline out of the schools. It's a bad situation in today's schools. It was a different world back then when we were kids."[19]

People of Bill Bradley's generation certainly could not see into the future to view a glimpse of how American society would change in several decades. Those kids back in the 1950s and 1960s were primarily focused on just making the most of their opportunities, both in and out of the classrooms. Part of Bradley's past and current successes were pragmatic in nature. He simply possessed a great ability to roll with the punches...to adapt to the changing times, trends, and situations. And then to land on his feet after being shaken about. It takes talent, but it also takes desire. Bill Bradley has both of those traits in abundance.

"I can tell you a story that sticks out quite a bit," said Marion Turner, who helped to coach the Palestine High School football team while Bradley attended the school. "I've always remembered this story. We were playing in the semi-finals in football, and it was the year that we went on to win the state championship. Anyway, things did not go too well in the first half of that game. In fact, we were behind on the scoreboard. As the team leaves the locker room before the second half, I'm standing in front of the head coach, and Bill was one of the last players walking out to the field. And he comes by, and he reaches over to the head coach and says, 'Coach, just remember… there's two halves.' And we won that game on the last play of the game. Bill threw a touchdown pass on that last play of the game.

"Some people would think that Bill was cocky, but that's not the case. He was just very confident. He's probably the fiercest competitor that I ever helped to coach. And I was fortunate enough to be able to coach him for two years."[20]

If one were to describe Bradley's confidence, you would also have to discuss his overall personality, and when doing that, you would probably never use the term one-dimensional. That is because there are so many visible sides to him that you would have to chat with him for several days—maybe even several weeks—to get to see all segments of his character and temperament. He is a survivor, which is readily evident, not so much from being able to walk after so many football collisions, but from several chapters of grief and sadness that he endured during his life. And then with each portion of Bill Bradley that you would observe, you would probably agree that it was more enlightening and more important than the previous one that you saw. His down to earth personage is probably the one that you would appreciate the most when spending some time with him. His sense of humor? That would probably be a close second place on the list.

"Yes, Bill is funny off and on," admits Susan Bradley, his wife of 22 years. "He just loves to tell stories. He can go on forever with those. For example, he'll ask me, 'Hey, do you have a minute?' And I'll say, 'Ah, well…do you mean an hour (laughing)?' I did not know that Bill was a former pro football player before I started dating him. I didn't really know much about him, actually. He said that he once coached with a friend of mine, and that guy ended up setting us up on a date.

"But with Bill, what you see is what you get. He treats everyone equally. I don't care who you are. Everyone is treated the same by him. He's a really genuine person."[21]

Bill has just as many compliments for his wife as she has for him. But that is not surprising. It takes a lot of hard work to stay married to one person for more than a couple of decades. For both of their parts, both Bill and Susan are willing to devote that hard work to each other. Moreover, the two are willing to accept each other's specific situations and stories in order to make their relationship a success.

"My wife is a football widow, and she's a wonderful lady," admitted Bill. "She doesn't know all of my football history, you know. But she has accepted it very well. I don't know what I would do without her. And I came into a kid's picture at ages two and four. See, I'm a stepdad, but they're like my real children. And I've made their real dad stay in contact with them. That's his birth children. He's married, and he used to come down here and watch Matt while Susan and I would go out and go places."[22]

Some of those places are nearby to his home...*very* close to his home in fact. And recall what his wife said about treating everyone the same? Well, Bradley certainly does that, as a clerk at the local convenience story will receive the same congenial smile and hand-shake and small talk from him as a well-known Hollywood star. And Bradley also has made and continues to make it a point to often help his neighbors. The requests that he fielded from his distant past to the current day to day can run the gamut from bailing hay for those who need his help on their farmsteads, to helping certain folks get ready to participate in an upcoming rodeo. Yes, rodeo.

"I was over at my next-door neighbor's down there driving a Kawasaki with a fake cow attached to it," explained Bradley. "Well the fake cow simulates a real cow coming out of the chute for roping practice. My neighbor is trying to rope a fake cow on wheels. You know how cowboys rope a cow coming out of the chute in a rodeo?

My neighbor has a little ranch here, and my job is to get up at daylight two or three days a week and drive the Kawasaki that's pulling the fake cow. And then my neighbor ropes it. And he just won like $1,000 last week roping cows."[23]

Despite giving a fake cow a Kawasaki ride, it is the sport of football which still owns the top spot as Bradley's activity of choice. It seems that his football experiences are never that far away from his mind and his heart. He enjoys reminiscing about his time as a player and as a coach, but he also as of late thinks about how he loves the game, and how much the sport has changed over the years. His personal take on the game is a reflective look at how he feels—and has previously felt—about the nature of football, its comparisons to the military, and to the financial aspects of the game.

"I miss playing football," Bradley admitted. "But I also miss the people. I miss the friends that I made out there...the lifelong friends that I made playing and coaching the game. That includes three different arenas...in high school, in college, and in the pros. We football players are just basically actors in a theater in the round. These people just build these pro athletes up as big-time heroes, and rightly so, but that's a different type of hero than say a soldier who fights in a war for the United States.

"In that and other respects, the game has gotten out of hand. Pro football...heck, even college football, generates a lot of money. If you play pro football, you have to be on a pro roster three years in order for you to become vested financially. It's more of a business now than it ever was before."[24]

The business world has indeed taken a strong hold on the world of sports. As time has gone by, Bill Bradley has come to grips with that fact firsthand. But both he and his friends have seen the United States mirror those changes. As previously mentioned, they have watched the country evolve into a different nation than it was when they were youngsters. The changes are evident for anyone who cares to take an honest look at the past, and then compares those previous eras to the present day. Now in the twilight in their years, Bradley and his friends often take the time to discuss the past, and to talk about how things have changed in their lifetimes. It can be a depressing picture that can also be both alarming and worrisome at times. But it is also a situation where there is not a whole lot that men Bill Bradley's age can do anything about. Those older folks nevertheless still try to look for a silver lining amidst the transformations, and amidst all the new computers and electronics and consumer gadgets on the market today (many of which few folks in their 70s in the small towns in the Texas Hill Country really have a huge interest in), and amidst all the changes in government and laws from those of decades ago.

The town of Palestine has also changed—at least a little bit—since the days of Bradley's youth. But in many ways, it is still the same. That is probably true of many small towns in rural America. The senior citizens get together and chat about their formative years, all the while knowing that the past is gone forever. Yet even so, a guy like Bill Bradley and his buddies are more than happy to discuss the happenings of the current day. Bradley often goes out of his way to sign autographs for his fans, and especially for youngsters today. Whenever he attends banquets or functions of the Eagles Hall of Fame, or the Texas Longhorns Hall of Fame, the lines of people awaiting his autograph are typically longer than the lines of other former players. Why is that? Because Bill Bradley appreciates the fans just as much as they appreciate him. It is a symbiotic relationship. It is all just a part of relating to each other. Moreover, the affability of his fans and of his friends can sometimes involve some incredibly unique stories.

"Bill stopped over my house last night, and we stayed up all night," expressed his longtime buddy, Curtis Fitzgerald. "We did so good the night before that I guess we decided that we owed it to ourselves, because I hadn't had a drink in four months. And so, the night before last he came over, and we had one drink, and we left at 9 p.m., and that's a record...seriously (chuckle). And then yesterday, he was leaving to go home. Well, he left five times, but he never did leave my front yard, and finally he said that he's gonna stay over (more laughter).

"So we went downtown and sat on a curb, and we saw several people that we hadn't seen in 20 years, and some of the others we got to be friends with. And then we would try to come home, because we ran out of things to drink. But then we had a blowout of the right front tire of Bill's truck. Bill was driving, and he lost control when he tried to stop. Well, he swerved off the road, but we pulled right up to the front door of a store. We were out there trying to change the damn blowout, and of course, everybody out there was helping us. We went in the store and bought six bottles of wine, and we got drunk again. We stayed up all night (more laughter). You know the doctors tell us to eat some fruit every day. And we consider wine to be our daily fruit. It's the fruit of the vine. It's like pain medication (persistent laughter). We ended up staying up all night. We got two hours of sleep. I was getting eight hours of sleep a night, but every time that Bill comes over, we start talking about our lives over the past 60 years, and this is the end result...being hung over in the morning. This is just what we've always done."[25]

It is important to know a couple of facts about this story. One, this is not really a unique incident. Not by a longshot. Bill Bradley has often experienced such friendly unplanned get-togethers throughout his life. He is a free spirit, after all. Yes, sometimes he and his pals enjoy having a drink or two. But they have earned the right to do so. They have lived into their 70s, and they have lived good lives, filled with hard work in their chosen fields. Two, this is Palestine, Texas. This is a town where most people are generally friendly and helpful to each other. It is how people get along. It is how strangers get to become friends. And it is how life gets lived to a special extent, where no one has a feeling of superiority. They do, however, have a feeling of equality...even when looking back in time over a bunch of years. It was not always an idyllic time back then, but the kids in Palestine in the 1950s and 1960s at least experienced lessons that they would take to heart. Lessons that would enable them to realize that life was often a struggle, but one that they would still nevertheless make the most out of.

"We talked about the differences of time last night," said Fitzgerald. "Listening to the folks downtown yesterday, we were talking about how lucky we were to have grown up in the time and the age that we did. Even so, our fathers did not have a great home life. My real dad didn't give us a great home life, and then my mom got remarried, and my stepdad was an alcoholic, so he and I didn't get along very well. And Bill didn't have the greatest home life either, but his dad was a great guy, and he really worked with Bill. He would make Bill come home from school every afternoon at 4 o'clock, and he made Bill work out and play baseball. No matter what he was doing, when it came to 4 o'clock, Bill had to break and run home to go to practice, or his dad would whip his ass."[26]

It did not take long for Bill and Curtis and all the other kids who grew up in Palestine during those years to realize that nobody—outside of possibly your parents—was actually looking out for you. There were simply no guarantees to be found in their lives, and perhaps that is the way that it should be. A person gains appreciation for what he acquires through his or her own hard work. It was that way many years ago, and to an extent, it is still that way today.

"We (Bill and Curtis) talk about how you had to make your own breaks back then," said Fitzgerald. "Nobody was going to give you anything back then. You had to earn whatever you got. When I was in the Army, from 1966 to 1972, I earned whatever I got. And everybody remembers where they were when they first got shot at. I know that I do. Now Bill did not get selected for the Army. He said it was because of one of his sports injuries. But I think that they didn't take him because of his mental incompetence (Author's Note: at this exact time, while Mr. Fitzgerald was chuckling, Bill Bradley stuck his head into the room where I was interviewing Curtis Fitzgerald, and exclaimed, 'I can hear you!')."[27]

Old friends often rely on humor to get by, and that humor provides the spice of life that everyone needs these days. Bradley,

Fitzgerald, and the rest of the Palestine fellows have that sense of humor, knowing that nobody takes things too seriously. Sometimes, these moments of banter are the moments that they all look forward to the most. Perhaps in its most foundational form, telling jokes to each other...often about each other...are part and parcel of the things that keep these guys close to each other, after all these years. Bill is a humble man, and he is cloaked in modesty. He can take a joke as well as anyone. But he can dish them out too, as this book has shown on numerous occasions. Bradley continues to recite the same words that the great Hall of Fame quarterback Bobby Layne once told him, "Don't ever let embellishment get in the way of a good story."[28]

This ending of Bill Bradley's story in written words is not *really* at an end, mind you. In fact, these last words are more representative of a new beginning. As was written in this book's preface and throughout the previous chapters, Bradley has had a lot of fun playing and coaching football...and living life. A *lot* of fun. That much is true, and it is also probably true that when Bill Bradley eventually travels on that one-way trip to Heaven, he will **continue** having plenty of fun. And furthermore, he will not be lugging around his "Super Bill" nickname any longer. I am betting that he will gladly trade that moniker in for the heavenly enjoyment and bliss that will be his for eternity.

In all actuality, Bill Bradley's fun and celebrations in Heaven will probably be off the charts. I mean, can you imagine the parties that he will have every day and every night in Heaven? Once he gets there on his very first day, I suppose that he will undoubtedly greet all his friends and relatives who preceded him to this new, ultimate, and forever paradise, with the obligatory hugs and kisses, and all gathered around the Cottonmouth Blues Wagon, which somehow showed up again for this moment. Hey, if dead people can come back to life to vote, then favorite old rusted-out Volkswagen buses can come back in this story to make an appearance too! Then the parties will start. And they will go on and on and on. Finally, late in the evening of Bill Bradley's first night in Heaven, some of his buddies might have the nerve to say to him, "We're tired Bill...we're going to bed. We'll continue this party sometime tomorrow." It is very likely to assume that Bill Bradley will stay true to his free-spirited nature in offering his response. "No, no, no!" he will probably exclaim. "This party is just getting started!"

NOTES

Chapter One

1. Interview with Bill Bradley on July 18, 2019.
2. *Ibid.*
3. Interview with Bill Bradley on July 3, 2019.
4. Interview with Bill Bradley on July 18, 2019.
5. Interview with Bill Bradley on July 3, 2019.
6. Interview with Bill Bradley on October 9, 2019.
7. *Ibid.*
8. Interview with Bill Bradley on July 18, 2019.
9. *Ibid.*
10. Interview with Bill Bradley on October 9, 2019.
11. *Ibid.*
12. Interview with Bill Bradley on July 18, 2019.
13. Interview with Bill Bradley on October 9, 2019.
14. Interview with Bill Bradley on August 21, 2019.
15. Interview with Bill Bradley on July 3, 2019.
16. *Ibid.*

17. *Ibid.*
18. *Ibid.*
19. *Ibid.*
20. *Ibid.*
21. Interview with Bill Bradley on March 19, 2020.
22. *Ibid.*
23. *Ibid.*
24. *Ibid.*
25. *Ibid.*
26. *Ibid.*
27. Interview with Bill Bradley on April 18, 2020.
28. Interview with Bill Bradley on July 3, 2019.
29. *Ibid.*
30. *Ibid.*
31. Interview with Bill Bradley on April 18, 2020.
32. Interview with Bob Stephenson on April 1, 2020.

Chapter Two

1. Interview with Bill Bradley on April 18, 2020.
2. Interview with Bill Bradley on August 21, 2019.
3. *Ibid.*
4. Interview with Bill Bradley on July 18, 2019.
5. Interview with Bill Bradley on April 18, 2020.
6. *Ibid.*
7. Interview with Bob Stephenson on April 1, 2020.
8. Interview with Bill Bradley on April 18, 2020.
9. Interview with Bill Bradley on July 18, 2019.
10. Interview with Bill Bradley on April 18, 2020.
11. Interview with Bill Bradley on October 9, 2019.
12. Flynn, John. "Intercepting Bill Bradley." *Football Digest*, June, 1973, 89.
13. Interview with Bill Bradley on October 9, 2019.

14. *Ibid.*
15. *Ibid.*
16. Interview with Bill Bradley on August 21, 2019.
17. *Ibid.*
18. Interview with Bill Bradley on July 18, 2019.
19. Interview with Bill Bradley on October 9, 2019.
20. Interview with Bill Bradley on April 18, 2020.
21. Interview with Bill Bradley on July 18, 2019.
22. Interview with Bill Bradley on April 18, 2020.
23. *Ibid.*
24. *Ibid.*
25. Interview with Bill Bradley on October 9, 2019.
26. *Ibid.*
27. Interview with Bill Bradley on April 18, 2020.
28. Interview with Bill Bradley on July 18, 2019.
29. *Ibid.*
30. Interview with Bill Bradley on March 19, 2020.
31. Flynn, John. "Intercepting Bill Bradley." *Football Digest*, June 1973, 89.
32. Interview with Bill Bradley on March 19, 2020.
33. *Ibid.*
34. *Ibid.*

Chapter Three

1. Interview with Bill Bradley on April 18, 2020.
2. *Ibid.*
3. *Ibid.*
4. Interview with Bill Bradley on October 9, 2019.
5. Interview with Bill Bradley on July 18, 2019.
6. Interview with Bill Bradley on April 18, 2020.
7. Interview with Bill Bradley on March 19, 2020.
8. Interview with Bill Bradley on April 18, 2020.

9. Interview with Bill Bradley on March 19, 2020.

10. Interview with Bill Bradley on April 18, 2020.

11. orbes, Gordon. "Bradley's Moon-Shot Punts Thrill at Eagles' Camp." *The Philadelphia Inquirer*, August 6, 1969.

12. Padice, Sandy. "Money, Football And Bill Bradley." *Philadelphia Inquirer*, August 20, 1969.

13. Interview with Bill Bradley on July 18, 2019.

14. Interview with Bill Bradley on May 18, 2020.

15. *Ibid.*

16. Brown, Hugh. "'Super Bill' Enhances Eagle Scene." *Pro Football Weekly*, December 4, 1969.

17. Lundgren, Hal. "Super Bill Revisited." *Houston Chronicle*, September 7, 1970.

18. Interview with Bill Bradley on August 21, 2019.

19. Interview with Bill Bradley on October 9, 2019.

20. *Ibid.*

21. Interview with Bill Bradley on May 18, 2020.

22. Interview with Bill Bradley on March 19, 2020.

23. *Ibid.*

24. *Ibid.*

Chapter Four

1. Interview with Bill Bradley on August 20, 2020.

2. Interview with Bill Bradley on May 18, 2020.

3. Didinger, Ray. "Pride Hurt Worse Than Knee." *The Evening Bulletin*, August 20, 1970.

4. Interview with Bill Bradley on May 18, 2020.

5. Didinger, Ray. "Pride Hurt Worse Than Knee." *The Evening Bulletin*, August 20, 1970.

6. Interview with Bill Bradley on May 18, 2020.

7. Didinger, Ray. "Pride Hurt Worse Than Knee." *The Evening Bulletin*, August 20, 1970.
8. *Ibid.*
9. Interview with Bill Bradley on May 18, 2020.
10. *Ibid.*
11. Interview with Bill Bradley on August 20, 2020.
12. *Ibid.*
13. *Ibid.*
14. Interview with Bill Bradley on May 18, 2020.
15. *Ibid.*
16. *Ibid.*
17. *Ibid.*
18. *Ibid.*
19. *Ibid.*
20. *Ibid.*
21. Interview with November 12, 2020.
22. *Ibid.*
23. *Ibid.*

Chapter Five

1. Interview with Bill Bradley on August 20, 2020.
2. Interview with Bill Bradley on March 19, 2020.
3. Didinger, Ray. "Bill Bradley Will Miss Ditka Today." *The Evening Bulletin*, October 28, 1973.
4. Interview with Bill Bradley on August 20, 2020.
5. Interview with Ed Khayat on November 27, 2019.
6. Interview with Bill Bradley on August 20, 2020.
7. *Ibid.*
8. Interview with Bill Bradley on May 18, 2020.
9. Interview with Bill Bradley on August 20, 2020.
10. *Ibid.*
11. *Ibid.*

12. Plarski, Don. "Cardinals flop again, 37-20." *Alton Evening Telegraph*, November 22, 1971.

13. Didinger, Ray. "League Leading Interceptor and Pressure Breaker." *The Evening Bulletin*, December 8, 1971, S1.

14. Interview with Bill Bradley on August 20, 2020.

15. Interview with Mickey "Mule" Hubert on April 27, 2020.

16. Interview with Marion Turner on April 20, 2020.

17. Interview with Bill Bradley on August 20, 2020.

18. Didinger, Ray. "Super Bill Lies Down on Job but Gets 11th Steal." *The Evening Bulletin*, December 13, 1971.

19. Shefski, Bill. "Super Bill Goes on Record With 10th Air Theft." *Philadelphia Daily News*, December 6, 1971.

20. Didinger, Ray. "The Saga Of Super Bill: 'I'm Just Me: I Do What Comes Naturally.'" *Gridiron Magazine*, December 20, 1971.

21. Interview with Bob Stephenson on April 1, 2020.

22. Didinger, Ray. "League Leading Interceptor and Pressure Breaker." *The Evening Bulletin*, December 8, 1971, S1.

23. Interview with Bill Bradley on August 20, 2020.

Chapter Six

1. Interview with Bill Bradley on October 7, 2020.

2. *Ibid.*

3. *Ibid.*

4. *Ibid.*

5. *Ibid.*

6. *Ibid.*

7. Interview with Bill Bradley on March 19, 2020.

8. Interview with Bill Bradley on October 7, 2020.

9. *Ibid.*
10. *Ibid.*
11. *Ibid.*
12. Forbes, Gordon. "Dear Bill, 'I Feel You and Tim Are Absolutely Right.'" *The Philadelphia Inquirer*, July 29, 1972.
13. Interview with Bill Bradley on October 7, 2020.
14. *Ibid.*
15. *Ibid.*
16. *Ibid.*
17. *Ibid.*
18. *Ibid.*
19. *Ibid.*
20. *Ibid.*
21. *Ibid.*
22. *Ibid.*
23. Interview with Bill Bradley on August 20, 2020.
24. Interview with Bill Bradley on November 12, 2020.
25. Greer, Tom. "Super Bill – Free As The Wind." *Pro! Magazine*, 1972.
26. Interview with Bill Bradley on March 19, 2020.
27. *Ibid.*
28. Didinger, Ray. "Bradley Is Wanted By Cowboys' Posse." *The Evening Bulletin*, November 21, 1972.
29. Ibid., "Super Bill Survives Destruction." *The Evening Bulletin*, November 27, 1972.
30. Forbes, Gordon. "Back to Conformity For Birds' Bradley." *The Philadelphia Inquirer*, August 6, 1972.
31. Interview with Bill Bradley on November 12, 2020.
32. *Ibid.*
33. Interview with T.J. Troup on November 13, 2020.
34. Greer, Tom. "Super Bill – Free As The Wind." *Pro! Magazine*, 1972.

Chapter Seven

1. Interview with Bill Bradley on August 20, 2020.
2. Perkins, Steve. "Free Spirits in The Right Spot," *Dallas Cowboys Weekly*, December 4, 1976.
3. Oates, Jr., Bob. "Safeties First...and Last." *Pro!* Magazine, September 22, 1974, 5B, 7B.
4. Interview with Bill Bradley on November 12, 2020.
5. Dolson, Frank. "Bradley Still Finds Some Fun in Game." *The Philadelphia Inquirer*, August 14, 1973.
6. Bernstein, Ralph. "A 'Team of Nobodies' Startles Dallas 30-16." *The Doylestown Daily Intelligencer*, 10-29-1973, 9.
7. Giordano, Paul. "Tom goes straight." *Bucks County Courier Times*, November 5, 1973, 48.
8. Eagles Public Relations Staff. "Bill Bradley." *Pro!* Magazine, November 18, 1973, 20.
9. Interview with Bill Bradley on March 19, 2020.
10. Associated Press. "Eagles' defense makes amends." *Delaware County Daily Times*, December 10, 1973, 16.
11. Didinger, Ray. "Super Ghost Looks For More Pickoffs." *The Evening Bulletin*, October 3, 1973.
12. Interview with Bill Bradley on March 19, 2020.
13. *Ibid.*
14. *Ibid.*
15. *Ibid.*
16. *Ibid.*
17. *Ibid.*
18. *Ibid.*
19. *Ibid.*
20. *Ibid.*
21. *Ibid.*
22. *Ibid.*

Chapter Eight

1. Interview with Terry Hanratty on June 10, 2020.
2. Interview with Bill Bradley on October 7, 2020.
3. Interview with Bill Bradley on November 12, 2020.
4. Interview with Bill Bradley on March 19, 2020.
5. Interview with Bill Bradley on October 7, 2020.
6. Interview with Bill Bradley on November 12, 2020.
7. Interview with Bill Bradley on October 7, 2020.
8. Interview with Phil Villapiano on June 4, 2020.
9. Interview with Mercury Morris on July 7, 2020.
10. Interview with Bill Bradley on October 7, 2020.
11. *Ibid.*
12. *Ibid.*
13. *Ibid.*
14. Interview with Bill Bradley on November 12, 2020.
15. Interview with Bill Bradley on December 9, 2020.
16. *Ibid.*
17. Interview with Bill Bradley on March 10, 2021.
18. Interview with Bill Bradley on December 9, 2020.
19. *Ibid.*
20. Forbes, Gordon. "Bradley Sniffs Playoffs After Eagles 2d Victory," *The Philadelphia Inquirer*, Oct. 1, 1974.
21. Klein, Dave. "The Specialist: Free Safety Bill Bradley." *Weekend Kickoff*, October 25, 1974.
22. *Ibid.*
23. Interview with Bill Bradley on December 9, 2020.
24. *Ibid.*
25. *Ibid.*
26. *Ibid.*
27. *Ibid.*
28. Interview with Bill Bradley on May 18, 2020.
29. *Ibid.*

30. *Ibid.*

31. *Ibid.*

32. *Ibid.*

33. *Ibid.*

34. *Ibid.*

35. *Ibid.*

36. *Ibid.*

Chapter Nine

1. Flynn, John. "Intercepting Bill Bradley." *Football Digest*, June 1973, 83-91.

2. Klein, Dave. "The Specialist: Free Safety Bill Bradley." *Weekend Kickoff*, October 25, 1974.

3. Interview with Bill Bradley on December 9, 2020.

4. *Ibid.*

5. Interview with Bill Bradley on May 18, 2020.

6. This is the NFL, *NFL Films*, October 5, 1975. Sabol, Ed, Executive Producer.

7. Forbes, Gordon. "Films Confirm Call on Bradley." *The Philadelphia Inquirer*, October 28, 1975.

8. Interview with Bill Bradley on October 9, 2019.

9. Zagorski, Joe. *The NFL in the 1970s: Pro Football's Most Important Decade.* Jefferson, NC: McFarland and Company, Inc., 2016, 157.

10. Interview with Bill Bradley on May 18, 2020.

11. *Ibid.*

12. *Ibid.*

13. Interview with Bill Bradley on August 20, 2020.

14. Interview with Bill Bradley on October 9, 2019.

15. Interview with Bill Bradley on August 21, 2019.

16. *Ibid.*

17. Interview with Bill Bradley on May 18, 2020.

18. Interview with Bill Bradley on August 20, 2020.
19. *Ibid.*
20. Interview with Bill Bradley on March 10, 2021.
21. Interview with Bill Bradley on May 18, 2020.
22. Interview with Bill Bradley on October 9, 2019.
23. *Ibid.*
24. *Ibid.*
25. Interview with Bill Bradley on December 9, 2020.
26. Interview with Bill Bradley on October 9, 2019.
27. Ibid.
28. Interview with Bill Bradley on December 9, 2020.
29. Interview with Bill Bradley on May 18, 2020.
30. Interview with Bill Bradley on December 9, 2020.
31. Interview with Bill Bradley on May 18, 2020.
32. *Ibid.*
33. Interview with Bill Bradley on October 9, 2019.
34. Interview with Bill Bradley on May 18, 2020.
35. *Ibid.*

Chapter Ten

1. Interview with Bill Bradley on May 18, 2020.
2. *Ibid.*
3. *Ibid.*
4. *Ibid.*
5. Interview with Ed Khayat on November 27, 2019.
6. Interview with Bill Bradley on December 9, 2020.
7. *Ibid.*
8. *Ibid.*
9. Interview with Bill Bradley on August 20, 2020.
10. *Ibid.*
11. Interview with Bill Bradley on December 9, 2020.
12. *Ibid.*

13. *Ibid.*
14. Interview with Bill Bradley on August 20, 2020.
15. Interview with Bill Bradley on December 9, 2020.
16. Interview with Ted Cottrell on January 11, 2021.
17. *bid.*
18. Interview with Bill Bradley on March 19, 2020.
19. *Ibid.*
20. *Ibid.*
21. Interview with Bill Bradley on December 9, 2020.
22. *Ibid.*
23. Ibid.

Chapter Eleven

1. Interview with Curtis Fitzgerald on October 17, 2020.
2. *Ibid.*
3. Interview with Bob Stephenson on April 1, 2020.
4. *Ibid.*
5. Interview with Mickey "Mule" Hubert on April 27, 2020.
6. *Ibid.*
7. *Ibid.*
8. *Ibid.*
9. *Ibid.*
10. *Ibid.*
11. Interview with Bob Stephenson on April 1, 2020.
12. Interview with Jackie Cherry on April 4, 2020.
13. Interview with Bill Bradley on October 9, 2019.
14. Interview with Bill Bradley on July 3, 2019.
15. Zimmer, Michael. "How Write You Are." *Pro!* Magazine, September 18, 1977, 3D.
16. *Ibid.*
17. Interview with Jackie Cherry on April 4, 2020.

18. Interview with Bill Bradley on July 18, 2019.

19. Interview with Curtis Fitzgerald on October 17, 2020.

20. Interview with Marion Turner on April 20, 2020.

21. Interview with Susan Bradley on January 6, 2021.

22. Interview with Bill Bradley on December 9, 2020.

23. *Ibid.*

24. Interview with Bill Bradley on July 18, 2019.

25. Interview with Curtis Fitzgerald on October 17, 2020.

26. Ibid.

27. Ibid.

28. Interview with Bill Bradley on March 19, 2020.

BIBLIOGRAPHY

Articles

Associated Press. "Four Draft Picks Sign With Birds." *The Sunday Bulletin*, July 6, 1969.
-----. "Eagles' defense makes amends." *Delaware County Daily Times*, December 10, 1973, 16.

Bernstein, Ralph. "A 'Team of Nobodies' Startles Dallas 30-16." *The Doylestown Daily Intelligencer*, October 29, 1973, 9.

Brown, Hugh. "Bill Bradley Has Finally Found the Right Position." *The Philadelphia Bulletin*, August 6, 1969.
-----. "'Super Bill' Enhances Eagle Scene." *Pro Football Weekly*, December 4, 1969.

Damer, Roy. "Kickers Are Up in Air – All-Stars Like It." *Chicago Tribune*, July 25, 1969.

Didinger, Ray. "Pride Hurt Worse Than Knee." *The Evening Bulletin*, August 20, 1970.
-----. "League Leading Interceptor and Pressure Breaker." *The Evening Bulletin*, December 8, 1971, S1.
-----. "Super Bill Lies Down on Job but Gets 11th Steal." *The Evening Bulletin*, December 13, 1971.
-----. "The Saga Of Super Bill: 'I'm Just Me: I Do What Comes Naturally.'" *Gridiron Magazine*, December 20, 1971.
-----. "Bradley Is Wanted By Cowboys' Posse." *The Evening Bulletin*, November 21, 1972.
-----. "Super Bill Survives Destruction." *The Evening Bulletin*, November 27, 1972.
-----. "Super Ghost Looks For More Pickoffs." *The Evening Bulletin*, October 3, 1973.
-----. "Bill Bradley Will Miss Ditka Today." *The Evening Bulletin*, October 28, 1973.

Dolson, Frank. "Bradley Still Finds Some Fun in Game." *The Philadelphia Inquirer*, August 14, 1973.

Eagles Public Relations Staff. "Bill Bradley." *Pro!* Magazine, November 18, 1973, 20.

Edwards, Roy. "No Strain, No Pain, No Sweat for Bradley." *The Dallas Morning News*, August 21, 1970.

Fisher, Jeff. "Big 33 Flashback – 'Super Bill' Bradley Leads Texas to Win Against Pennsylvania in 1965." *High School Football America*, April 21, 2018.

Flynn, John. "Intercepting Bill Bradley." *Football Digest*, June, 1973, 83-91.

Forbes, Gordon. "Bradley's Moon-Shot Punts Thrill at Eagles' Camp." *The Philadelphia Inquirer*, August 6, 1969.
-----. "Two Eagles Get Surgery For Knees." *The Philadelphia Inquirer*, August 19, 1970.
-----. "Dear Bill, 'I Feel You and Tim Are Absolutely Right.'" *The Philadelphia Inquirer*, July 29, 1972.
-----. "Back to Conformity For Birds' Bradley." *The Philadelphia Inquirer*, August 6, 1972.
-----. "New Eagle Pact Puts Smile on Bradley's Face." *The Philadelphia Inquirer*, September 14, 1972.
-----. "Bradley Sniffs Playoffs After Eagles 2d Victory," *The Philadelphia Inquirer*, Oct. 1, 1974.
...... "Films Confirm Call on Bradley." *The Philadelphia Inquirer*, October 28, 1975.

Giordano, Paul. "Tom goes straight." *Bucks County Courier Times*, November 5, 1973, 48.

Greer, Tom. "Super Bill – Free As The Wind." *Pro!* Magazine, 1972.

Klein, Dave. "The Specialist: Free Safety Bill Bradley." *Weekend Kickoff*, October 25, 1974.

Lundgren, Hal. "Super Bill Revisited." *Houston Chronicle*, September 7, 1970.

McCarthy, Mickey. "Super Bill." *The Atlanta Constitution*, June 24, 1969.

Oates, Bob, Jr. "Safeties First...and Last." *Pro!* Magazine, September 22, 1974, 3B-7B.

Padice, Sandy. "Money, Football And Bill Bradley." *Philadelphia Inquirer*, August 20, 1969.

Perkins, Steve. "Free Spirits in The Right Spot." *Dallas Cowboys Weekly*, December 4, 1976, 7.

Plarski, Don. "Cardinals flop again, 37-20." *Alton Evening Telegraph*, November 22, 1971, 11.

Shefski, Bill. "Super Bill Goes on Record With 10th Air Theft." *Philadelphia Daily News*, December 6, 1971.
-----. "Superman is Back." *Pro Quarterback*, July,1972, 39-41.

Zimmer, Michael. "How Write You Are." *Pro!* Magazine, September 18, 1977, 3D-7D.

Books

Campbell, Donald P. *Sunday's Warriors: The Philadelphia Eagles' History, 2nd Edition*. Philadelphia: Quantum Leap Publisher, Inc., 1995.

Dent, Jim. *The Kids Got It Right*. New York: Thomas Dunne Books, 2013.

Zagorski, Joe. *The NFL in the 1970s: Pro Football's Most Important Decade*. Jefferson, NC: McFarland and Company, Inc., 2016.

Interviews

Bill Bradley, July 3, 2019; July 18, 2019; October 9, 2019; August 21, 2019; March 19, 2020; April 18, 2020; May 18, 2020; August 20, 2020; October 7, 2020; November 12, 2020; December 9, 2020; March 10, 2021.

Jackie Cherry, April 4, 2020.

Curtis Fitzgerald, October 17, 2020.

Terry Hanratty, June 10, 2020.

Mickey "Mule" Hubert, April 27, 2020.

Ed Khayat, November 27, 2019.

Larry Miller, April 5, 2020.

Eugene "Mercury" Morris, July 7, 2020.

Bob Stephenson, April 1, 2020.

T.J. Troup, November 13, 2020.

Marion Turner, April 20, 2020.

Phil Villapiano, June 4, 2020.

Video

This is the NFL, *NFL Films*, October 5, 1975. Sabol, Ed, Executive Producer.

INDEX

ACKNOWLEDGMENTS

I was truly fortunate to get an opportunity to write a biography about a man who really should be much more famous than he currently is. Bill Bradley often gets confused with the former New York Knicks basketball player and former New York Senator of the same name. The Bill Bradley that this book details is a former pro football player, and an incredibly unique character with numerous accomplishments in his own right. Bill spent many hours over the course of a couple of years answering my hundreds of questions. Each of his answers seemed to me to be more interesting than the one before. The entertainment value from many of his stories is worth its weight in gold, and you will get to read about many of them in this book. I am truly indebted for all his help with this project. I only hope that I have done him justice with my efforts within these pages.

Another person who greatly deserves my thanks is Jon Kendle, the chief historian of the Ralph J. Wilson Pro Football Hall of Fame Research Library, in Canton, Ohio. Jon went out of his way to provide me with many different articles and newspaper clippings detailing Bill Bradley's years with the Philadelphia Eagles. His help really gave this book a stronger understanding of Bradley's achievements throughout his NFL career.

It is probably true that everyone living in Philadelphia knows Ray Didinger. The long-time *Philadelphia Bulletin* football writer, Eagles beat writer, and sports talk radio host, has reported on more Eagles games than anyone else in the history of the team. As a fellow football writer hailing from near Philadelphia, I consider Ray to be legendary in his own right. Like me, Ray also considered Bill Bradley to be one of the most unique athletes that the city has ever seen, so he was a natural choice to write the foreword for this book. I thank him immensely for contributing such a wonderful and entertaining introduction on "Super Bill."

I would also like to thank my friend T.J. Troup, a long-time college football coach, and a current pro football author and pro football film analyst. Coach Troup came through for me once again, as he shared with me his sagacious knowledge of Bill Bradley's career and his style of play throughout the 1970s. In fact, when Troup was a young player in high school and college himself, he often studied Bill Bradley, to better understand how to succeed in the defensive backfield. Thanks once again, Coach!

I would also like to thank Tricia Gesner of Associated Press Images, for helping me to obtain the front cover for this book. I would also like to thank my friend Matt Hudson, for contributing a photo of me he took for the back cover.

A big thanks goes out to Deborah Kevin of Highlander Press for her willingness to see the worth in publishing Bill Bradley's incredible biography. Thanks also to Kristy Crippen for introducing me to Ms. Kevin, and to Kristy's husband, Ken Crippen, for his support and friendship over the years.

Thanks also goes out to my friend Chris Willis of NFL Films, who has always made his research library available to me to study numerous films of former players like Bill Bradley. Chris is a renown pro football writer in his own right, and his numerous books on the sport run the gamut from the Columbus Panhandles in the 1920s to the San Francisco 49ers of the 1980s. Thanks once again for your help Chris!

Bill Bradley's family members have helped to shape his life in many ways. As their esteemed representative, I would like to thank Bill's wife Susan, who was willing to spare some of her time to chat with me about her husband and their family. I hope that I did not overly surprise her when I barged into the back door of their house in

Texas, back in March of 2021, while Bill was toweling off after one of his Epsom salt baths. It was indeed my great honor to interview her.

I would also like to thank Bill Bradley's friends, colleagues, and former coaches and teammates who have generously given me moments of their time to discuss their free-spirited and always entertaining friend. They include (in random order): Ed Khayat, Ted Cottrell, Curtis Fitzgerald, Bob Stephenson, Jackie Cherry, Larry Miller, Mickey Hubert, and Marion Turner. These men have remained friends with Bill Bradley for many years, and their wonderful memories of the man have lent great insight into Bradley's character...and into many anecdotes of his lively past.

Last but never least, I would like to thank my late parents, Stephen and Natalie Zagorski, for giving me a great childhood, filled with wonderful and enjoyable memories. My love to them always.

ABOUT THE AUTHOR

Photo credit: Matt Hudson

Joe Zagorski is a U.S. Army veteran, a former schoolteacher, a former park ranger, and a former sportswriter for two newspapers in Pennsylvania. He is a member of the Pro Football Writers of America (PFWA) and the Pro Football Researchers Association (PFRA). He is also an associate member of the NFL Alumni Association.

Zagorski's first book, *The NFL in the 1970s: Pro Football's Most Important Decade*, was rated by the Library Journal as one of the Top 10 Football Books in America in 2016. His second book, *The Year the Packers Came Back: Green Bay's 1972 Resurgence*, explored one of the most unique teams in modern NFL history. It was published in 2019. A year later, his third book, *America's Trailblazing Middle Linebacker: The Story of NFL Hall of Famer Willie Lanier*, recounted the exploits of the first fulltime African-American middle linebacker in pro football history. In 2021, Zagorski won the Pro Football Researchers Association's Ralph Hay Award for Lifetime Achievement for Pro Football Research and Historiography. Also in 2021, he finished writing his first screenplay, entitled *Town Teams*.

Zagorski was born and raised in Pottstown, Pennsylvania. He currently lives in Oak Ridge, Tennessee.

ABOUT THE PUBLISHER

Highlander Press, founded in 2019, is a mid-sized publishing company committed to diversity and sharing big ideas thereby changing the world through words.

Highlander Press guides authors from where they are in the writing-editing-publishing process to where they have an impactful book of which they are proud, making a long-time dream come true. Having authored a book improves your confidence, helps create clarity, and ensures that you claim your expertise.

What makes Highlander Press unique is that their business model focuses on building strong collaborative relationships with other women-owned businesses, which specialize in some aspect of the publishing industry, such as graphic design, book marketing, book launching, copyrights, and publicity. The mantra "a rising tide lifts all boats" is one they embrace. Learn more at https://highlanderpress books.com.

facebook.com/highlanderpress

instagram.com/highlanderpress

tiktok.com/highlanderpress

linkedin.com/highlanderpress

www.ingramcontent.com/pod-product-compliance
Lightning Source LLC
Chambersburg PA
CBHW051609120626
46551CB00014B/1723